The Jesuits and Religious Intercultural Management in Early Modern Times

Human Capital, a Global Mindset, and Missionary Work in Japan and Peru during the Sixteenth and Seventeenth Centuries

Frank Jacob
Nord University, Norway

Series in World History

VERNON PRESS

Vernon Press 2025. This book is licensed under a Creative Commons Attribution 4.0 International license (CC BY 4.0) which is the most open licence available and considered the industry 'gold standard' for open access. This license allows you to share, copy, distribute and transmit the text; to adapt the text and to make commercial use of the text provided attribution is made to the authors and a full reference to book as follows:

Frank Jacob, *The Jesuits and Religious Intercultural Management in Early Modern Times: Human Capital, a Global Mindset, and Missionary Work in Japan and Peru during the Sixteenth and Seventeenth Centuries*, Vernon Press, 2024.
https://vernonpress.com/book/1889

More information about the CC BY license is available at
https://creativecommons.org/licenses/by/4.0/

Published in Open Access thanks to the financial support from Nord Universitet.

Copyright, attributions and/or permissions for third party material included in this book may differ, and are noted, as appropriate.

www.vernonpress.com

In the Americas:	In the rest of the world:
Vernon Press	Vernon Press
1000 N West Street, Suite 1200	C/Sancti Espiritu 17,
Wilmington, Delaware, 19801	Malaga, 29006
United States	Spain

Series in World History

Library of Congress Control Number: 2023949197

ISBN: 979-8-8819-0193-6

Also available: 978-1-64889-809-9 [Hardback]; 978-1-64889-849-5 [PDF, E-Book]

Cover design by Vernon Press.
Background image: *China Monumentis, qua sacris qua profanes* by Athanasius Kircher. Public domain. https://commons.wikimedia.org/wiki/File:Athanasii_Kircheri..._China_monumentis_(1667)_%22Frontispicio%22_(22629197626).jpg
Map: *1590-1602 Nova Hondius*. Public domain. https://commons.wikimedia.org/wiki/File:1590_1602_Nova_Hondius.jpg

Every effort has been made to trace all copyright holders, but if any have been inadvertently overlooked the publisher will be pleased to include any necessary credits in any subsequent reprint or edition.

Table of Contents

	List of Figures	v
	List of Tables	vii
	Acknowledgements	ix
Chapter 1	**Introduction**	1
Chapter 2	**Literature Review**	13
Chapter 3	**Research Model and Outlook to the Methodology**	33
Chapter 4	**The Cases**	39
	4.1. The Jesuits: A Short Introduction	
	4.2. Japan	
	4.3. Peru	
Chapter 5	**Successful Intercultural Management and Early Modern Proselytization**	137
Chapter 6	**Management-Related Recommendations**	147
Chapter 7	**Conclusion**	153
	Works Cited	157
	Appendices	189
	9.1. Appendix 1: Jesuit Missionaries in Japan 1549-1614	
	9.2. Appendix 2: Jesuit Missionaries in Peru (1568-1605)	
	List of Abbreviations	221

List of Figures

Fig. 1.1:	Relevant research fields.	6
Fig. 3.1:	Operationalization of the project.	34
Fig. 3.2:	Schematic depiction of the research model.	36
Fig. 4.1:	Ignatius of Loyola, painting by Peter Paul Rubens (1577-1640).	40
Fig. 4.2:	Alessandro Valignano, ca. 1599.	48
Fig. 4.3:	Number of Jesuits in Japan between 1553 and 1614.	76
Fig. 4.4:	Number of Jesuits in Peru between 1569 and 1601.	125
Fig. 5.1:	Jesuits in Japan who spoke Japanese.	137
Fig. 5.2:	The percentage of Jesuits who spoke Japanese in the respective periods.	138
Fig. 5.3:	Jesuits in Peru who spoke an indigenous language.	139
Fig. 5.4:	The percentage of Jesuits who spoke an indigenous language in the respective periods.	140
Fig. 6.1:	The percentage of indigenous Jesuit fathers in Japan and Peru according to available data.	150

List of Tables

Tab. 2.1:	The development of cultural management research (Barmeyer, 2018, 31-32).	19
Tab. 2.2:	Research approaches toward cultural aspects of management (Barmeyer, 2018, 32-33, in reference to Adler, 1983).	20
Tab. 2.3:	SME categories used and recommended by the European Commission.	28
Tab. 3.1:	Description of the main aspects of the present book.	33
Tab. 4.1:	The first ten Jesuit Order provinces.	42
Tab. 4.2:	The number of Jesuits within the first century of the order's existence (Hartmann, 2008, 30).	44
Tab. 4.3:	Number of padres and irmãos serving in Japan between 1553 and 1614 (including available data for Japanese padres and irmãos).	77
Tab. 4.4:	Jesuits who served in Japan between 1549 and 1563.	78
Tab. 4.5:	Jesuit padres who served in Japan in 1587.	79
Tab. 4.6:	Jesuit padres who served in Japan in 1614.	81
Tab. 4.7:	Number of padres and hermanos serving in Peru between 1569 and 1601 (including available data for Peruvian padres and hermanos).	125
Tab. 4.8:	Jesuits who served in Peru between 1568 and 1575.	126
Tab. 4.9:	Number of Jesuits in Peru in 1591 according to location (MP 4, 1966, 674).	128
Tab. 4.10:	Jesuit padres who served in Peru between 1576 and 1599.	129
Tab. 4.11:	Jesuit padres who served in Peru in 1601.	131
Tab. 5.1:	Combined Data for Japan and Peru	141

Acknowledgements

This book is a revised version of a DBA thesis, originally titled "Religious Intercultural Management and the Value of Human Capital and a Global Mindset: A Historical Case Study of the Jesuit Missions in Japan and Peru in the Sixteenth and Seventeenth Centuries," that was submitted to and accepted by the joint doctoral program in Business Administration by the Université Jean Moulin Lyon 3 and the Business Science Institute (BSI), Luxembourg in 2021. I would like to thank my supervisor, Prof. Dr. Dr. Thomas Gergen, who supported this endeavor since its early stage. Furthermore, I would like to thank Prof. Dr. Anne Bartel-Radic for her critical and constructive comments during the three years of the program and the final examination while I was working on the topic and for finding fruitful ways to connect historical sources to management theory. I would also like to thank Prof. Dr. André Reuter and Prof. Dr. Lars Meyer-Waarden for their important insights and steady encouragement during the courses, presentations, and casual meetings. In addition, I would like to thank Prof. Dr. Ulrike Mayrhofer and Prof. Dr. Alain Burlaud for their efforts during the examination and oral defense of my thesis. I gained considerably from the input I received from the named colleagues, as well as from talks with Prof. Dr. Michel Kalika and other staff members at the BSI. Exchanges with the other members of my cohort at the institute's meetings between 2018 and 2021 were similarly enlightening, and I would like to express my gratitude for their support as well.

Turning a thesis into a book is always a challenging process, and although this doctoral thesis was not my first one, it was still quite an endeavor. I would like to thank Blanca Caro Duran and Argiris Legatos from Vernon Press for their support during the book production. The latter was also made possible by the comments and remarks of two anonymous peer reviewers, whom I would like to thank for important input as well. The final book was made much better due to their helpful and mostly constructive suggestions and recommended adjustments. Special thanks also go to Anthony Wright, who usually proofreads my English manuscripts.

The publication of this book in open access was made possible through financial support from Nord Universitet, Norway, for which I also wish to express my gratitude. Over the years, my colleagues there also provided me with advice and important comments, for which I cannot express enough gratitude. Last but not least, I would like to thank my family for their steady support and love. Without them, books such as the present could not exist.

Chapter 1

Introduction

Contemporary companies and top-level managers can learn a lot by looking to the past, and they should. While small and medium-sized enterprises (SMEs) are without any doubt "key players in national economies and are increasingly integrated into global value chains" (Dominguez & Mayrhofer, 2018a) and, in addition, "form an important part of nearly every country" (Prange & Zhao, 2018), similar 'business structures' were important for the expansion of religious orders during the 16th and 17th centuries as well. They have been leading economic globalization in the last decades (Dominguez & Mayrhofer, 2018c, 195), and it seems obvious that their role cannot be overemphasized (Bijaoui, 2016). The members of "[t]he Society of Jesus dreamt of both its own universalism and that of Christianity" (Hosne, 2013, 1) and therefore its expansion, like modern-day SMEs, into culturally different – in their historical context even completely unknown – regions of the world. It is hardly a surprise that today, in addition to their economic potential, SMEs often also act as cultural bridges, with managers being influenced by their work in geographically and culturally different environments (Pauluzzo & Shen, 2018) and vice versa. SMEs consequently must also be considered an institutionalized form of intercultural management whose managers need global management competencies (Bücker & Poutsma, 2010), especially since the internationalization of such enterprises usually demands their managers to be culturally flexible or open-minded. In this regard, they are confronted with similar problems as the Jesuit missionaries, who, in the 16th century, began to globalize the work and influence of a religious order. They acted as intercultural managers, in the truest sense of the word, as they could neither rely upon a lingua franca nor on existent knowledge about the regions of the world in which they began to work.

The study of 'historical companies' is often recommended for business students, as "[c]ase studies provide a detailed and organized analysis of historic business decisions and implementations" (Business Case Studies, 2019). Furthermore, as the present study will show, there is much knowledge to be gained from historical case studies, especially since the categories for intercultural management to be determined or separated are much clearer. Jesuits arriving in a foreign environment in the sixteenth century really had to face an unfamiliar culture, and they often could not rely on anything but their own skill set, i.e., their human capital, and their own global mindset, including a necessary dogmatic flexibility, to spread the word of the Bible and to secure a large number of converts.

A comparative longitudinal qualitative analysis of the Jesuit Order in two different areas, namely Japan and Peru, during the sixteenth and seventeenth centuries, will therefore provide a good understanding of important factors, i.e., the role of human capital and a global mindset, for successful intercultural management.

The Topic

Established in 1534, the Society of Jesus and its members were very active in expanding the influence of the religious congregation across the globe. They were consequently agents of early modern globalization, establishing a global network of self-sufficient provincial orders (Barthel, 1991; O'Malley et al., 1999; Friedrich, 2018). Representatives of the religious order therefore needed to act like modern businesses, especially SMEs (Dominguez & Mayrhofer, 2018b), and develop similar strategies for the work of their intercultural teams. One could, however, ask why a historical case study is relevant for considerations related to business administration. That religious orders developed their own forms of governance and relevant management practices to expand their influence, not only in a religious but also in an economic sense, has been emphasized before (Wirtz, 2020). The analysis of historical cases in business studies is not new, especially since long-term studies can fully grasp economic developments and structural changes (le Bris, Goetzmann & Pouget, 2017), while complete data sets spanning centuries are often available for the study of these developments and changes.

As Bartel-Radic et al. remark, the "global business environment is increasingly complex" (2015, 2), but the Jesuits of the sixteenth and seventeenth centuries very often faced similar problems to those companies face in a globalized world economy today. Like modern companies, the Jesuit Order had to rely on multinational and multicultural teams (Maloney & Zellmer-Bruhn, 2006; Jenster & Steiler, 2011) during their attempt to spread Christian beliefs around the globe and to secure their own mission financially (Thanh, 2016, 2018). The Jesuits were consequently managers in a twofold sense: they managed their missionary work while providing the monetary means to achieve their religiously motivated goals. Like modern-day global companies, the Jesuits had to use intangibles, especially the human capital of their missionaries, to develop successful management structures that would secure the order's interests in different regions of the world as well as their financial independence in a foreign environment. Necessary skills needed to be identified and applied by the missionaries to make sure that the goals of the order in the specific region of missionary activity could be secured in a process similar to those applied by global companies in the early twenty-first century (Bartel-Radic et al., 2015, 2).

Nevertheless, the organization founded by Ignatius of Loyola (1491-1556) also faced quite different realities during this mostly successful period of expansion (Feld, 2006). One example of a problematic environment of Jesuit expansion, which recently reached a larger audience through Martin Scorsese's film *Silence* (2016), is Japan (An'no, 2014). This negative example of Jesuit interaction with local authorities was, as I will argue, related to a lack of human capital and multicultural management skills. The case of Japan will therefore be compared with the congregation's relatively successful work in the order's province of Peru (Roemer, 1946; Cushner, 1980; Martin, 2001; Hosne, 2013), which spanned a longer time period than the order's activities in Japan. The analytical comparison will take a look at the managerial and business structures that were established. Afterward, why the missionaries were successful in Peru while they were expelled or killed in Japan will be discussed. The timeframe for the attempted comparison covers the sixteenth and seventeenth centuries because a deeper analysis of the society's activities in East Asia and Latin America within this timeframe will show how the men in charge reacted to the local diversities and which business strategies were favored. The longer time span will also allow an analysis of trends and impacts related to management decisions, as they were based on the existence or lack of human capital. Through a study of the Jesuits in charge, i.e., the higher management level, it will be possible to identify the existence of human capital and to evaluate its impact on the success[1] of the intercultural management of the Jesuits in Japan and Peru.

Research Field, Relevance, and Value

It seems to be quite well known in management-related research that "intercultural task performances" (Presbitero, 2021), and thereby "cultural intelligence" (Şahin & Gürbüz, 2020), deserve special attention, but historical approaches related to Management and Organization Studies (MOS) have hardly dealt with interculturality and how managers dealt with it in different time periods. Although it was stated years ago that "management history has the potential to add value to the management curricula" (Smith, 2007, 522), a particular focus on managerial skills as an expression of interest in intercultural performance is lacking, which is why the research this book presents offers new insights into the historical dimension of intercultural management, including results that can be applied by modern-day managers and organizations, especially expanding SMEs, as well.

Previous works in the fields of management and organizational history highlighted that management practices have been determined by their specific

---

[1] Success is understood here with regard to the conversions achieved by the missionaries and the existence of the mission as well as its numerical growth in its geographical context.

times, e.g., with regard to the existence of new technologies (Karsten, 2014), and faced "cultural barriers" due to globalization (Schwarzkopf, 2013) that could have a negative impact on managerial and organizational performances. However, with a few exceptions that highlight the potential of such research (Saka-Helmhout, 2011), larger longitudinal historical comparative studies with a focus on intercultural management and its related aspects have not been undertaken yet – the *Journal of Management History*, to name just one example here, shows no hits in its database for the term "intercultural." Regardless of this obvious deficiency, numerous works have discussed the possibility of applying historical methods and perspectives to questions related to management and organizational research (Harvey & Press, 1996; Taylor, Bell & Cooke, 2009; Decker, 2013; Coraiola, Foster & Suddaby, 2015; Godfrey, Hassard, O'Connor, Rowlinson & Ruef, 2016; Pfefferman, 2016; Wadhwani, 2016; Wadhwani & Decker, 2017; Stutz & Sachs, 2018).

Considering the interdisciplinary use of historical as well as management and organization theory to study management performances and successful intercultural management in different historical contexts, one also has to consider the "three epistemological dualisms derived from historical theory to explain the relationship between history and organization [as well as management] theory" that Rowlinson, Hassard & Decker (2014) emphasized:

1) in the dualism of explanation, historians are preoccupied with narrative construction, whereas organization theorists subordinate narrative to analysis;

2) in the dualism of evidence, historians use verifiable documentary sources, whereas organization theorists prefer constructed data; and

3) in the dualism of temporality, historians construct their own periodization, whereas organization theorists treat time as a constant for chronology.

In recent years, management and organization scholars, as well as business historians, have tried to elaborate the opportunities and challenges for an interdisciplinary approach (Bucheli & Wadhwani, 2015), and it became evident that "the historical discipline provides an alternative to the dominant science paradigms in organization studies" (Van Lent & Durepos, 2019, 429). Scholars often point out that there has been a "historic turn" in MOS (Mills & Novicevic, 2020, 18-25), especially since the "past decade has witnessed the growth of a body of work on how, if at all, business historians can bridge the gap between the discipline of history and MOS" (Van Lent & Durepos, 2019, 429) The value of historical perspectives in these fields of study have therefore not only been identified (Maclean et al., 2016; Suddaby, 2016), but their value is now more often stressed as an important aspect for the course of future research (Üsdiken & Kipping, 2021). The research presented in this book consequently addresses this point while offering a novel and seminal comparative historical longitudinal case study on the intercultural management performances of Jesuits in Japan and Peru during the sixteenth and seventeenth centuries. While having chosen a historical topic, the results will address issues managers in current-day globalizing SMEs have to deal with, and therefore, the presented insights possess a practical value that goes beyond the time period of the original events.

For the approach of the present study, the Jesuit Order will be considered to have been an early modern form of an expanding SME (see Chapter 2). The order has previously been identified as an expanding "enterprise" (Alden, 1996), and scholars have emphasized that its history "illustrates how, even in early modern times, people in charge of managing organizations ... could rely upon a huge amount of information" (Macintosh & Quattrone, 2010, 94). The Jesuit Order has also been considered a suitable case study for the analysis and discussion of management accounting and control systems (MACS) (Ibid., 10-17), especially due to the collection of data on its members (Ibid., 14-16) and the control mechanisms supporting the organization's hierarchical structure (Ibid., 10).

The present book intends to evaluate the order's success with regard to intercultural management in Japan and Peru and will add to several research fields, namely:

1. Studies related to the successful performance and internationalization of SMEs in general (Oviatt & McDougall, 1994; 2005; Knight & Cavusgil, 1996; Lefebvre & Lefebvre, 2001; Zhou, Wu, & Luo, 2007; Russo & Perrini, 2010; Louart & Martin, 2012; Hagen, Denicolai, & Zucchella, 2014; Rask 2014; Subhan, Mahmood, & Sattar, 2014; Hilmersson & Johanson, 2016),

2. Studies considering the role of (language) education or learning as an element for successful intercultural management (Furuya, Stevens, Bird, Oddou, & Mendenhall, 2009; Bartel-Radic & Lesca, 2011; Bartel-Radic, 2013; Kawalilak & Lock, 2018; Godwin-Jones, 2019), and

3. Studies highlighting the role of a global mindset for the successful internationalization of SMEs within the global economy (Levy et al., 2007; Scarino, 2010; Ng, Tan, & Ang, 2011; Hruby, 2013; Eriksson, Nummela & Saarenketo, 2014; Hruby, 2014; Elo, Benjowsky & Nummela, 2015; Torkkeli, Nummela & Saarenketo, 2018; Hruby et al., 2019).

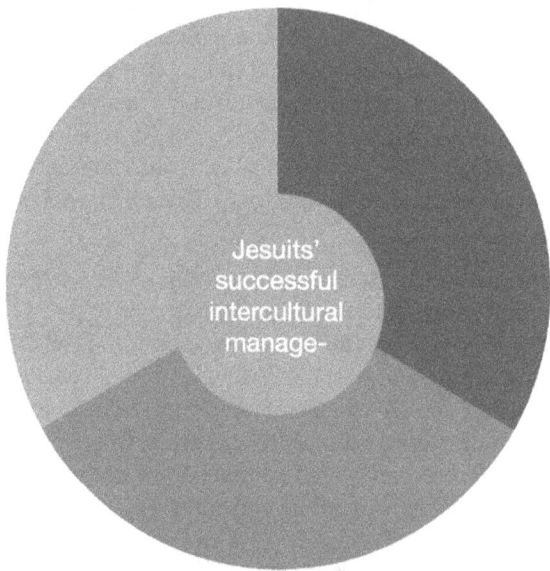

● Intercultural management, human capital and language skills
● Global Mindset
● SMEs global expansion and successful internationalization

Fig. 1.1: Relevant research fields.

The comparative longitudinal qualitative analysis of Jesuits who acted as 'managers' in early modern Japan and Peru will shed light on the named aspects and, due to a long historical time frame, allow more detailed and, without any doubt, relevant recommendations for current-day companies whose managers face similar issues with regard to securing the necessary capabilities of international management teams that can perform in the best interests of global companies (Bartel-Radic, 2006). In addition, the comparative historical longitudinal qualitative analysis al-lows clearer determinations for intercultural management, especially concerning the relevant cate-gories, namely proof of the existence of human capital and a global mindset (for a discussion of qualitative methods, see Dubois & Gadde, 2002; Flyvbjerg, 2006; Gibbert, Ruigrok, & Wicki, 2008; Welch, Piekkari, Plakoyiannaki, & Paavilainen-Mäntymäki, 2011).

Problematization

What role did human capital and a global mindset play in the success of intercultural religious management, especially in the case of the Jesuit management structures of the sixteenth and seventeenth centuries under analysis? In response to this question, the present study will provide a deeper insight into two very important factors of global, i.e., intercultural, management that also determine the growth and performance of SMEs in the twenty-first century, namely human capital and a global mindset, by intensively analyzing two historical case studies that emphasize the importance of these two elements for successful intercultural management during the period of early globalization and the establishment and internationalization of early modern SME structures. While it is historical with regard to its subject of study, this book will be able to provide important insights that can be used to better understand the value and importance of human capital and a global mindset, as well as their implication as necessary preconditions for more balanced intercultural management and SME expansion by modern-day companies and intercultural teams. Similar problems exist in the global world economy and can be avoided by a strategy that takes the measures that secured success in the past into account while avoiding decisions that led to failure. Since a successful management structure is able to determine a company's success, not only financially but also with regard to innovation (Chemmanur, Kong, Krishnan, & Yu, 2019), it is even more important to learn from past management structures to secure future-oriented strategies concerning successful management, especially intercultural management, for companies in the days to come.

The Case of the Jesuit Order

The primary target of the following study is to find out how early modern management structures, in the specific case of the Jesuits, were established and how business-related decisions were determined with regard to the existence and evaluation of human capital and a global mindset. In other words, the core question for international business research, namely the determinants of the success or failure of businesses (Bartel-Radic, 2013, 239), will be central to the following analysis. By having access to intercultural competencies on the personal level, i.e., the missionaries themselves, the Jesuits as an organization gained additional intercultural competencies which they could use to expand their influence and missionary work further (Bartel-Radic, 2013, 240). In the case of the Jesuits, one would have to emphasize what is claimed for modern companies as well, namely that "international experience and intercultural interaction, supported by geocentric international human resource strategies, are key factors in the organizational development of intercultural competence" (Bartel-Radic, 2013, 239).

The Jesuits were first and foremost interested in spreading the Christian religion, as P. F. Willert emphasized in an almost hagiographic way:

Churches and shrines were the trophies of their bloodless victories, or if not bloodless, purchased by the blood of their own martyrs; not the din of battle, but the music of holy bells marked their progress; not broken hearts, but healed consciences; not cities plundered, and women ravished and infants wantonly slain, but well-ordered towns, and virgins dedicated to God, and little children delivered from oblations to devils and brought into the family of Jesus and Mary. Such were their labours of which every region of the earth was full. (1887, 338)

However, they were not only successful in gaining new believers for the Christian Church, but they were also adapting techniques of intercultural management that allowed them to easily reach possible converts in different geographical regions (Duignan, 1958, 725-726). There was no unity among the Christian orders when it came to missionary practices, but the Jesuits "led the movement for accommodation and adaptation" (Duignan, 1958, 725), which means they accepted the existence of diversity and were willing to accommodate it, as long as it made their missionary activities easier: "Experience with pagans and nonbelievers did not merely help the Jesuits to develop methods of directing cultural change, but forced them to adopt a position of relativism in order to deal with the diversity of conditions encountered" (Duignan, 1958, 726).

All in all, the Jesuits "were able to work to win the souls of men with tact and forbearance, not with rudeness and impatience" (Duignan, 1958, 726). We know of a case in India, to name just one example, where Roberto de Nobili (1577-1656) studied the Brahmin traditions and language and followed the relevant religious and cultural rules, which made it much easier for him to win the trust and eventually belief of many people in India, who willingly followed his argument to convert to Christianity (Duignan, 1958, 727). He consequently combined language skills and dogmatic flexibility, showing how human capital and a global mindset would lead a form of intercultural management to success, i.e., the existence of converts. Similar examples are known from China, but these Jesuit approaches to and interpretations of missionary work also led to struggles with other orders, whose members were unwilling to comply with such intercultural forms of missionary work, and especially the global mindset of the Jesuit missionaries, since the former believed in European superiority: "Intriguers, rebels, hypocrites, casuists, have all been terms applied to the Jesuits. They have been attacked for tolerating, and compromising with, heathen customs and accused of profaning Christianity by adapting pagan rituals to Christian uses" (Duignan, 1958, 730).

These few examples already make it clear that the Jesuits were quite capable of adjusting their missionary approach to the existent preconditions in a specific region (Healy, 1958). The Jesuits would also be involved in local trade developments and become agents of a transnationalization of early modern trade relations, especially in relation to the trans-Pacific silver trade, which, in a way, also connected Japan and Peru (Cauti, 2005, 254-262).

The Jesuits' successes were made possible due to their possession and application of human capital and a global mindset, which was established by their missionary training, which, in contrast to other orders, allowed them to adopt local elements to make the Christian message more attractive to the indigenous population. With regard to education and the creation of human capital, the Jesuits followed similar steps to those that modern-day companies need to take: 1) recruitment and selection, 2) training and development, and 3) performance appraisal (Jain & Ahuja, 2019, 269-270).

In Japan, where their mission began with the arrival of Francis Xavier (1506-1552) in 1549 (Vlam, 1979, 48), the Jesuits tried to educate Japanese disciples, especially in Latin and Portuguese, since there was an obvious need for language training, as this was one of the most important human capital-related skills for successful missionary activity. While the Jesuits had achieved the conversion of around 750,000 Japanese by 1600 (Boxer, 1951, 180-187), they were unable to provide sufficient missionaries for this immense number of believers, especially since mass conversions were usually the consequence of the baptism of a local feudal lord (*daimyō*). Xavier's early assumption that Japan would provide a very fruitful ground for Jesuit missionary activities was consequently too enthusiastic (Ellis, 2003, 157).

Although the Jesuits had recognized the importance of language (Vande Walle, 1996) and had begun to print the first dictionaries for the training of and use by the missionaries (Correia, 2003, 80-81),[2] there was a numerical incapacity that made their activities problematic. In addition, the mass conversions of subordinates to a local daimyō might have increased the number of believers on paper but not in reality, where the new Christian communities would have needed spiritual guidance for their religious development (López-Gay, 2000). Another infrastructural problem was the lack of official financing, which is why the Jesuits had to get involved in the silk trade between Macao and Japan in order to secure sufficient financial income to cover their missionary activities in the country (Cushner, 1967, 361). They consequently had to face similar problems to SMEs that expand toward and enter foreign markets today.

---

[2] Correia cites a letter from Father Diogo de Mesquita to the Rector of Manila College, Nagasaki, 28 October 1599, Roman Archives of the Society of Jesus, Japonica-Sinica, 13 II, fl. 349.

Beyond these existing problems, the Jesuits also had to deal with an internal struggle over the value of intercultural approaches to their religious management, which represents a discourse about a global mindset. Visitor Alessandro Valignano (1539-1606) struggled with Superior Francisco Cabral (1529-1609) over the strategies and techniques that were supposed to be used by the Jesuits during their missionary activities in Japan. While Valignano was in favor of intercultural approaches based on the training of Jesuits and Japanese disciples with regard to language and culture, Cabral opposed the adoption of foreign elements into the Jesuit mission. This clash was an early modern expression of the struggle over the value of human capital and the global mindset concerning a new intercultural approach to management (Hoey, 2010).

Japan was not the first Jesuit mission that eventually failed (Gradie, 1988), but, in contrast to the Peruvian case, the Jesuit missionaries were obviously able neither to gain the trust and support of the local authorities nor to create a solid community of believers or converts among those who would determine the fate of the country in the centuries to come.

It is, therefore, an interesting and promising endeavor to compare the two cases that Cauti considered to be "two incompatible models" (2005, 299-319), especially with regard to the existence and application of human capital and a global mindset by individual Jesuit missionaries as well as the order as such in their specific cultural and political environments. The study will show which impact factors, besides the genuine interest of the Jesuits, played a role in and were responsible for the success or failure of the structures established. It will, therefore, look in particular at the role of persons within the decision premises of organizations (Luhmann, 2011, 222-255). Volker Kessler has previously considered the writings of Ignatius of Loyola as a "forerunner to modern management techniques of decision-making" (2019, 106): "In his Spiritual Exercises Ignatius presented a holistic model for decision-making that integrates spirituality, intuition, emotions and reasoning" (Ibid., 116). This study will show the extent to which his successors and disciples alike reacted with regard to their mission-related decisions in accordance with Loyola's recommendation to make decisions "when sufficient clarity and understanding is received through experience of consolations and desolations, and through experience of discernment of different spirits" (Loyola, 1951, Sp.Ex. 176, cited in Kessler, 2019, 107-108).

At the same time, the book will analyze the local environments of expansion and therefore provide insight into the problems that expanding and internationally active corporations might deal with in our own days (Koschorke, 1998). The proposed comparison will consequently highlight how local parameters need to be taken into consideration for current business decisions, especially those

Introduction

related to the internationalization of SMEs (Dominguez & Mayrhofer, 2018b). Of course, Japan and Peru are culturally different regions and were even more so in the 1500s and 1600s. How the Jesuit agents reacted toward these existent preconditions will be of special interest. An analysis of their strategies will highlight how highly they evaluated existent or necessary human capital and the demands for a global or, to be more precise, globalized mindset. Therefore, taking these elements together, the analysis will eventually show how intercultural management worked in the sixteenth and seventeenth centuries and that it was quite similar to modern forms of such a management format. It will also explain why it failed in Japan while it seemed to work much better in Peru.

There exists plenty of literature about the Society of Jesus in several different languages (Shore, 2007), including in some leading journals like the *Journal of Jesuit Studies* (Brill) and the book series *Jesuit Studies* (Brill). Of course, this book will also refer to recent studies written in Portuguese, Spanish, and Japanese. Regardless of the historical coverage of Jesuit activities, no research has tried to connect the data available for the named cases from a management perspective. This will be provided for the first time in the present study with its focus on human capital and a global mindset as preconditions for successful intercultural management.

Chapter 2

Literature Review

The following chapter intends to provide a review of the literature in the previously mentioned fields of study that are relevant to the present book:

1) intercultural management, human capital, and language skills,
2) the global mindset, and
3) the global expansion of SMEs.

Regardless of the fact that we are currently living in a globalized world, cultural differences continue to exist, especially within organizational structures and companies (Barmeyer, 2018, 9). Globalization or internationalization, therefore, almost naturally provides the context for all research related to intercultural management (Barmeyer, 2018, 17) and the internationalization of SMEs (Chetty, Ojala, & Leppäaho, 2015; Zhang, Ma, Wang, Li, & Huo, 2016; Ahi, Baronchelli, Kuivalainen, & Piantoni, 2017; Dominguez & Mayrhofer, 2018c; Prange & Zhao, 2018; Sestu, Majocchi, & D'Angelo, 2018; St-Pierre, Lacoursière, & Veilleux, 2018), which are often represented in culturally different environments by global teams (Bartel-Radic, 2006; Maloney & Zellmer-Bruhn, 2006). The Jesuits, as early agents of globalization, had to deal with questions related to such intercultural management since the missionaries would usually come into contact with representatives of different cultures who needed to be persuaded to convert to Christianity.

Like modern companies, the Jesuits first needed to identify the existent otherness before they could try to address it (Barmeyer & Frankling, 2016a). Competencies and resources can only be channeled toward these needs once they have been identified. The "handling [of] cultural otherness" (Barmeyer & Frankling, 2016c), therefore, usually begins on an individual level but needs to be incorporated as an official company policy to become successful or to have a positive impact.

The Jesuits are consequently considered an early modern religious company whose aim was to convert as many people to Christianity as possible while creating structures allowing them to finance these activities. Intercultural management was necessary to achieve these aims, as the Jesuits were acting as foreign managers in a culturally and politically different environment. Individuals' human capital was eventually decisive for the success or failure of the established management structures in culturally different regions, namely the order's provinces of Japan and Peru.

In these provincial case studies, individuals from different cultural contexts met, and in these cases, it is, in contrast to our modern times, more than obvious from the first meetings that "[g]lobalization brings together places and people" (García Echevarría, 1999, 48). Globalization, at the same time, stimulates processes to be changed (Ibid., 50-58) and demands special reactions from companies and international organizations in particular (Ibid., 59-65). The internationalization of organizations, like the Jesuits in the early modern period, therefore, according to Barmeyer (2018), provides a threefold context of interculturality:

1) A macro context in relation to a company's or organization's overall internationalization and globalization (Ibid., 17-19),

2) A meso context for international organizations (Ibid., 20-26), and

3) A micro context for international management (Ibid., 27-30).

A closer look at the latter is of particular interest to the present study of intercultural management by the Jesuits in Japan and Peru during the sixteenth and early seventeenth centuries. Regardless of such perspectives, Dominguez and Mayrhofer (2017) emphasized that the internationalization of companies is not always a stringent process, and global success often depends on more than just the micro context as such. Specific management and marketing strategies demand changes due to a change in local and/or global contexts (Ivens & Mayrhofer, 2003), especially when strategies fail to address a culturally different context. The fact that companies and their respective entry-mode strategies might fail due to national and cultural prejudices by the company's management (Mayrhofer, 2004) makes it obvious that managers have to think about cultural differences and interculturality, just as the Jesuits had to do more than 400 years ago.

Managers need to develop cultural sensitivity because "[d]ecision making, project planning, conducting a meeting and giving feedback to a member of staff are examples of universal management activities, yet they all become more challenging when managers are working across corporate and/or national cultural borders because they may be achieved in culture-specific ways" (Holzmüller, 1997, 263). Holzmüller further outlined why interculturality demands culturally sensitive management to secure a company's success in a culturally different context:

> When people encounter not just a foreign language and a different communication style but different ways of acting and managing, this can be very burdensome. In a tourist situation, interactional differences

often result in only passing discomfort, but in business, much more is usually at stake. The success of the company's or client's business, the harmony of significant relationships, the jobs of staff and colleagues and/or indeed one's own, are among the things which may be endangered through culturally influenced, dysfunctional management interaction. (Ibid.)

Considering the possible impact – negative or positive – of interculturality, it is therefore not surprising that numerous studies have focused on company performances in relation to society (Whitley, 1999; Maurice & Sorge, 2000) and, just as importantly, to culture (D'Iribarne, 1994; 2009; Hofstede, Hofstede & Minkov, 2010). That not only the managerial level of a company or organization is impacted by cultural aspects has also been emphasized by Barmeyer and Mayrhofer, who argued that "the history of a country, its identity and related set of values constitute a framework of reference which conditions and gives meaning to the stakeholders' social practices, even within the organization and its actors" (2014, 430). D'Iribarne et al. (2020, 1-3) similarly emphasized the importance of culture for modern management decisions, and it is not surprising that it was of special importance for the managerial work of the Jesuits in the sixteenth and seventeenth centuries as well.

While management itself can usually be closely tied to the specific cultures of its origin (Ibid., 13-14), it is not only the cultural origin of a company that defines successful intercultural management. Barmeyer, Bausch, and Mayrhofer recently pointed out that

> [o]rganizations are increasingly permeated by interculturality, and their actors are becoming more intercultural in their work and practices. Although globalization has, to some extent, led to harmonization and standardization in social, cultural, and economic spheres, cultural diversity remains present in organizations. These differences can neither be denied nor minimized.... (2021, 1)

They also highlighted that "interculturality plays a central role within and between organizations, and actors need new approaches of how to deal with cultural diversity" (Ibid.). In other words, companies and organizations that do not accept the importance of interculturality will automatically lose chances to penetrate new and handle existent global markets successfully. Like many other aspects with regard to managerial procedures within companies, interculturality also needs to be managed, as it "emerges from cultural diversity and reflects the processes and outcomes of diverse groups. If not managed in an appropriate way, interculturality can be irritating and conflicting due to diverging values, expectations, norms, meanings and interpretations of actors" (Ibid.). To avoid problems based on different cultural contexts, it is important to prepare managers for intercultural activities.

Grosskopf and Barmeyer (2021, 2) made it clear that interculturality is sometimes hard to pay tribute to as an analytical category for researchers, as an analysis of cross-cultural management practices would also necessitate an intercultural approach. Thomas stated that "[c]ulture as an orientation system structures a specific field of action for the individual belonging to that society, thereby creating the conditions for the development of independent forms for mastering the individual milieu" (1988, 149, cited in Fink & Meierwert, 2004, 65). Cultural standards, as formulated in the national contexts of a particular manager, eventually determine their cross-cultural interactions (Fink & Meierwert, 2004, 65). It is consequently not surprising that the study of culture in relation to management aspects became more important due to the rise of the multinational corporation (MNC), "an artifact of modern society that may translate the theories of one culture into practice in others" (Lane, 1980, 62). Business problems in a more and more globalized world were often related to "cultural insensitivity" (Ibid.), and companies were interested in avoiding them. Due to the interest in these issues, "remedies usually focus[ed] on increasing sensitivity to the host culture to improve managers' interpersonal communication skills" (Ibid.). However, Lane has emphasized that management systems' relations to culture were often unclear, and since culture as a category was hard to work with, some companies – like the Jesuits in the present case – had to deal with problems first before further research could stimulate understanding and thereby a possibly more successful management strategy that addressed the specific necessities of the culturally different space into which one wanted to expand. Furthermore, companies had the possibility to address cultural issues using different administrative subsystems (Lane, 1980, 64):

a) **Strategy**: This is the way in which an organization chooses to relate itself to its external environment. It encompasses such things as the firm's chosen niche in its industry and the control of critical factors for competing successfully in that niche, the way in which the firm develops resources, and the mode in which the political and social environments are "read" and approached.

b) **Structure**: This is the division of labor, hierarchy, and integrating mechanisms used by the firm.

c) **Measurement Systems**: These are the task-related information and control systems and the employee performance appraisal and evaluation systems.

d) **Reward Systems**: This is the firm's constellation of job assignment, compensation, sanction, and promotion practices.

e) **Selection and Development System**: This includes recruiting, selection, training, and development practices.

Administrative systems apply whenever managers attempt to link their company or organization to the specific context they act in, as they also do between the company and its employees as well as the latter and their respective tasks, but they demand more or less intercultural sensitivity as well according to the cultural space they are operating in (Lane, 1980, 64). Simply put, the more cultural differences exist within the existent administrative systems, the more intercultural competences are demanded of the leading managers. This makes intercultural management a basic necessity for the success of a globally operating company.

Intercultural management, following the definition of Engelhard (2018), "is part of international management. In contrast to the latter, intercultural management is not aimed at coordinating the company vis-à-vis its entire environment (economic, technical, legal environment, etc.) but exclusively at the environmental segment of 'culture.' The aim of intercultural management is the successful handling of management problems in interculturally overlapping situations." Culture as such works as a "communicatively conveyed, dynamic orientation system that provides basic assumptions about human existence, values, norms and symbols" (Ibid.), but which can be perceived according to national or regional differences and therefore must be defined by interculturally successful managers in and for their respective context of operation, which does not mean that they automatically have to adopt foreign cultural values or deny their own ones. They do, however, have to act in a mode of awareness with regard to these differences.[1]

Barmeyer, Bausch, and Mayrhofer outline in this respect that "[i]ntercultural management ... considers all the processes that emerge between actors from different cultures. While comparing cultures, it also considers the underlying dynamics and outcomes of intercultural interaction, whether positive or negative. It thus takes into account both the interaction of individuals and the

---

[1] Thomas (2014) defined cross-cultural management, a term also used in the literature, as follows: "Cross-cultural management is the study of management in a cross-cultural context. It includes the study of the influence of societal culture on managers and management practice as well as the study of the cultural orientations of individual managers and organization members. At the individual level, individuals' values as well as their understanding of and reactions to their cultural context and experience figure prominently."

evolutionary character of social systems" (2021, 4). From a managerial perspective, the global and multinational operations of companies or organizations – within them, cultural aspects also determine the development of power relations (Barmeyer & Mayrhofer, 2010; 2020) – make interculturality inevitable and therefore demands relevant strategies to transplant an existent company-related management and operational culture to a market or sphere of operation based on different cultural norms. According to Engelhard (2018), companies and leading management representatives can develop different strategic plans to achieve this aim:

1. **Monocultural strategy**: The corporate culture of the home base is transferred to the foreign branch, as a result of which one sees one's own corporate culture as dominant compared to the foreign one and, through appropriate management activities, ensures that a corporate culture that is identical to that of the parent company is created in its foreign branches.

2. **Multicultural strategy**: Subsidiaries develop their own corporate culture and adapt it according to their own national culture. The result is a situation in which the subsidiaries might even have a completely different corporate culture to the parent company.

3. **Mixed culture strategy**: A cultural mix takes place between the subsidiaries and the parent company, resulting in a uniform corporate culture. In contrast to pure monoculturalism, which amounts to a cultural export from the parent company to the daughters, cultural synthesis takes place here.

Considering these strategies, it is not surprising that theories related to aspects of intercultural management were and are often formulated in relation to functional area-specific concepts (Engelhard, 1997), although culture did not play a prominent role in management-related research early on (Tab. 2.1).

Although in-depth research related to questions of intercultural management is relatively young, the field became more important after the 1960s, especially since it does not consider management solely to be a business-related issue but also as a "culture-related field of shaping" (*kulturabhängiges Gestaltungsfeld*, Barmeyer, 2018, 31) for company strategies and organizations. With regard to the research foci on culture and management, there are numerous possibilities at hand, of which intercultural management is probably the most sophisticated and ambitious (Tab. 2.2).

Tab. 2.1: The development of cultural management research (Barmeyer, 2018, 31-32).

Time Period	Starting Level	Stage	Approach
Pre-1960		"Cultural ignorance" of business management	Culture as a non-existent phenomenon
Since 1960	Macro level	Cross-cultural management	Culture-free management approach Culture-bound management approach (national culture as an independent variable)
Since 1970		Comparative management	Correlation between national culture and managerial behavior
Since 1980	Micro level	Research related to business culture	Research/influencing of business culture without national context
Since 1990	Macro and micro level	Cultural integration	Correlations between managerial and national culture
Since 2000	Global level	Cultural pointillism	Consideration of small cultural units that determine different perceptions of culture
Since 2010	Embedded micro level	Cultural situativity	Companies frame their own individual culture depending on strategy and context

Tab. 2.2: Research approaches toward cultural aspects of management (Barmeyer, 2018, 32-33, in reference to Adler, 1983).

Research	Cultural reference of the studies	Approach regarding similarity or difference	Central research question
Close	Studies with regard to single cultures	Assumed similarity	How do people act in relation to work in organizations or companies?
Ethnocentric	Studies with regard to a second culture	Search for similarities	Can theories from one's own national context be applied in foreign cultural contexts?
Polycentric	Studies with regard to many cultures	Search for differences	How do managers and employees work in a specific country?
Comparative	Studies for the comparison of (many) different cultures	Search for similarities and differences	To what extent is the behavior of managers and employees different or similar across cultures?
Geocentric	Studies in international management	Search for similarities	How do international organizations function?
Synergetic	Studies in intercultural management	Use of similarities and differences as resources	How can intercultural actions be managed in national or international companies and organizations?

In an analysis of two leading management journals, namely the *International Journal of Cross Cultural Management* and *Cross Cultural and Strategic Management*, between 2001 and 2018, Barmeyer, Bausch, and Moncayo (2019) showed that studies in cross-cultural management mainly focus on corporate culture, human resource management, and cultural dimensions. These studies tend to follow "four major research paradigms: positivist, interpretivist, postmodern, and critical" (Romani, Barmeyer, Primecz & Pilhofer, 2018, 2). These paradigms are based on the following assumptions:

1. The **positivist** paradigm in cross-cultural research defines cultures as self-contained, separate, and stable phenomena comprised of distinct characteristics that can be observed, measured, and manipulated (Ibid., 3).

2. Shared sense-making of experience stands at the heart of **interpretive** studies of culture. Cultures are seen as interpretive frameworks that are shared within a group by those with a common socialization yet who also differ in their social positions and opinions (Ibid., 4).

3. Similar to interpretive work, studies inspired by **postmodernism** emphasize a local understanding. They value context-specific, rich descriptions of cases while including stronger assertions on ambiguity, fluidity, and constant transformation, as well as immanent contradiction (Ibid., 5).

4. Studies in the **critical** paradigm share the emphasis on the relationship between power, knowledge, and theory with research that results from a postmodern inspiration. However, in contrast to postmodernism, critical theories are inclined to draw upon grand narratives because they focus on power dichotomies, oppression, and reproduction of the status quo, investigating how power structures (e.g., social, economic, military, and political) influence management (Ibid., 7).

Regardless of the mentioned developments and diverse approaches toward the interrelationship between culture and management, there were also conflicts concerning the importance the former should have in management research. While Oberg (1963, 142) emphasized the role of cultural differences, England and Lee (1974) supported the convergence hypothesis,[2] and Negandhi (1975) argued that there are socio-cultural variables that determine management policies. At the same time, many studies were in fact national studies that did not focus too much on cultural differences (Kelley & Worthley, 1981, 165). With regard to the importance of the latter, two different comparative management models developed, namely that of Farmer and Richman (1965), which described culture as one of the major variables for the effectiveness of a company's or organization's management, and that of Negandhi and Prasad (1971), which considered management philosophies to be independent factors within companies or organizations. Later studies attempted to combine both

---

[2] For a survey of this hypothesis, see Rassekh (1998).

models (Kelley & Worthley, 1981, 167-169), although until the 1980s, as mentioned above, many studies remained cross-national rather than cross-cultural at their level of analysis (Negandhi, 1983, 19).

Furthermore, many studies have considered intercultural aspects to be a disadvantage for companies and organizations for a long time, while recent works tend to emphasize that intercultural management can have a positive effect as long as the managers in question receive some kind of training, which has been considered to provide a possibility to increase business efficiency in culturally different operational contexts (Kiryakova-Dineva & Hadzhipetrova-Lachova, 2017). Companies and organizations that operate on a global market realize and accept the necessity for a constructive interculturality that, according to Barmeyer, Bausch and Mayrhofer (2021, 4), develops in the following three steps:

1. Awareness and understanding of culture and cultural differences,
2. Gaining experience through examples and practices, and
3. Designs and options for strategic action.

Due to the fact that "intercultural management is framed by the context of internationalization and globalization[,] people and organizations from different countries and continents interact in the political, social, and economic field of a global world" (Ibid., 8), especially since a lack of intercultural sensitivity might severely damage the business and management performance of the respective company or organization.

Considering these necessities, there is a crucial debate about convergence or divergence as guiding principles in intercultural management (Barmeyer & Mayrhofer, 2008; 2020). The two central questions related to these debates are the following: "Do global transfer and diffusion processes lead to the gradual approximation of people and organizations across the world, that is, are they becoming more uniform? Or do specific nations and cultures come up with their own ways of dealing with cultural diversity, maintaining their uniqueness?" (Barmeyer, Bausch & Mayrhofer, 2021, 11). The impact of the two factors can often be identified for single managers, as "individuals are influenced by the two mechanisms of alignment and differentiation as well as the convergence and divergence of cultural influences, which lead to value changes in society" (Ibid., 12).

The named issues and questions, however, become naturally more pressing for companies that have a strong international business interest because they are "embedded in intra- and inter-organizational networks with a variety of actors marked by different cultural backgrounds" (Ibid., 13; see also Buckley, 2018). Although there are three different types of market entry modes a company can choose from for its initial penetration into a foreign and culturally different market – namely, export activities, strategic alliances, and wholly-owned subsidiaries (Barmeyer, Bausch & Mayrhofer, 2021, 13) – its management will without any doubt be confronted by "intercultural challenges in cross-border operations" (Ibid., 14-16).

Research on intercultural management consequently not only offers multiple aspects and methods to analyze a company's or organization's intercultural performance (Barmeyer, 2018, 115-138) but also a possibility to strengthen its business efficiency in more and more internationalized and globalized markets. Regardless of the debates about "culture-bound" or "culture-free" (Hickson, Hinings, McMillan & Schwitter, 1974; Maurice & Sorge, 2000), convergent or divergent business practices in the past (D'Iribarne et al., 1998; Inglehart & Welzel, 2005), companies and organizations have to deal with a certain level of interculturality at multiple levels of their respective organizational systems and practices because global businesses cannot evade a certain degree of interculturality today (Barmeyer, 2018, 9). In actual working situations, this interculturality might cause problems and misunderstandings that hinder a company or organization from achieving its goals; however, there is also a constructive understanding of interculturality, which offers chances to improve business performances (Ibid., 9-10; see also Barmeyer & Franklin, 2016b). While the constructive side of intercultural management has long been ignored or its synergetic effects treated rather marginally (e.g., Gannon & Newman, 2002; Peterson & Søndergaard, 2008; Smith, Peterson & Thomas, 2008; Bhagat & Steers, 2009) and the negative consequences of interculturality have been stressed (Stahl & Tung, 2015; Chanlat & Pierre, 2018), recent works have focused particularly on constructive intercultural management (CIM) (Barmeyer, 2018; Barmeyer, Bausch & Mayrhofer, 2021).

CIM studies consider intercultural management as an "option to shape intercultural cooperation" (Barmeyer, 2018, 14), and CIM per se is understood as the "conscious dealing with cultural specifics and cultural diversity in organizational contexts, where, through mutual adaptation and development processes, it is possible to constructively use specifics as enriching and complementary resources in such a way that added value is created for the organizations and their actors" (Ibid.). It is therefore also assumed, in contrast to former negative perspectives on interculturality, that "cultural diversity can also lead to synergy and complementarity, in the form of creativity and innovativeness" (Barmeyer, Bausch & Mayrhofer, 2021, 1). New approaches toward CIM must almost naturally "consider interculturality and cultural differences as a *resource* and take an explicit *constructive* approach to cultural diversity. We call this new approach *constructive intercultural management*" (Ibid., emphasis in original). New approaches consequently also have to be "based on the humanistic, idealistic and normative conviction that humans, whether in their functions as managers or consultants, are able to learn and develop" (Ibid., 2), because intercultural interactions can and often do produce positive outcomes for companies and organizations as well (Barmeyer & Franklin, 2016b; Mayrhofer, 2017; see also Franklin, 2007; Spencer-Oatey & Franklin, 2009). That the Jesuits in Japan and Peru in the sixteenth and seventeenth centuries were confronted with cultural differences, some of which even outweighed those that contemporary companies or organizations encounter in more globalized markets, makes the study of Jesuit missionary work as an early modern form of intercultural management, in some cases as early forms of CIM, particularly interesting. The cultural diversities being even stronger than in the globalized twentieth and twenty-fist centuries also allows us to focus on some aspects that were particularly important for the success or failure of intercultural management practices in the two geographical contexts of early modern globalization, missionary history, and management history.

Human capital is one intangible on which a company's success is based. Of course, the modern-day category of human capital cannot easily be transferred to former times, but with regard to the current approach, it is probably the most promising to use as a theoretical frame. Armstrong defines human capital as all human abilities, whether innate or acquired attributes, whose value could be augmented by appropriate development investments (2006, 29-52). Bonfour has also already emphasized the necessity "for an integrated multidisciplinary reflection on the place of intangibles in the modern strategic analysis" (2007, 5). Since we are living in a society in which the economy reflects a "growing importance of creative workers," it is not surprising that "[t]he irruption of intangibles in the strategic field underlines the importance of competences and knowledge assets as a strong basis for the identity of the company, and thus for its competitiveness" (Bonfour, 2007, 6). In the case of the Jesuits, as emphasized above, it was human capital, as one of the company-related intangibles – even if not fully in the modern sense of the word, as they were not capitalized like today –, of the individuals and the intercultural missionary approach by the order as a whole that could determine the success of the mission (Nonaka & Reinmoeller, 1999, 22). A detailed analysis of the existent human capital and the skills that were successfully applied by missionaries in Japan or Peru will also present further insights into and illumination of the modern necessities of internationally active companies, especially SMEs.

The human capital of interest here could be the capacity to talk, read, or write in a foreign language, as well as social capacities like diplomatic skills. Cañibano et al. (1999, 11-12) defined intangibles as follows:

> "Intangible resources" which include "assets" and "skills" [i.e.,, human capital] are understood in a dynamic sense, that is companies are

undertaking activities to acquire externally or produce internally those resources, and also to measure and manage them. Although the activities undertaken are always costly, companies are not always able to measure and keep track of those costs. In general such costs are considered as "intangible investments" which can be defined as a set of expenditures (sometimes not expressed in financial terms), that may or may not appear in the corporate financial reports, and either give rise to new "intangible resources" or allow a more efficient use of existing ones. These "intangible resources" are likely to increase the future value of the company, in general and its innovation capacity in particular.

According to Sánchez et al. (2000, 312), companies define important intangibles, like human capital, in three steps:
1. The identification of intangibles,
2. The measurement of intangibles, and
3. The monitoring of related resources and activities.

With regard to human capital in particular, Wohltmann (2018) argues that this is produced through learning and training based on the spending of resources and learning-by-doing processes. In the case of the Jesuits, these processes were not centralized, as they might be in modern companies, but were instead often ad hoc reactions to specific needs in a particular geographical and chronological context. Human capital is also attached to individuals. That means that for successful intercultural management, the capabilities of single managers – in the present case, single Jesuits – were decisive.

For the Jesuits who were sent to Japan or Peru in the sixteenth and seventeenth centuries, one of the most essential intangibles that would increase their human capital as intercultural managers was their language skills. The overall human capital of a Jesuit missionary might, of course, have relied on other intangibles, e.g., social or diplomatic skills, as well, but considering the necessity to explain the basics of the Christian religion to foreigners who speak a different language, the capacity to communicate with the Japanese or indigenous people of Peru was probably the most important (Piekkari & Zander, 2005; Barmeyer, 2018, 193-199).

Scarino (2010, 324) emphasized the role of language, especially with regard to its cultural component, which "frequently comprised a generalized body of knowledge about the target country and its people, ranging from literature and the arts (high culture) to aspects of everyday life." It is therefore important to take a closer look at the language skills of the Jesuits in the respective cases, as their capacity to speak with possible converts in their own language seems to be an important aspect of determining the role of human capital in a broader sense for the success of intercultural management in the early modern period. The diversity of the Jesuits, who can be considered a global team of managers in many ways, further stimulated the development of intercultural competencies, as such teams in particular seem to develop them through their interactions within the framework of international companies (Bartel-Radic, 2006). The Jesuits were already fluent in more than one language (one being Latin, one the language of their home region/country, and maybe another language related to previous assignments), which shows that their intercultural competence seems to have been a prerequisite for their missionary work in more peripheral regions of the world. Those who had thereby shown intercultural competence, something that has been considered particularly important for successful company performance in a foreign market for decades (Black 1990; Müller 1996), were eventually sent to further missions, as the later data evaluation will also highlight.

Beyond their practicability and use in everyday business, it was consequently the study of foreign languages that must have stimulated the global competence, the global mindset to be more precise, of the Jesuit managers in question (Little & Thorne, 2017; Godwin-Jones, 2019). As internationalization is a rather complex and diverse task, it is safe to say that the capacity to communicate with the possible targets of their mission must have increased the chances of the Jesuits spreading their new religious beliefs in Asia and Latin America.

The internationalization of SMEs also demands a global mindset, which has been emphasized as an important factor for the success of market entry strategies and enterprises' expansion to culturally different markets. A global mindset, in this regard, is defined as the cognitive capacity to understand and link different cultures (Hruby, 2014). Managers who possess such a global mindset are considered particularly efficient for achieving the aims of expanding SMEs as well as larger companies (Hruby, 2013; Hruby et al., 2019). The term 'global mindset' is usually applied "either as a characteristic of top management in multinational companies that leads to better global leadership … or as a feature of SME managers that leads to successful entrepreneurial internationalisation" (Torkkeli, Nummela & Saarenko, 2018, 9). It has an impact on the decision-making process of leading managers and is therefore often considered to be a prerequisite for those who orchestrate the international expansion, especially in an SME-related context.

Regardless of greater emphasis in recent research, the global mindset remains a debated aspect of SME-related research (Andresen & Bergdolt, 2017), although it has been deemed essential for globally acting managers by some (Oviatt & McDougall, 1995; Nummela et al., 2004; Eriksson, Nummela & Saarenketo, 2014). According to Torkkeli, Nummela, and Saarenko, global mindset "[a]s a concept ... integrates the manager's openness to and articulation of multiple cultural and strategic realities on global and local levels and his/her ability to manage geographically spread operations despite this diversity" (2018, 9). Managers must therefore be able to identify existent cultural dynamics (Fang, 2010) and apply or use "culture-specific knowledge" (Hofstede, 1980) to plan entry strategies, cooperative approaches, and the continuing expansion to and exploitation of culturally different markets. If managers are aware of the existence of cultural differences and open to accepting their existence as an important factor in strategic decisions, they are supposed to be more successful with regard to their overall performance (Elo, Benjowsky, & Nummela, 2015). A global mindset, or what has also been referred to as "cultural intelligence" (Ramsey et al., 2016), must consequently "be considered a meta-capability required for successful internationalisation" (Torkkeli, Nummela, & Saarenko, 2018, 10; see also Eriksson, Nummela, & Saarenketo, 2014). If SMEs strengthen the awareness of their leading managers, they consequently increase their own success rates (Levy et al., 2007) and secure the companies' long-term success in culturally different environments.

The positive role of expanding SMEs in the global economy has been emphasized by the following two arguments (Beck, 2013, 23):

1. SMEs stimulate innovation and growth beyond their own performance, and
2. successful SMEs reduce poverty on a global scale because they create new labor opportunities in the regions they expand to (on the resource mobilization of SMEs, see Subhan, Mahmood & Sattar, 2014, 161).

At the same time, "they are constrained by institutional and market failures" (Beck, 2013, 23). This ambivalent situation regarding the performance of SMEs has increased interest in the topic since the 1990s (Oviatt & McDougall, 1994; Knight & Cavusgil, 1996), especially since a growing number of companies had to globalize their business strategies in the last several decades (Laanti, Gabrielsson, & Gabrielsson, 2007; Sumati, 2011). Most companies therefore act as "multinational firms" (Gomes & Ramaswamy, 1999) and are consequently interested in recommendations for a successful intercultural management strategy in contrast to traditional companies, which at one point expanded their market due to their success 'at home.' Furthermore, one can also observe an increase in the number of so-called born global (BG) firms (Oviatt & McDougall, 1994) that begin their international expansion immediately after their founding. Considering that most companies around the globe can be characterized either as micro, small, or medium-sized enterprises (Beck, 2013, 23), SME management, in particular, has to face global challenges now. Moreover, as has been shown by Zhou, Wu, and Luo, "international entrepreneurial SMEs are capable of exploiting global opportunities more rapidly and efficiently" (2007, 673). These enterprises, especially due to the differences that separate them from larger firms (Russo & Perrini, 2010), simply need to be innovative to remain competitive (Lefebvre & Lefebvre, 2001) and, therefore, also rely on the best possible management skills to successfully expand in culturally different market contexts.

Regardless of the increased research interest in SMEs, the issue of their definition creates problems. In the European Union (EU), 99% of all businesses are SMEs. They are defined in the EU recommendation 2003/361 and are usually separated according to staff headcount and annual turnover or balance sheet total (European Commission, 2021). The European Commission accordingly uses the categories laid out in Table 2.3 for micro, small, or medium-sized companies.

Tab. 2.3: SME categories used and recommended by the European Commission.[3]

Company Category	Staff Headcount	Turnover	Balance Sheet Total
Micro	<10	≤ € 2 m	≤ € 2 m
Small	<50	≤ € 10 m	≤ € 10 m
Medium-Sized	<250	≤ € 50 m	≤ € 43 m

However, this definition is not a universal one, and this "lack of a common definition of SMEs highlights their heterogeneity and attests to the importance of getting [a] better understanding of the main peculiarities of these companies across the world" (Dominguez & Mayrhofer, 2018a, 1). While companies with less than 500 employees in North America are considered SMEs (Berk, 2017, 13), in China, the number is usually less than 1,000. The Jesuits, who acted in small teams when a new 'market entry' was underway, can consequently be considered to range between micro and small enterprises, although the order's capacity in some world regions was medium-sized if not larger in later periods. Regardless, the definition seems to fit, especially when one considers the existent varieties related to these definitory categories (Lawrence, 2012; Beck, 2013; Chin & Lim, 2018).

---

[3] "These ceilings apply to the figures for individual firms only. A firm that is part of a larger group may need to include staff headcount/turnover/balance sheet data from that group too" (European Commission, 2021).

When one takes into consideration that the Jesuits acted like SMEs when they worked toward the globalization of Christianity, it is almost ironic that these company structures are particularly important in these regions today, as they have become developing hubs of the world economy (Hallberg, 2001). SMEs continue to play an important role today in countries like Brazil, China, and Malaysia, as well as Latin America and the Caribbean region (Siu & Liu, 2005; Lawrence, 2012; Roofe & Stone Roofe, 2016; Zhang, Ma, Wang, Li, & Huo, 2016; Rasiah & Thangiah, 2017; Chin & Lim, 2018).

In contrast to older SMEs, which, according to the Uppsala model (Johanson & Vahlne, 1977) and the innovation-related model (Cavusgil, 1984), did not internationalize immediately after their establishment and instead chose markets based on their geographical and cultural proximity (Prange & Zhao, 2018, 209-210), newer SMEs, so-called BG SMEs, defined as "young, small and medium-sized, entrepreneurial firms that, from or near founding, obtain a substantial portion of total revenue from the sale of outputs in multiple countries" (Knight & Cavusgil, 1996), begin to globalize/internationalize immediately after their foundation (Cancino, 2014, 143). They consequently internationalize much faster and use existent knowledge and networks to penetrate new markets (Andersson & Wictor, 2003; Hermel & Khayat, 2011). Considering that SMEs consequently have the choice between gradual and immediate internationalization, the Jesuits' activities fall into the second category, although they could not initially rely on a large amount of knowledge about their new 'market' of interest and therefore represent an intermediate level between an older SME and a BG SME.

The Jesuits, therefore, at the beginning of a new venture, had to deal with issues that often cause modern SMEs' market entries to fail, namely limited resources and a lack of experience in that region (Lu & Beamish, 2001; Brouthers, Nakos, & Dimitratos, 2015; Oehme & Bort, 2015). At the same time, the Jesuits had to face the "uncertainty of doing business with markets in which there are many cultural differences and institutional constraints" (St-Pierre, Lacoursière, & Veilleux, 2018, 176), which SMEs struggle with today as well. Asian markets are considered to be particularly risky in this regard. Like the Jesuits in the 16th century, SME managers and executives have to decide today where to launch their global expansion or market penetration attempt. "Transaction cost economics argues that to minimize uncertainty, enhance flexibility, and reduce costs, firms should target host countries that are geographically, socially, culturally, and/or economically similar to their home country" (Cui, Walsh & Zou, 2014, 68), but the realities and the possibility to create maximum gain demand or dictate that such actions should be ignored and instead press SMEs onto markets that are much riskier as they are culturally different. The market entry, and if it is a successful one, depends on taking cultural differences seriously into consideration (Johnson & Tellis, 2008), and although many SMEs try to avoid such an entry into a market they consider too risky, an entry into a region or country that is considered culturally closer and "easier" does not automatically guarantee success (Cui, Walsh, & Gallion, 2011). Cui, Walsh, and Zou also emphasized that the latter markets might also be "saturated and the competition may be too intense for SMEs with limited resources" (2014, 68), so a culturally more different and difficult yet relatively uncontested market could offer more gains, regardless of the possibly higher risk involved.

An SME that intends to accept this risk must nevertheless be aware of aspects to be considered for a successful internationalization strategy (Cavusgil & Zou 1994; Zou & Cavusgil 2002). A market entry, and this was understood by the Jesuits, who gathered information in the regions they intended to expand their missionary work to, depends on valuable information about the market, which can be hard to gather properly due to several forms of distance, i.e., geographical, cultural, or economic (Kalafsky, 2017, 1135). It is consequently no surprise that SMEs' "management practices tend to be highly contextualised," and, as the present study will show, so were the Jesuit management strategies in the sixteenth century. Successful intercultural management that addresses a foreign and culturally different market has to find ways to answer to the specific needs or local contexts and risks of these markets (Li & Quian, 2008). It is therefore essential to seek local partners who are able to provide "local knowledge," i.e., a proper insight into the market that is supposed to be opened up (Sestu, Majocchi, & D'Angelo, 2018, 66). Such markets are not easy to deal with, as the risks for the expanding SMEs are possibly increased by a "lack of international experience" and the "psychic distance between home and host countries" (Ibid., 67). The latter risks may vary, depending on the reasons for the SME to enter a culturally different market, namely

1) resource-seeking investments,
2) market-seeking investments,
3) efficiency-seeking investments, or
4) asset-seeking investments. (Dunning, 1992, cited in Sestu, Majocchi, & D'Angelo, 2018, 63-64)

What is particularly important, regardless of the SME's aims and size (Chiao, Lo, & Yu, 2010; Majocchi, Mayrhofer, & Camps, 2013), is the market entry and the entry mode into the foreign market (Root, 1977; Rasheed, 2005; Aharoni & Brock, 2010) because "[s]electing the mode of international market entry is, alongside the market entered, among the most important decisions an internationalizing firm has to make" (Ahi, Baronchelli, Kuivalainen, & Piantoni, 2017, 1). Hennart and Slangen (2015) point out that entry mode decisions and

Literature Review

the relevant processes are often still unknown, although it is clear that the aim of such a decision is the internationalization of an SME's business (Chetty, Ojala & Leppäaho, 2015). The main factors in the process, however, are known and have been debated in the literature (Ahi, Baronchelli, Kuivalainen, & Piantoni, 2017, 3):

1) information scarcity (Gabrielsson & Gabrielsson, 2013; Child & Hsieh, 2014)
2) resource availability (Evers & O'Gorman, 2011)
3) decision-maker's leadership characteristics and interpretations of the environment (Oviatt & McDougall, 1994; Child & Hsieh, 2014)
4) entrepreneur's prior knowledge, experience, and business and social networks (Evers & O'Gorman, 2011)
5) hybrid governance structures in SMEs, in which decisions are made with partners (Nummela et al., 2014)
6) goal setting (Gabrielsson & Gabrielsson, 2013)

Next to these aspects, speed also plays an important role in a market entry (Casillas & Acedo 2013; Casillas & Moreno-Menéndez 2014; Hilmersson & Johanson, 2016), and this can be fast when an SME also uses local knowledge instead of trying to gather all necessary insight by itself. The Jesuits were very often fast because they both provided a global mindset necessary for an expansion in a culturally different environment and relied on the knowledge provided by "local agents" who supported them during the entry period. In this regard, the Jesuits resembled international new ventures (INVs) that "operate internationally from their inception and internationalize faster than traditional models predict" (Hilmersson & Johanson, 2016, 68). The "host country" for an SME expansion must also fit the latter's "exploration and exploitation strategies" (Cui, Walsh, & Zou, 2014), and cultural diversity is usually considered an obstacle for the best possible match in this regard. The Jesuits were able to address this through the innovation of their missionary strategies, which needed to be adjusted to the respective local contexts, highlighting that the idea that expanding SMEs have to adapt and innovate their own internationalization policies to be successful is not something new at all (Louart & Martin, 2012; Hagen, Denicolai, & Zucchella, 2014; Rask 2014). Expanding SMEs must consequently also take care of the management of innovation as part of their internationalization processes (Kunttu & Torkkeli, 2015, 84).

As "internationalization in SMEs is a complex phenomenon" (Zhou, Wu & Luo, 2007, 674) that relies early on upon networks and the exchange of knowledge (Ellis, 2000) – Zhou, Wu, and Luo (2007) also recommend considering the role of social networks for the successful internationalization of SMEs (see also Adler & Kwon, 2002) –, it is important not to forget the role of local foreign intermediaries (Ellis, 2000; Ellis & Pecotich, 2001), e.g., translators, who play an important role in a successful market entry of an expanding SME.

Taking the previous aspects for successful intercultural management into account, one has to emphasize that managers who can combine human capital, and language skills in particular, with a global mindset that allows them to apply the necessary flexibility to address different cultural settings, especially those culturally far away from their home country, and to achieve the expected results in a more and more global world. SMEs that intend to expand globally will consequently need to pay attention to managerial skills related to and determined by human capital, language skills, and a global mindset. Entry into foreign and often culturally different markets dictates a precautious selection process and subsequent measures to establish sufficient awareness of existing interculturality and the means to overcome obstacles that could be presented by cultural diversity. Considering the presented literature in the different fields of research, it is important from a management perspective to increase the number of culturally aware managers, especially within the higher company management.

Only if such measures are applied will an expanding SME's local management be flexible enough to guarantee the successful penetration of a so far unknown market without endangering the company's success due to a lack of intercultural sensitivity. The combination of human capital in general, language skills in particular, and a global mindset will allow the leading managers of expanding SMEs to change and adapt the latter's strategy if necessary, and probably in a rather proactive manner.

Chapter 3

Research Model and Outlook to the Methodology

As mentioned before, the present book provides a comparative historical documentary analysis and a longitudinal case study (Bartel-Radic & Lesca, 2011) of the Jesuits' missionary activities in the order's provinces of Japan and Peru in the sixteenth and seventeenth centuries, and it will especially consider the role of human capital and intercultural management on the success of these activities. These two examples have been chosen in order to evaluate the role of the named factors better: while the Japanese government undermined the position of the religious congregation in Japan and eventually became very hostile, the Peruvian case was instead one of success for the missionary and educational approach of the Society of Jesus. The following study will consequently study this question through the lens of organization and management theory. Nevertheless, the context of each case will be presented to highlight the cultural space in which the missionaries' activities took place and to make sure that it is better understood by an unfamiliar reader.

Tab. 3.1: Description of the main aspects of the present book.

Research Question	What impact did human capital and a global mindset have on the success of Jesuit missionary work in sixteenth- and seventeenth-century Japan and Peru?
Definitions	Human capital (first and foremost language-related skills); global mindset (based on previous experience and dogmatic flexibility)
Method	Comparative historical longitudinal case studies for two order provinces
Data collection	Data collection for more than 200 individuals in Japan and Peru who were active in three different periods (entry period, consolidation period, period of decline)

Research Design

Considering the above-mentioned paradigms for cross-cultural research, the present study does not per se intend to follow a positivist one, as the author does not consider culture to be a static element, although the diversity between the Jesuits and the indigenous population in Japan and Peru can be considered more intense than would be the case today. Since cultures are "interpretive frameworks" and since this becomes visible in both cases, the main paradigm that is applied is the postmodernist one, as both cases are studied in their local context, taking into account the everyday interaction, i.e., communication, between the Jesuits and the people they intend to convert. The presented study consequently follows an interpretive-postmodern paradigm.

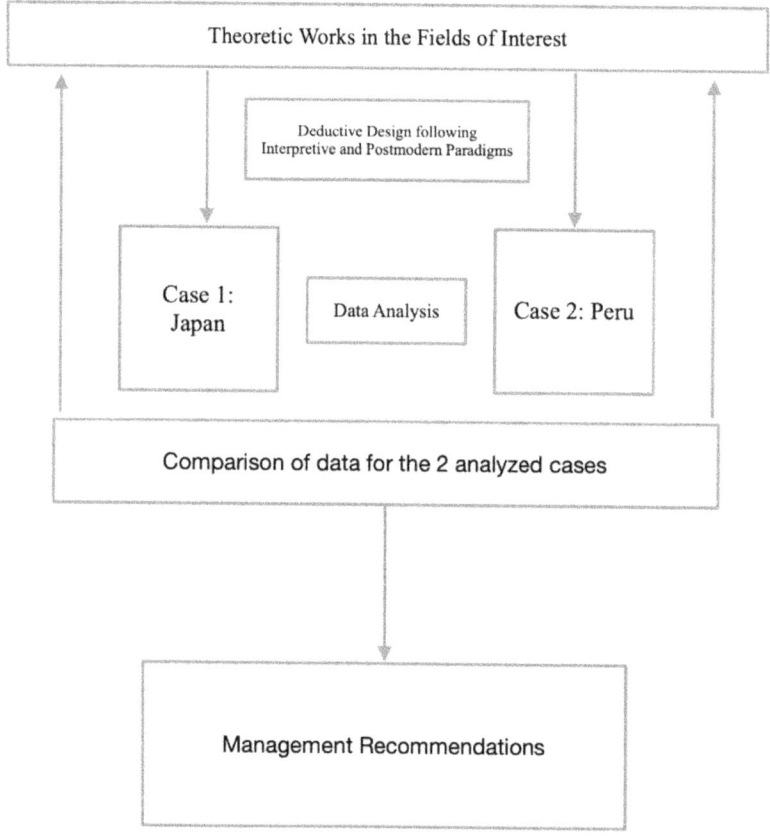

Fig. 3.1: Operationalization of the project.

The research design itself is deductive, as it is assumed that the combination of human capital, in particular, language skills, and a global mindset are important factors in securing successful intercultural management. The two detailed case studies of the Jesuits' missionary work in Japan and Peru in the sixteenth and seventeenth centuries are used in an effort to prove this assumption.

Research Model and Chosen Cases

As mentioned above, the analysis of the Jesuit missions in Japan and Peru will provide a longitudinal case study of religious and economic management in the early modern period since "[t]he prospects of profit and the truths of Christianity became linked, often uncomfortably, as merchant imperialists and Christian clergy engaged a world of diversity" (Tutino, 2021, 11. Also see Winnerling, 2014). The two Jesuit provinces have been chosen as they offer culturally different spaces that had no direct organizational connections and, therefore, allow a comparative analysis that looks at Jesuit experiences with and strategies toward interculturality. The factors of interest, i.e., the human capital and interculturality of the missionary teams, will first be gathered in their chronological context through a historical documentary analysis. The sources available will be used to condense qualitative data that will then be used to establish and better define the named factors. These will then be placed in relation to their overall impact on the missionaries' success in Japan and Peru. A comparison of the success of the missionaries in relation to human capital and intercultural management in the two specific contexts will then generate better insight with regard to the value of these two components of international management. The human capital (language skills, previous experience on missions in culturally different environments) of interest will be collected for the individuals of interest as far as available, but assumably, these will mostly be members of the higher management level.

It will also be necessary, following the theoretical considerations of Bartel-Radic and Lesca (2011), to highlight the role of the teams' variety and the existence of human capital in the work of the intercultural teams as such, which will be analyzed over a long time period. Consequently, the role of human capital on external factors and their interrelationship with intercultural competence, possibly leading to successful intercultural management, will be taken into consideration.

It is consequently also argued that the existence of human capital allows better and more effective intercultural team processes. This is supposed to impact the missionaries' effectiveness (i.e., successful intercultural management) when acting as intercultural teams in culturally different environments. One of the most important intangibles is the language capacity of the team members. As

Church-Morel and Bartel-Radic confirm, one "can also consider the degree and the nature of the language diversity and language skills of the team" when determining the "degree of cultural diversity of a team" (2014, 20). For missionaries, language skills seem to be particularly important and are considered of special interest.

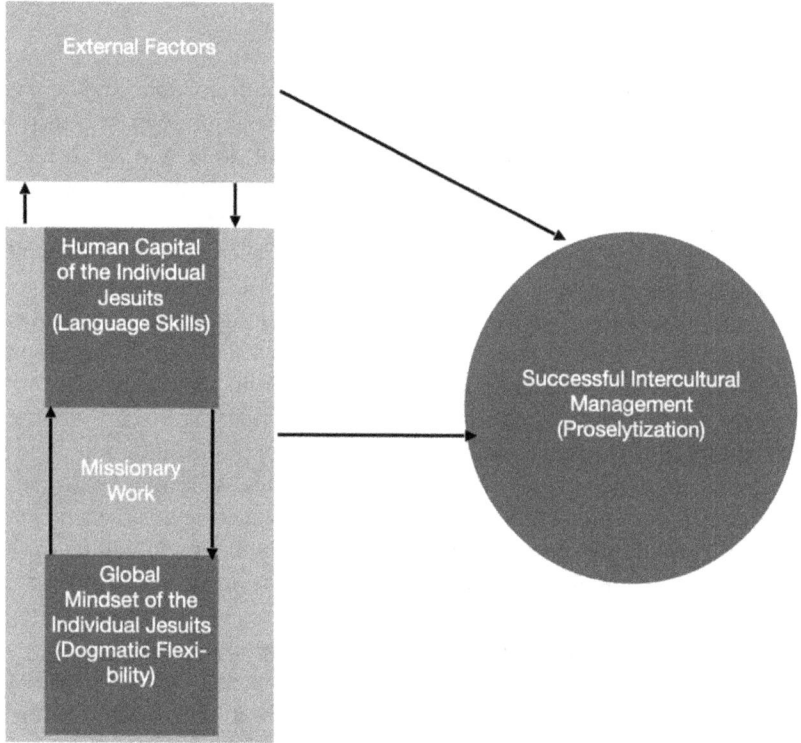

Fig. 3.2: Schematic depiction of the research model.

It is consequently also argued that the existence of human capital allows better and more effective intercultural team processes. This is supposed to impact the missionaries' effectiveness (i.e., successful intercultural management) when acting as intercultural teams in culturally different environments. One of the most important intangibles is the language capacity of the team members. As Church-Morel and Bartel-Radic confirm, one "can also consider the degree and the nature of the language diversity and language skills of the team" when determining the "degree of cultural diversity of a team" (2014, 20). For missionaries, language skills seem to be particularly important and are considered of special interest.

Methodology

The presented study will apply a comparative longitudinal case study to identify the role of human capital and a global mindset in the success of intercultural management in geographically distant and, according to the Uppsala model, inconvenient spheres of expansion (Johanson & Vahlne, 1977).

The main foci of this book are consequently twofold: identifying the human capital and global mindset as presented by the intercultural teams of the Jesuits on the one hand and the local cultural context on the other:

The Jesuits

1. The actors' human capital, first and foremost, the existence or lack of language skills and their global mindset;
2. The actions reflecting intercultural management by the Jesuits in charge, as requested by the overall organization's strategy;
3. Local ad hoc as well as strategic responses to intercultural problems by the Jesuits, and how far these correspond with the human capital and global mindset of the actors or the intercultural management policies of the organization.

The Local Perspectives

1. The believers and new converts and their reactions toward the human capital presented by the Jesuits;
2. Local elites and their reactions toward Jesuit intercultural management;
3. The economic and political geography and its impact on human capital and intercultural management opportunities.

Once these two main elements for the success or failure of the overall Jesuit intercultural management in the regions in question have been analyzed, recommendations with regard to modern-day SME strategies, especially for the planning of global entries into new markets, will be provided. The comparative longitudinal qualitative analysis will provide a clear insight into globalization processes and allow better and data-related conclusions to be made about the necessity for language education or a global mindset when it comes to the selection of leading managers for global teams in the future.

Data Analysis

The data analysis for the present study is twofold as well. In a first step, the active teams and their managers in Japan and Peru will be identified (see Appendices 9.1-6). The data necessary for this first step will be extracted from the *Monumenta Historica Japoniae* (MHJ, vol. 1), which provides the relevant data for Japan for the years between 1549 and 1654, and the *Monumenta Peruana* (vols. 1-8), which contains the pertinent data for Peru for the years between 1565 and 1604. Once the leading and documentable Jesuits, i.e., the higher management level for the missions, have been identified, existent sources, either published by themselves or documents related to their work available through source editions (Polgár, 1986, 427-473) or Jesuit archives, will be used as a basis for the intended comparative longitudinal qualitative analysis. Since this kind of data collection cannot be adjusted through additional information acquisition, the data set is limited to a certain degree, which is why only the higher management personnel can be taken into consideration.

The individual Jesuits in the respective time periods will also be presented in the book's appendices. The overall evaluation of Jesuit intercultural management, its failure or success, and the latter's relation to human capital, global mindset, or external factors will be provided in detail in the main part.

According to the historical data from the two longitudinal case studies and the respective qualitative analyses, the present book will eventually provide data-related recommendations with regard to current SME management strategies, especially ones clearly related to intercultural forms of management and expansion.

Chapter 4

The Cases

In this chapter, an analysis of the two cases of Jesuit missionary work in Japan and Peru will be presented after a short introduction to the Jesuit Order. This analysis will then be followed by detailed data on the Jesuit fathers (padres) who were active in the respective contexts in the different periods, i.e., entry period, consolidation period, and period of decline. Some important managers will then also be described in detail before the findings related to the data are briefly summarized.

4.1. The Jesuits: A Short Introduction

In 1540, Pope Paul III (1468-1549) announced the official acceptance of the Jesuit Order, a "totally new type of [religious] order" (Hartmann, 2008, 7) and, in fact, a "controversial new society" (Alden, 1996, 3-23). In contrast to other religious orders, the Jesuits were particularly flexible with regard to their missionary work and, therefore, advanced to become a "versatile shock troop of the Catholic Church" (Ibid.). In contrast to this flexibility of their missionary mindset, the structure of the society was very hierarchical, and a lot of information and data was produced and circulated to keep this structure in place (Friedrich, 2009a; Friedrich, 2009b). It was due to this character of the Jesuits that the order was very successful in its global expansion and played an important role in the globalization of Christianity after Christopher Columbus (1451-1506) arrived in the so-called "New World" in 1492 (Paul, 2014, 43-88) and Vasco da Gama (ca. 1469-1524) reached India in 1498 (Contente Domingues, 2003). At this time, the Jesuits participated in and intensified the colonization of hitherto unknown parts of the world. As the order was very strict with regard to the selection of its novices, it soon represented a kind of "Catholic elite" (Hartmann, 2008, 7) whose members were actively involved in expanding the influence of the Pope and the Catholic Church in almost all parts of the globe.

Ignatius of Loyola was the central figure in the establishment and early development of the Jesuits (Rahner, 1979; Guillermou, 1993; Tylenda, 2001; Marcuse, 2008; de Ribadeneira, 2014). After a military career and a kind of "spiritual awakening experience" after being severely wounded during the Battle of Pamplona in 1521, Ignatius laid down his sword and continued his life in poverty, following a religious path. After a pilgrimage to Barcelona and the Holy Land, at the age of 33, he decided to learn Latin to be able to apply to a university as a student. Ten years later, in 1533, he finished his degree at the

University of Paris. By that time, he had already gathered friends around him who would later help him to form the Jesuit Order, e.g., Pierre Favre of Savoy (1506-1546) and Francis Xavier (1506-1552). In 1537, the friends reached Rome and received permission from Pope Paul III to make a pilgrimage to Jerusalem (Olin, 1979). Due to political reasons, Ignatius and his friends, who had been ordained as priests in Venice, returned to Rome to take care of sick people and proselytize among the city's Jewish population. In 1538, Ignatius eventually conducted his first Holy Mass.

Fig. 4.1: Ignatius of Loyola, painting by Peter Paul Rubens (1577-1640).

It might have been his years of experience that provided him with an advantage in his demand to establish the new Jesuit Order, a task for which he received the Pope's permission in 1540, and in April of the following year, his followers and friends elected Ignatius as the order's General, a position he kept until his death in 1556. It is worth mentioning here that the order had enemies from the beginning, especially since its leading figure had been accused by the Inquisition multiple times before the order was founded. Although never considered guilty, Ignatius had been attacked before and would draw anger, e.g., from Cardinal Gian Pietro Carafa, who later became Pope Paul IV (1476-1559) (Quinn, 1981), toward the order as well, especially since the Jesuits represented competition for older religious orders at this time.

Until his death, Ignatius was able to grow the order substantially, and while there were only 40 Jesuits in 1540, their number had reached around 1,000 in around 50 branches by 1556. In addition, almost 30 Jesuit academies had been founded by that time, securing the education of and by the order's members, a number that would grow further in the following centuries (Fig. 7) (Grendler, 2019).

However, the Jesuits were not only interested in educational issues but also intended to expand the order's influence in the known and as yet unknown parts of the world. The order grew fast and, under Igantius's leadership, also expanded its influence around the globe relatively quickly. Soon, Jesuits would be active on all known continents and thereby extend the missionary activities of the Catholic Church. As the order's General, Ignatius had already established ten Jesuit provinces by 1557 (Tab. 4.1).

The Jesuit Order would continue this expansion in Europe, e.g., in the British Isles and Ireland (Kelly & Thomas, 2019; McCoog, 2019), and other parts of the world in the years after Ignatius's leadership had ended when the order's influence steadily increased. The first generations of provincial "managers" nevertheless already shows that the Jesuit Order would rely on a form of intercultural management from early on. While the provinces in Portugal and Spain were run by two "locals," namely Simão Rodrigues (1510-1579), born in Vouzela, Portugal, and Antonio Araoz, a Spanish Jesuit, respectively, the Spaniard Francis Xavier (1506-1556) was sent to India, Jerónimo Doménech (1516-1592), another man from Spain, ran the province in Sicily, while the Frenchman Paschase Broët served for some years in Italy before later being assigned the province in France. While the Dutch Jesuit Petrus Canisius (1521-1597) served in the German province, the Spanish Jesuit Andrés de Oviedo (1518-1577) was sent to Ethiopia. The early period of the Jesuit Order's expansion therefore highlights that the organization relied upon men from different cultural backgrounds, who were often sent to provinces that were different from their own cultural background. In many provinces, we can consequently observe forms of "intercultural management," and it can be said without any doubt that, at different stages of their career, several leading Jesuit "managers" would be able to increase their competencies with regard to the diverse contexts of their missionary work.

Tab. 4.1: The first ten Jesuit Order provinces.

Order Province	Date of Foundation	Provincial	Reference
Portugal	1546	Simão Rodrigues	Alden (1996)
Spain	1547	Antonio Araoz	Casalini & Pavur (2016: 55-59)
India	1549	Francisco Xavier	Fernando (2016); Županov (2016)
Italy (excluding Rome)	1551	Paschase Broët	Padberg (1997)
Sicily	1553	Jerónimo Doménech	Anonymous (1768)
Brazil	1553	Manuel de Nóbrega	McGinness (2018)
France	1555	Paschase Broët	Avon & Rocher (2017)
Lower Germany	1556	Bernard Oliver	Johnston (2016)
Upper Germany	1556	Petrus Canisius	Brodrick (1950); Oswald & Rummel (1996); Haub (2004); Leinsle (2014)
Ethiopia	1557	Andrés de Oviedo	Wolde Aregay (1998); Pennec (2003)

The success of the order was based on two things: 1) a centralized organization that was led by Ignatius from Rome, and, at the same time, 2) a certain degree of flexibility concerning the methods the Jesuits could apply to their missionary work (Hartmann, 2008, 17). Regardless of these early successes, Ignatius was not very successful with regard to the order's finances, and, often, money remained a problem. This also stimulated independent actions by the order's provincial leaders to secure a local income. Consequently, the Jesuits were not only active as missionaries but would often also develop an economic agenda. This fact further highlights the character of the global missionary ventures of the Jesuit Order as those of an expanding company that was not solely interested in the Christian mission. It would also need financial assets to finance its provincial activities and the respective structures.

The Jesuit Order was also something totally new with regard to the demands made by its members. While older orders usually centralized their members in monasteries, prayed together, and shared the same clothing, the Jesuits were relatively liberal about such demands. This aroused criticism and suspicion from other religious orders and often led to conflict (Tronu Montane, 2015), but it also provided the order with more flexibility, especially when adaptations needed to be made in different cultural contexts (Zampol D'Ortia, 2020). The order's members were relatively flexible, and the focus on the individuum – in a way representing the ideals of the Renaissance – supported Ignatius's agenda. Members of the order had to commit themselves by their vow to serve the order and the Pope in any region of the world. Mobility was thereby granted by the acceptance of new members, who, vice versa, were willing to serve wherever they were sent. If the comparison is allowed here, the Jesuit Order thereby presented a kind of early modern and Catholic "Foreign Legion," and it has recently been emphasized that the transoceanic voyage can also be considered as an essential ritual, a "rite de passage into missionary manhood" (Strasser, 2020, 79-112).

The religious management of the order allowed its members to act quickly, establish new order provinces, and have dogmatic flexibility with regard to their appearance, but the way they presented Christianity in the new spheres of their work also made their missionary attempts relatively successful. Early on, Ignatius had therefore created a new "international type of order" (Hartmann, 2008, 20). Although the centralized structures demanded strict obedience, Jesuits only had to follow orders if they were in compliance with the Christian order and rules, in particular, the Ten Commandments. All in all, the local developments were closely related to the order's provincials and their decisions, as distance played a more important role than it does today. It consequently took longer for changes with regard to existent problems to be able to be addressed by the central authorities, especially once the Jesuit Order had begun to spread its work and influence across continents (Quattrone, 2004).

Peter C. Hartmann (2008, 22-26) describes the structures of the Jesuit Order and refers to them as those of a "centralist world order" (*zentralistischer Weltorden*) whose representatives were active missionaries for the Catholic Church in all known parts of the world. The order's "troop" was very international in character, and members from all parts of Europe were sent abroad, where they encountered new cultural settings and had to adjust their missionary agenda to reach possible converts, using different languages and cultural codes to successfully preach the message of the Bible and the story of Jesus Christ and the Lord. The internationality of the order and its structures was quite modern, considering that the Jesuits expanded their influence like modern-day companies tend to extend their access globally to international markets. Further similarities can be emphasized since the order's provinces needed to be self-financed and could not expect financial support from Rome, where Ignatius, as described earlier, was often struggling with financial problems himself.

Another of the aspects that stimulated the Jesuit success with regard to the conversion of non-Christians in all parts of the world was the emphasis of the order on the presentation of Jesus as well as Christianity as a comforting institution and pastoral care as an essential element to provide consolation for believers. Ignatius put an emphasis on two aspects that should determine the work of the Jesuits, i.e., the glory of God and the common good (Hartmann, 2008, 29), and he thereby established or paved the way for a certain "Jesuit culture" (O'Reilly, 2020, 378) the men of the order were supposed to follow in the centuries after his death. In addition to their pastoral care, the Jesuits also began to establish colleges and universities early on to educate young men according to these new values and the order provided in particular for possible future members (Donnelly, 2006, 32-63). That the Jesuits replicated such educational attempts in the non-European world, e.g., in Latin America (Klaiber, 2009) in general and Peru in particular (Ghelarducci, 2020), made and still makes them particularly attractive as co-operational partners in many regions of the globe. It is therefore not surprising that the number not only of converts but also of Jesuits increased tremendously within the first 100 years of the order's existence (Tab. 4.2).

Tab. 4.2: The number of Jesuits within the first century of the order's existence (Hartmann, 2008, 30).

Year	Number of Jesuits
1540	40
1556	1,000
1570	3,000
1590	6,000
1640	15,000

Of course, the Jesuit success was related to the foreign expansion of the European powers from the late 1400s, but the order and its members actively influenced these developments as well. It is this interrelation between religiously motivated missionary work, the expansion of territorial rule, i.e., colonialism, and the economic penetration of foreign and culturally unfamiliar regions that makes the Jesuits comparable to modern SMEs and their attempts to increase their influence in such markets. Since this book intends to analyze the success of the Jesuit Order's intercultural management and the role of the human capital of the provincial 'top managers' in Japan and Peru, it seems to be in order here to outline some of the similarities relating to present-day SMEs to emphasize the analytical possibilities from a modern-day managerial perspective.

4.2. Japan

In East Asia, the Jesuit Order's expansion followed that of the Portuguese Empire (Alden, 1996). Henry the Navigator (1394-1460) laid the foundations for the success of Portugal's sailors who reached the Cape of Good Hope in 1488 and paved the way for Vasco da Gama's journey to India (da Gama, 2009), where the latter arrived ten years later. From there, the Portuguese Empire spread its influence across the Indian Ocean and established a regional harbor and trade post network in Southeast Asia (Newitt, 2005; Sousa Pinto, 2012), gaining extensively from the trade in the region, and the export of luxurious goods – silk, spices, porcelain, tea, etc. – would fill the pockets of European traders in the centuries to come (Disney, 2010; Canepa, 2016). The Portuguese had succeeded in "systematically establishing a network of factories and fortresses all over the world, directly or indirectly connected with Lisbon by regular maritime routes" (Loureiro, 2000, 155), and the Jesuits would eventually gain from this network in the order's Asian context, just as the Jesuit missionaries in Latin America had initially gained from the presence of Spanish conquistadors and colonial authorities. As mentioned before, a willingness to travel was essential for members of the Jesuit Order, and many young men realized the possibilities this would present to them, especially since "Jesuits were supposed to spend the rest of their lives on the selected missionary fields. This meant that they were completely set on dedicating their life to religious tasks" (Ibid., 156), but at the same time they also received a chance to do something challenging, away from the cultural sphere of their upbringing. The motives for such an important decision were, without any doubt, diverse, and the outlook for future adventures might only have been one of them. Regardless of this fact, as Boscariol emphasized, "given the embryonic stage and the reduced number of individuals involved, the missionaries sent to these missions had a similar background and an equivalent educational formation," while their destination in some culturally unfamiliar space demanded "that their rules would need to have some flexibility, being adaptable to the distinct realities encountered" (2017, 62).

Early on, the Japanese case was considered a positive example of the Jesuits' missionary work in faraway regions of the world, especially since it provided some insight with regard to the necessities of some kind of "cultural acclimatization" or "acculturation" (Alberro, 1992; Alves Filho & Milton, 2005) by the missionaries. In that sense, the Jesuits in Japan resemble managers of a modern-day SME who are sent to a culturally unfamiliar space, where they often face the same problems as the Jesuits hundreds of years before. A look at this historical case will consequently also allow some recommendations to be made for currently expanding SMEs with a special interest in Asian markets. It was and is important that the people responsible for a successful expansion, i.e., business and mission managers alike, were and are dogmatically flexible and culturally open. In the case of the Jesuits, these were actually essential preconditions expected from the order's leadership; however, these demands would not always be fulfilled in the respective foreign context. However, "in different territories we can recognize missionaries who demonstrated not only a distinct talent but also disposition to learn the indigenous languages, as others who tried to adapt their behavior and style in order to follow the precepts of the local culture" (Boscariol, 2017, 65). Nevertheless, as Boscariol correctly emphasizes, "this kind of initiative was organic precisely in the attitude of those missionaries working outside Europe, as it was an approach that only could flourish in a completely different context from the one of their origin" (Ibid.). The study of such an "organic case" can therefore offer valuable insight for future SME-related strategies as well, and the experiences gathered by the Jesuits in their East Asian provinces give valuable insight into the problems that could be faced in the twenty-first century in this region as well, especially with regard to the tasks required for successful intercultural management.

The missionary work by the Jesuits in Japan consequently offers valuable knowledge, especially since it shows that there was not a centralized strategy in existence yet, but the respective representatives of the Jesuit Order had to address existent problems. At the same time, however, their success was also determined by external factors, as the following closer analysis will show. Considering the work of the missionaries in the regions far away from the clerical centers of power in Southern Europe, it is not surprising that the provincial authorities, while acting on behalf of the Catholic Church, needed to get involved in economic ventures as well, because they needed to finance their own activities without any support from Rome, particularly during the early years of the Jesuits' activities in East Asia, when the latter could not expect economic support either from the Order General or the Pope. Regardless of these obstacles, the order successfully established a "worldwide presence, with 372 colleges and 123 residences for its

The Cases

estimated 13,000 members" (O'Malley, 1994) in 1615. It is ironic that this first climax of Jesuit influence around the world was achieved when the Japanese authorities banned the order from Japan, and missionaries who did not leave the country were soon persecuted and killed.

Beforehand, however, the Jesuits had not only been successful in converting a large number of Japanese – ca. 300,000 – but also in engaging with and gaining from the existent trade networks that connected Japan with Macao on the one hand and Manila on the other (Campos, 2007, 96; Tronu Montane, 2012a: 257; Tremml-Werner, 2015). Japan was gradually included in a more and more global trade system, and the Jesuits could use this development for their own economic purposes, although this involvement also caused some issues, e.g., the trading of Japanese slaves (Ehalt, 2017). However, the order's financing in Japan could only be secured by sharing trade profits, especially the ones related to the *nao do trato*, the galleon that regularly sailed from Macao to Japan (Moran, 1993, 43-44). Years without this trade opportunity clearly show the extent to which the Jesuits' existence in Japan was not only a question of successful proselytization but also of a successful business operation (Ibid., 44).

Next to the silk trade network established between Macao and Japan, where the Jesuits had their own establishments as well, the occupation of Manila by the Spanish Empire in 1571 expanded the Jesuits' trade possibilities even further, as galleons would now also sail between Manila and Acapulco in Mexico (Nueva España) and create opportunities for further income. The exchanges can be explained quite simply: "The Spaniards and the Japanese had silver and wanted Chinese silk, and the Chinese were always ready to trade silk and other things for silver from either Nagasaki or Manila. There was no such commodity that the Philippines wanted from Japan or Japan from the Philippines, but there was a considerable amount of trade between Nagasaki and Manila in the last years of the sixteenth century and the first of the seventeenth" (Ibid.). The union of the two Iberian kingdoms in 1580 also made trade relations less competitive, although the administration in the Southeast Asian region remained separated. For the Jesuits, however, this union increased the pressure from other religious orders (Pérez, 1920; Schütte, 1967, 178-179), whose representatives now pressed for access to the previously exclusively Jesuit spheres of influence, namely in China and Japan, where Spanish friars appeared in 1580 and 1584 respectively to challenge the missionary ambitions of the Jesuits there (Moran, 1993, 46).[1]

---

[1] The present part of the book follows, if not otherwise indicated, Moran (1993). In the 1590s, Augustinians, Franciscans, and Dominicans arrived in Japan as well, although their numbers never surpassed a quarter of the Jesuits (Schütte, 1967, 175).

Fig. 4.2: Alessandro Valignano, ca. 1599.

The involvement of the Jesuits in the Macao-Japan silk trade aroused criticism not only from outside but also from the missionaries themselves. In a report from June 1584, the Visitor to the Province of India, Alessandro Valignano, who for a long time was the most powerful and influential Jesuit in East Asia and who would show a special interest in Japan as well, is said to have critically described the Jesuits of Macao as "pampered, self-indulgent, and living in a style hard to reconcile with the spirit of their vow of poverty. As symptoms of this decadence he mentions servants, pets, silks, fine bedding, frequent baths and changes of underclothing, eating fruit between meals, singing, unnecessary talking, and visits from outsiders" (Ibid., 48). On the other hand, the criticized Jesuits offered a report in which the Visitor was partially blamed because he was supposed to be "holy, helpful and co-operative, but also as a man who is in his element when dealing with great personages about weighty matters, but tends to neglect the details essential to organized religious life, among which he lists rules, the bell (summoning the religious to his various duties), silence, dress, and order" (Ibid.). This dispute highlights that there were already tensions within the order itself, which would have a decisive impact on the success of the missionary work of the Jesuits in Japan in later years as well.

The trade interest of the Jesuits with regard to the Macao-Japan silk trade and its structural organization "was developed around a simple organization chart in which the priest who was in Macau as a Prosecutor was responsible for the annual shipment of silks and other products necessary for the mission from Japan, while, on the Japanese side, another Father Prosecutor took over the management of the business" (Campos, 2007, 101). Luís de Almeida (ca. 1525-1583), one of the Jesuits who would be in Japan during the entry period but could also look back on some successful trade activity in the region before joining the order, came to Japan in 1552 after having been active in India since the late 1540s. Three years after first coming to the country, the merchant Almeida "visited the kingdom of Bungo and, impressed and deeply moved by the results obtained by the Jesuit priests, applied to join the Company. He learned the Japanese language, toured various regions of the country, and did a remarkable job at the hospital he founded in Funai, thus introducing Western medicine into Japan" (Campos, 2007, 102). This example already shows how close the interrelation between trade, expansion, and religious missionary work was, particularly during the early years of the Jesuit activities in Japan.

At the same time, the Jesuits in Japan had to react to the volatile political situation (Ibid., 74-91), which changed a lot between 1549, when Francis Xavier first arrived on the shores of the island country, and 1614, when the order's missionaries were forced to leave again. The Japanese political order was, in a way, in turmoil when feudal lords, after the weak Ashikaga shogunate eventually ended in 1573, struggled even more for expansion and power, but power was eventually centralized by the three unifiers, Oda Nobunaga (1534-1582), Toyotomi Hideyoshi (1537-1598), and Tokugawa Ieyasu (1543-1616). Consequently, the period of the Warring States (*sengoku jidai*) was determined by the rivalries among the Japanese feudal lords, rivalries that were sometimes also expressed through conversions to Christianity (Imai, 1971; Nagahara, 1978). The Jesuit Order was therefore drawn into politics, and the successes achieved with regard to local missionary work could be destroyed again by changes within the political order quite fast. Once the country was unified and centralized under Tokugawa Ieyasu's rule, anti-Christian acts initiated by Toyotomi Hideyoshi intensified or were properly enforced.

In addition, the geographically peripheral position of the Jesuits made communication with other provinces, not to mention with Rome, quite problematic. To send a letter from Europe and receive a response could take five to six years, which is why multiple copies of letters were often sent on different routes. The Jesuits in Japan were in "closer" contact with Macao and India than with the European center (Moran, 1993, 42). Valignano, in particular, seems to have used multiple routes to get responses as fast as possible because he became frustrated in 1591 when he received eight letters from Europe that had been written between 1587 and 1589 (Ibid., 45). Communication, especially when compared with modern-day possibilities to exchange knowledge, ideas, and information, was rather slow in the 1500s and 1600s. This also means that the Jesuit Order had to rely on the people acting on its behalf in the faraway regions of the world, e.g., Japan. While the missionaries that went abroad had all received the same guidelines, it was eventually their local experiences that determined what they would make out of these guidelines, and these thereby provide insights into similarities and differences with regard to the strategies for the missionary work applied and the successes achieved, as well as to the local developments in a somewhat peripheral region:

> [T]he project for the conversion of populations outside the European context was fueled by guidelines common to the different mission territories – instructions that, over time, came to be confronted with repercussions and resulting from them, both from Europe and from other existing missions. That said, by contrasting completely different experiences, we may be able to identify the sharing of many points within the discourse that was disseminated and in the interpretation that was made about the natives. (Boscariol, 2016, 91)

It must also be emphasized, as researchers like Ebisawa Arimichi (1910-1992) have done before, that the contacts between the missionaries and the Japanese people stimulated an exchange of Christian and local religious ideas (Ebisawa 1944, 1960, 1971), often creating quite symbiotic interpretations as they were not uncommon in Peru either.

While the Jesuits, as mentioned before, were not the only missionary order active in Japan (Pérez, 1923; Álvarez-Taladriz, 1973; Delgado García, 1985;

Zamora, 1997) during the "Christian (*Kirishitan*) period" (Amaro-Bebio, 2016, 3), as the years between 1549 and 1640 are referred to, they were without any doubt the most influential and visible. In particular, since the "Christian facilities" – a term Amaro-Bebio uses "not only [for] churches, but other built and non-built structures, such as chapels, colleges, residences, hospitals, cemeteries, large crosses and altars on open spaces" (2016, 3; see also Pacheco, 1977; Arimura, 2014) – were often run by the Jesuits, their existence was quite openly displayed, first and foremost in Nagasaki, which between 1569 and 1620 was probably the most openly Christian place in the whole of Japan (Toyama, 2011; Hesselink, 2015). The ties between Japanese and Western culture were, however, not only forged in public spaces, where elements of different religions were mixed, e.g., in architectural structures like "the architecture of the Jesuit College of São Paulo in Nagasaki after the 1600s, in which the spatial organization of the main building is a compromise between Japanese architecture and the requirements of European Jesuit colleges" (Amaro-Bebio, 2016, 4) but also in other "cultural practices" (Rogge, 2013), e.g. art or music (Redondo Bonet, 2011; Fukahori, 2016).

Considering the meticulousness of the Jesuits and the fact that they produced countless letters (Tōkyō Daigaku Shiryō Hensanjo, 1990-1996) and reports – often multiple copies of the same one –, the researcher is provided with rich and valuable material, although the lack of sources from the perspective of the converts, especially ordinary Japanese Christians, has been emphasized before (Higashibaba, 2001). Regardless of the problems related to these one-sided sources (Ferro, 1993, 139), whose translative nomenclature is not always clear (Amaro-Bebio, 2016, 25), and the "rather complex hermeneutical problems" (Loureiro, 2000, 158) they cause, they offer important insights into the work of the Jesuits in Japan as well as into the internal struggles that existed, despite the hierarchical structure of the order (Amaro-Bebio, 2016, 23). The sources allow us to reconstruct the Jesuits' activities, especially those related to the leading Jesuits in Japan, who are (Ibid., 19; Sarmento de Matos, 1989):

1. the superiors Francis Xavier (1548-1551), Cosme de Torres (1551-1570), Francisco Cabral (1570-1581), and Gaspar Coelho (1581-1582),
2. the vice-provincials – Japan had become a vice-province in 1582 – Gaspar Coelho (1582-1589), Pedro Gomez (1589-1599), and Francisco Pasio (1599-1610),
3. the provincial – in 1610, the status of Japan was changed to a province – Valentim de Carvalho (1610-1617), and
4. the most important Jesuit for Japan, the Visitor (Padre Visitator) Alessandro Valignano (1574-1606).

These men were most important for the development of the Jesuit Order and its work in Japan during the different periods of their missionary work there, which will now be taken into closer consideration to explain how a relatively successful mission ultimately faced expulsion and the deaths of many of its representatives.

The Entry Period

When Francis Xavier arrived in Japan for the first time in 1549, he was not alone but accompanied by, among others, Anjirō, a Japanese whom he had met in Goa and who was extremely important for the initial contact, which must be considered "a fascinating episode in the history of cultural interaction" (Tronu Montane, 2012b, 9). From Kagoshima, where they arrived, they would spread Christianity mostly in Kyūshū and the west of Honshū, with the first region and Nagasaki later being the strongholds of Christian converts in Japan – even after the expulsion of the Jesuits, Christian communities would stay active there, although hidden (Ogawa, 2010; Nofuji & Uchijima, 2017). While Xavier was "much impressed by the intelligence of Japanese people and he repeatedly states in his letters that Japanese people are quite rational and that they do not believe anything unless they are convinced of the rationality of the doctrines that are presented to them" (Yamamoto, 2012, 250), how far this was the reality or solely his impression remains unknown. Considering that he could not communicate with the Japanese without Anjirō, it must remain unclear as to whether hope was the origin of Xavier's impression or if actual experiences made him come to such a conclusion.

It was Anjirō who also translated important texts for Xavier, which the latter would find quite useful during his trip to Japan. Together with Cosme de Torres and Juan Hernandez, who had accompanied Xavier and Anjirō, initial contacts were successfully made with local rulers, whose replies and reactions to the newly arrived Christian missionaries seem to have been relatively positive. Shimazu Takahisa (1514-1571) was the first important daimyō (Niina, 2017) whom Xavier talked to, while Anjirō translated for the Jesuit (Amaro-Bebio, 2016, 30). The meeting shows how important material culture was during the early missionary activities (Debergh, 1980; 1984), as Xavier needed to arouse a positive interest in Christianity without having the possibility to rely on a well-known corpus of texts or scripture in such a case:

> The Jesuits showed them an altarpiece with an image of Mary holding the baby Jesus, which caused a strong impression in Takahisa. He kneeled down in reverence to the image and ordered all of his vassals to do the same. ... The Jesuits showed Takahisa some beautifully illuminated manuscript Bible, which also impressed him. As a result,

Takahisa allowed his vassals to become Christians, and some were baptized. (Amaro-Bebio, 2016, 30)

It is obvious from this first meeting that the room for interpretation on both sides was quite large, and it is furthermore not surprising that "[t]he early modern Japanese Church developed syncretistic practices in which Roman Catholicism came to function similarly to Buddhism and Shintō" (Fujitani, 2016). Along with the daimyō, Xavier was also able to meet one of the leading Buddhist monks, namely the one that led the temple of Fukushouji, i.e., an important religious representative, with whom he had the chance to discuss religious questions (Amaro-Bebio, 2016, 30), especially those related to Buddhism, which Xavier had studied before reaching Japan (App, 1997a; 1997b). Since Anjirō was the only medium to communicate through, it must be taken into consideration that he had the knowledge and possibility to add his own interpretation to the actual translation, so one must be careful not to overestimate the reports of these early talks. Overall, the first mission to Japan was a success, especially since local authorities were in favor of the Jesuits who had reached the Japanese shores.

In the next years, and especially during the entry period (Morris, 2018, 93-99), the success of the missionary approach was actually very closely related to the positive attitude of local rulers toward the Jesuits. Influential daimyōs like Ōtomo Sorin (1530-1587), also known as Ōtomo Yoshihige, in Chikugo supported the Jesuits and not only made the first conversions possible but also often demanded their subordinates to embrace the new religion (Laures, 1959/60, 380-381). When Belchior de Moura baptized Japanese in Chikugo in the late 1570s, he was able to do so because Ōtomo Sorin had supported such conversions, and other cases point to the same precondition for successful proselytization (Kigama, 2014). The fact that the Jesuits, however, relied on the goodwill of the daimyō made their missionary work vulnerable, too. When a local ruler expanded his territory, the Jesuits' activities could expand as well, while they were in danger if a daimyō lost his influence or territory to others who were not in favor of Christianity in general and the Jesuits in particular (Laures, 1959/60, 382-384). The attitude of the feudal elites toward the Jesuit Order was consequently very important, which is why many works have focused on this particular relationship (Gonoi, 1983; 1990; 2002; Takase, 1993; 1994; 2013; Murai 1998; 1999; 2000).

These relationships were essential to start the missionary work in the first place, and when Ōtomo Sorin donated land to the Jesuits in 1556, it was only then that they were able to begin building a church in the north of Kyūshū (Tronu Montane, 2012b, 28). When the Jesuits began their work in Nagasaki, the authorities had provided them with an old temple building as a place to work from before the building was rebuilt step by step and turned into a church (Compañía de Jesus, 1575, 284). In addition, it would take the Jesuits a couple of years before their language capacities had improved, but it was still not easy to translate the Christian terms into proper Japanese without causing confusion for converts familiar with more Buddhist terminology (Amaro-Bebio, 2016, 33). While the feudal lords protected the Jesuits in some regions, they were not secure from anti-foreign resentment by the Japanese population: "In general, [they] were constantly exposed to aggressions, and in their letters, we can find many instances in which Japanese people would spit on their faces while they were preaching, groups of children threw stones at them, people would shoot arrows or fire arquebus shots at their sleeping rooms at night, or try to burn their houses" (Amaro-Bebio, 2016, 33). That the lack of an accurate translation of Christian practices was an obstacle to successful conversions becomes clear when one takes a look at the Jesuit hospitals, where the Jesuits tried to take care of the sick. This kind of work was considered to be done only by socially low-ranking or degraded people, so only a few poor people reacted positively to this essential element of Jesuit work. Therefore, a lot of explanatory work was needed at first to make the Japanese understand the meaning of this act of caregiving to others, especially with regard to its role within the Christian religion (Ibid., 34). The first few years of the entry period were spent establishing the basic facilities needed for the Jesuit work in Japan, and larger numbers of converts would not be achieved – daimyōs like Ōtomo Sorin supported the Jesuits, yet did not initially convert themselves – before the consolidation period, when the Jesuit Order, under Valignano's influence, intensified its activities and became more important.

The Consolidation Period and the Influence of Alessandro Valignano

The missionary strategy of the Jesuits of Japan was sometimes not very careful, as Gaspar Vilela's (1526-1572) actions show. In 1569, Vilela "was invited by one of Ōmura Sumitada's Christian vassals to visit him in a fishing village located on the coast of Hizen. After converting the lord's retainers and burning the Buddhist temple, Vilela built a Christian church under the invocation of 'Todos os Santos' (All Saints)" (Curvelo, 2001, 23). This shows that there was not too much awareness about cultural differences, and, in some cases, a quite aggressive conversion policy was applied by some Jesuits. Larger numbers of converts were nevertheless the exception, not the rule, and were usually related to the baptism of a daimyō or lower feudal lord. When Ōtomo Sorin was baptized in 1578, some of his vassals would soon follow his lead and support the work of the Jesuits in the following years (Cieslik, 1959, 39; 1962). In 1579, however, the arrival of Visitor Alessandro Valignano on a ship from Macao would change the situation (Frois 1976, 3, 128). In his position as Visitor, Valignano held high authority and power in his hands and only needed to report to the order's General in Rome (Moran, 1993, 3; on the role of the Visitor, see Danieluk, 2019). Everard Mercurian (1514-1580) was the fourth General – after Ignatius Loyola, Diego Laynez (1512-1565) (Oberholzer, 2015), and Francis Borgia (1510-1572) – and he appointed Valignano in 1573 as "'visitor of the East Indies', with authority over all Jesuit missions and all Jesuits from the Cape of Good Hope to Japan" (Ibid.). Claudio Aquaviva (1543-1615) became General once Mercurian died in 1580, but he would be the only one Valignano had to fear, and considering the long time letters took in those days, the new Visitor had all the time and power necessary to change the missionary strategy in East Asia in general and in Japan in particular.

Valignano stayed in Japan until 1582, when he left, accompanied by four Japanese students, who were sent to Rome to present the success of the Jesuits in the East Asian country. This mission, which will be discussed later in more detail, also acted as a diplomatic mission, as the "four Japanese Christian boys from noble Kyushu families," who represented the result of Valignano's and his fellow Jesuits' educational efforts, "carried letters to the Pope from the lord of Bungo and two other Christian lords" (Ibid.). They returned to Japan, together with Valignano, who in the meantime had been in India, via Macao, in 1590, and the Visitor stayed for another two years. He returned to Japan for the last time in 1598 and left the island country on 15 January 1603.

The Neapolitan Valignano was appointed in the first place in the hope, of Mercurian and others, "that under him the Indian mission would be less dependent on Portugal and more directly in touch with Jesuit headquarters in Rome, and his insistence on taking Spanish and Italian as well as Portuguese Jesuits with him when he sailed for the Indies in 1574 did not endear him to the senior Portuguese Jesuits" (Ibid., 49). Valignano had a global mindset from the start of his mission (Nejime, 2014) and considered the Jesuit Order not an expansive instrument of an Iberian kingdom but a community of men eager to spread Christianity in the name of the Lord and the Pope. In his *Sumario de las cosas de Japón* (1583), Valignano explained why he considered Japan to be particularly important for this aim in the East Asian context:

1. It is a very large country, and the people are white, cultured, prudent, and subject to reason.
2. Japan is the only oriental country in which the people have become Christians for the right reasons.
3. In Japan, and only in Japan, the Christian converts include some of the highest in the land.
4. The Japanese have a natural inclination to religion, and hold their Buddhist priests in high regard. We, who teach the truth and have the

help of grace as well as of reason, can expect a higher degree of respect and obedience.
5. The Japanese mission, unlike all other missions, will eventually be self-supporting in both manpower and revenue, as the Buddhists are. ...
6. We are now very well established in Japan, and have overcome the worst of the difficulties. We have many here who know the customs and the language, and many Japanese [Jesuit] brothers. ...
7. Lastly, it seems that Our Lord has reserved this great enterprise in Japan for the Society alone, since other religious orders should not and probably will not be able to go there. And with the Society in charge of Christianity, more will be brought to salvation in Japan in time than in any other place, and my conclusion is that the Society must devote all possible attention to this great work. (Valignano, 1954; translation cited in Moran, 1993, 51-52)

What is important is that Valignano, for the first time, developed a clear agenda for Jesuits who were active in Japan, and he "reformed the mission in ways that broke fundamentally and decisively with the approach to the propagation of the Christian faith by missionaries under the authority of the Spanish and Portuguese crowns" (Ross, 1994: xi).

In contrast to his colleagues in Peru, he could do so, as neither the Spanish nor Portuguese crown had any authority in Japan, and the space within which the missionary activities took place was not controlled by any other authority. Valignano was also "adamant that Japan and China were not lands to be conquered, and he insisted that any attempt at such an adventure would be to the detriment of the missionary outreach of the Church" (Ibid.). Consequently, in his letters and reports, he "insists that Japan was not like Mexico or Peru" (Ibid.), although similar problems, especially with regard to language capabilities and the necessity for a global mindset, applied, as later internal struggles would prove. Nevertheless, Valignano wanted to secure a successful mission, first in Japan, and later also in China (Liu, 2011), and therefore, "[t]he creation of a truly Japanese and Chinese Church was his aim, and he viewed the imperial pretensions of both Portugal and Spain as a threat to that end, not an aid" (Ibid., xiii). Every time the Visitor was in Japan, he tried to improve the work of the Jesuit Order there, and even if he spent time in Goa or Macao, Valignano was always kept informed about events in Japan. Regarding his overall regional aims, Japan seemed to hold a key position within the perspective of Valignano, who deemed the conversion of the country's people to Christianity as an essential element for the success of the Jesuits in the region (Amaro-Bebio, 2016, 20).

Valignano initially wanted to educate young Japanese boys and men to prepare them for a later role within the Jesuit Order and as priests in Japan, "but had recommended that none should actually be ordained until Christianity had taken firmer root in Japan and there were kingdoms wholly Christian, with Church jurisdiction over clerics" (Moran, 1993, 52). However, the Visitor was not so sure about access to the order for Japanese, who were "clever, honourable and noble, and the Society needed their mastery of the Japanese language," but who, on the other hand, he perceived as "deceitful, secretive, untruthful, and inclined to vice" (Ibid.). Maybe it was due to some further actual experience that he eventually decided that "love and concord between the Japanese and European Jesuits" was an essential precondition for the success of the missionary work, which is why he put forward the argument, partly also stimulated by a dogmatic struggle with the provincial Cabral, that the Japanese students and novices must be treated "with gentleness, showing a high regard for their talents, sympathizing with them in their difficulties, and on no account belittling them, calling them negros, or using other offensive or angry words to them" (Ibid.). Cabral, who was in charge as the provincial leader of the Jesuits until 1581, when Valignano made him leave the island, was against a Japanese priesthood and is reported to have treated the Japanese quite harshly and without any understanding for the existent cultural differences. The struggle between him and the Visitor consequently represents a struggle between dogmatic inflexibility and openness, between a narrow and a global mindset. The conflict between the two men would not be solved in 1581, but for Japan, Valignano's victory resembled a new course, one that fully accepted the cultural differences as they existed in the island country and had to be faced by any Jesuit missionary who wanted to achieve successful conversions there.

The Visitor had realized that the Japanese could not be forced into conversion – an important difference with regard to the Peruvian case – and Valignano was simply flexible enough to realize that the Jesuits were not backed by a colonial power in Japan. Accordingly, "[s]ince the Japanese were too proud and too clever ever to allow themselves to be ruled by foreigners, the only way to establish the Church in Japan was to educate native Japanese, and then leave it to them to run things themselves in their own way" (Ibid., 54). If that was to be achieved, however, the Jesuits had to accept their own foreignness in the Japanese context, and, therefore, they had to learn and better prepare the missionaries for their interactions with the possible converts. Nothing was to be achieved in Japan by force. The Christian faith had to be attractive, and the Jesuits needed to be admired, not only as well-educated but also as well-behaved men who preached a message worth listening to. It is therefore unsurprising that Valignano was involved in many discussions about the level of "cultural adaptation" (Ibid.) that was supposed to be achieved by the Jesuits, and just one example concerning food will highlight the dimensions of the problem. The Visitor "forbade the raising of pigs and goats, the slaughtering of cows, the drying and selling of hides, at all Jesuit establishments in Japan. Hens and ducks might be kept, but only if enclosed and never permitted to enter the house. The missionaries were normally to eat Japanese food, with Japanese cooking, service, and table manners," especially because "greasy dishes, dirty kitchens, table manners uncouth or clumsy by Japanese standards … were hindrances to missionary work" (Ibid., 54-55).

It was Ōtomo Sorin who pointed the Visitor in the right direction, as he outlined that the Christian fathers rarely followed the necessities of Japanese etiquette and were thereby considered to be inferior because "if absurd, boorish or disgusting behaviour was an embarrassment to allies it was welcome ammunition to hostile observers, such as those who spread the persistent rumours that the carnivores were also cannibals" (Ibid., 55). Valignano reacted to such problems with a handbook he had compiled in the early 1580s for Jesuit missionaries in Japan (Valignano, 1946; on this work, see Radulet, 1994). Furthermore, Valignano paid close attention to language-related aspects:

> [The] Visitor noted that correct or polite Japanese speech had to take account of the social position of the speaker, the person spoken to, and the persons or things spoken about. Such distinctions of rank as the Jesuits had did not correspond to the Japanese distinctions, so it was difficult to determine what would be correct speech or behaviour where the missionaries were concerned. His characteristically bold solution was to assign Japanese-style ranks to his men, each of whom was to know his place and role, and to speak and act his part. (Moran, 1993, 56)

These reactions emphasize that Valignano was probably one of the more culturally sensitive Jesuits, whose global mindset allowed him to pay close attention to existent cultural diversity and also made him address relevant aspects to achieve better intercultural management. The Visitor consequently developed what is often referred to in the relevant literature as an "accommodative method" or "cultural adaptation" (Elison, 1973, 54-84; Tronu Montane, 2012c, 1617). Valignano consequently "reformed the Japanese mission and designed a very innovative missionary policy to evangelise the Japanese more effectively" (Tronu Montane, 2012c, 1617), and this policy would have a tremendous impact in many regards, e.g., on applied funeral rites (Ibid.), on an attempt to replicate the hierarchical orders presented by and within the Buddhist system of Japan, which, however, was not successful (Moran, 1993, 56-57), and on a more culturally oriented preparation for missionaries who were supposed to work in Japan (Loureiro, 2000, 161).

Language played an important part as well, as Jesuits who spoke Japanese were considered much more effective than those who did not (DI, 10, 246-247).

Indeed, Valignano was "a man with vision" and, therefore, "fully reorganised the Jesuit mission in Japan and it was there where he first introduced his innovative ideas and missionary principles" (Tronu Montane, 2012b, 23) that would later be taken up by Matteo Ricci (1552-1610) in China (Collani, 2010; Hsia, 2010; Hosne, 2014; Wong, 2017; Mignini, 2019). These principles "aimed at enhancing the missionary policy and solving the economic, organizational, and social problems of the Jesuit Japanese mission" (Tronu Montane, 2012b, 23), and the number of members and converts indeed grew substantially, when compared to the entry period, while Valignano was actively involved in the Japanese business of the Jesuits. His important work *Il cerimoniale per i missionari del Giappone: Advertimentos e avisos acerca dos costumes e catangues de Jappão: importante documento circa i metodi di adattamento nella missione giapponese del secolo XVI* (Valignano, 1946), usually referred to simply as *Advertimentos*, documents the Visitor's attempts to establish his ideas, i.e., the "accommodative method" (Tronu Montane, 2012b, 23) as the fundamental principle for the Jesuits' future activities in Japan.

Valignano demanded the Jesuit padres and irmãos (brothers) in Japan to follow his lead with regard to this new attitude toward the missionary approaches, and, as Amaro-Bebio emphasizes,

> the whole idea behind the notion of "cultural adaptation" was that the Jesuits wanted Christian religion to be seen as "respectable," "dignified" or "prestigious" in the eyes of the Japanese. In the opinion of Valignano and other Jesuits, the Japanese population was often convinced that the ideas behind Christian religion were "more logical" than the ones of Buddhism and Shinto; however, they refused to convert, because foreigners were seen as lowly people with uncivilized or uneducated behaviors. (2016, 18)

For the Japanese, being identified as close to the Jesuits and, thereby, Christianity could have caused serious social damage to their own position, which is why the missionaries, according to Valignano's perspective, needed to become as Japanese as possible so as not to be considered "foreign" but a real alternative to Buddhism or Shintō. For him, the situation seemed to be clear, as "it is quite one-sided and ridiculous that the European priests, who want Japanese people to change their traditional way of thinking and acting according to the Christian way, do not change their own customs and continue to act in the way that appears vulgar and barbarous to Japanese people" (Yamamoto, 2012, 253). The Visitor consequently intended to involve the local people in the work of the Jesuits much more, and he also wanted to produce books that would inform them about Christianity in Japanese, which is why a printing press was later imported, on which such books were produced (Ebisawa, 1991, 200-202).

Two seminaries for the sons of the Japanese aristocracy were established, and two colleges would later continue their education to prepare them for work as Jesuits, but the latter plan could not be fulfilled due to political changes in the late 1580s. The seminary of Arima, however, remained quite successful, regardless of the political centralization under Toyotomi Hideyoshi and Tokugawa Ieyasu, and during its more than 30 years of existence, it educated quite a large number of young students (Cieslik, 1959, 41-42). In 1603, the college at Nagasaki introduced a Japanese-Portuguese dictionary, the *Vocabulario de Lingoa de Iapam* (Rodrigues, 1976), which contained, with a supplement published a year later, more than 30,000 words (Yamamoto, 2012, 254). This work, like many other publications, such as the *Arte de Lingoa de Iapam* (Rodrigues, 1604-1608), documents the efforts that had been invested since the 1580s to bring the Jesuit Order and its missionaries as close to the Japanese as possible (Cooper, 1973; 2001; Ehalt, 2009). However, this could not be achieved without problems, especially since Valignano's very flexible approach toward the means to reach the aims of the Jesuit Order was not shared by all Jesuits. The struggle with Cabral, for example, would cause trouble, and the internal disputes also weakened the positive perception of the missionaries active in Japan.

Valignano was familiar with the reports about Japan sent by Xavier and other Jesuits who had reported their experiences during the entry period before he became the Visitor and responsible for the Japanese business of the order himself. When he arrived in 1579, however, Valignano was quite surprised by the realities presented to him. Although some daimyōs had converted to Christianity, the overall situation in the island country was far from favorable for the Jesuits: "The difference between what I have found through experience in Japan and what I learned about it in India and China from the information I was given ... is like the difference between black and white" (letter by Valignano, Kuchinotsu, 5 December 1579, Roman Archives of the Society of Jesus, Japonica-Sinica, 8, I, fl. 242, cited in Moran, 1993, 34). Valignano was, in a way, shocked that the real situation had not been clearly described in the reports and argued that such a misleading style should not be replicated in the future (Moran, 1993, 35). The criticism was directed toward the provincial, Cabral, who had been the leading Jesuit in Japan since 1570. Cabral obviously did not possess a global mindset, as he had also prevented the missionaries from adequately learning Japanese (DI, 17, 272-275).

Cabral, who maintained a harsh attitude toward the Japanese students and novices, did not understand what Valignano attempted to achieve when the

The Cases

latter planned to establish three seminaries serving Japanese students first and foremost – two for boys aged 10-18 years and one for older ones who were supposed to become novices later – in Arima and Azuchi in 1580. The Visitor understood the essential role the Japanese had played as preachers, actually being able to communicate with their countrymen and women and translating the Christian message for Japanese ears more accurately. The students were taught Latin, literature, including classic Japanese texts, and music (Moran, 1993, 12; Yamamoto, 2012, 252). Like in other culturally different contexts, education was supposed to pave the way to the hearts and minds of the people who should sooner or later be converted to Christianity. The graduates would continue their path in Usuki or Funai, where a novitiate and a college, respectively, were soon established.

Cabral, on the other hand, must have been furious about such changes, as the provincial usually "discriminated [against] Japanese people," especially since "[h]e thought that the only way to spread Christianity in Japan was to gain the favor of the 'daimyos' ... by the profit of the trade with European countries and to use the influence of the daimyos to convert the common people" (Yamamoto, 2012, 252). Cabral instead believed in proselytization from above and did not want to seek contact with the common people. He therefore also did not favor the idea of Japanese priests who would become part of the Jesuit Order. The struggle between the two mindsets, i.e., Valignano's global mindset, open to change, and Cabral's limited views and dogmatic inflexibility, was eventually only solved when the Visitor dismissed the provincial. In 1583, Cabral was appointed as the superior in Macao, a decision that might also have been made possible by the complaints about him from other Jesuits. Regardless of his opposition to Valignano, Cabral was able to move up the ranks and became the provincial in Goa in 1592. Regardless of his reappointment, Cabral continued what had turned into a "personal crusade" against the missionary work in Japan, and Valignano later accused him of "an extraordinary hostility to Japan, of exaggerating and criticizing the income of the Japanese vice-province, of dissuading Jesuits in India from going to Japan, and of maintaining that missionary effort and manpower spent on Japan is effort and manpower wasted" (Moran, 1993, 15). For the Visitor, Cabral's position was unbearable and sabotaged the success of the Jesuits in Japan, as the latter's "methods were wrong, and he antagonized both Jesuits and non-Jesuits" (Ibid., 21).

One has to be careful not to trust all Valignano's statements about the situation, as his personality might also have played a role in the development of the dispute. Valignano was a formidable person, and when he met Oda Nobunaga in Kyoto in 1581, he left quite an impression as the Visitor, who did not speak Japanese but could rely on the Jesuit padre Luís Fróis (1532-1597) as a capable translator, was able to stimulate the missionary work of the order in

Japan. At the same time, Valignano tried to control the spread of information about the Japanese events to Europe when he prevented his translator from sending a manuscript, namely his magnum opus, the *História de Japam* (Fróis, 1976-1984), to Rome. The Visitor also criticized the vice-provincial Gaspar Coelho, whom he described as "old and weak, does not know the language of the country, has little or no theology, and lacks authority and stature" (Moran, 1993, 21). Valignano probably struggled with the fact that a change to the existent structures, regardless of his powerful position, was not possible without Jesuits who shared his vision for the country. Considering the fact that Valignano was an early modern "workaholic" whose text production was prolific, his obsession with Japan could also have led to a low tolerance for the real situation in the island country.

In the past, an "[a]bility in foreign languages, as well as service within the order – and of course virtue – were matters taken into account in judging suitability for profession, but qualifications in the humanities and other recognized academic disciplines, in philosophy, and especially in theology, were of primary importance" (Ibid., 22). A doctrinal change in this regard would have demanded time, but Valignano seemed quite impatient, although, as mentioned before, he did not speak Japanese himself, nor could he take confessions in the language. His agenda and aims might therefore have overestimated the actual possibilities in the Japanese context, and wishful thinking was confronted with the realities of missionary work in an environment that would become hostile during the Visitor's final visit. However, he continued on his chosen course, and he even overruled orders from Mercurian or Aquaviva if he thought them to be unreasonable, especially with regard to the silk trade between Japan and Macao. The newly determined course of the Jesuits' strategy in Japan, however, had to take local issues and developments into closer consideration, as the missionaries were not acting in a vacuum.

The relationship between the Jesuits and Portuguese merchants in the 1580s was important in strengthening the financial capacities of the order in Japan (Gonoi, 2002, 344-357; Sousa, 2010, 23-30). One such influential donor, Captain Bartolomeu Vaz Landeiro, spent quite a lot of money to have churches built in Japan. However, alongside such support from external interest groups, Valignano had to pay much attention to the local situation, i.e., the demands and needs of the local feudal lords. In 1580, he tried to persuade Arima Harunobo (1567-1612) to convert to Christianity, but there was a danger that Ryūzōji Takanobu (1530-1584) would invade Arima. In this situation, the daimyō of Arima might have liked the idea of being baptized, as he considered this an act to secure the military support of the Portuguese, especially since some of his fortresses had already fallen into the hands of the enemy (Sousa, 2010, 23-24). Fróis remarks that "As the daimyō of Arima found himself in such a predicament and as it seemed to him that he had no other choice but join the Church and the daimyō of Omura, who was the brother of his father, he wished to become a Christian very soon, and asked the Father to baptize him urgently" (Fróis, 1976-1984, 3, 136, cited in ibid., 24).

Fróis assumed that it was one of the Buddhist monks who had urged Arima to seek an alliance with the Christians but for military and not for religious purposes, "as this was the only chance he stood of being able to maintain his dominions" (Sousa, 2010, 25). The whole situation put Valignano in a dilemma, as Arima's baptism could have harmed further Japanese conversion rates if he was defeated after his baptism as a Christian lord. A military defeat would have led to the assumption that the high-ranking convert had been punished for his decision, although if the invasion was successfully resisted, his act could also be positively interpreted. To quote Fróis once more:

> [A]s things were in turmoil and unstable in Arima, and every day more fortresses were rebelling, it seemed to Father Visitor Alessandro Valignano that it would not be convenient to baptize the daimyō of Arima, lest, if he were to be defeated, as would probably happen, the pagans might say that such thing had happened because he had become a Christian, as they usually say when similar cases happen with Christian daimyōs in Japan, in wars and changes, which in Japan are always not only continuous but also unexpected. (1976-1984, 3, 136-137, cited in ibid.)

Local developments consequently always influenced the success rate of the Jesuits' activities in Japan, as another example might further highlight.

Daimyō Ōmura Sumitada (1533-1587) gave the Jesuits a land concession in Nagasaki, which might have expressed his interest in trade with the Portuguese rather than his love for the Christian missionaries and their god (Sousa, 2010, 27; on the foundation of Nagasaki, see also Pacheco, 1989). The harbor, which was economically important from the 1560s due to this concession of land, further linked the Jesuits to the Macao trade as well as the daimyō to the respective trade routes that were quite valuable, especially since the wars of the period often needed to be financed by the income such a link could provide as well. The city had grown, and by 1579, it counted 400 houses, while some Portuguese had settled there and married Japanese women as well (Curvelo, 2001, 23). The community consequently needed Christian services for its Portuguese inhabitants. It was in 1580 when the city was officially given to the Jesuits, although the sovereignty of the received territory remained in Ōmura Sumitada's hands. It was agreed that "the Portuguese would pay him an annual due, part of which was to be spent on the priests' maintenance, and the other on the city's military fortification and on the feudal Christian lords" (Curvelo, 2001, 24). This arrangement, however, did not last long, as the city was eventually turned over to Shimazu Yoshihisa (1533-1611), who had invaded the Ōmura territory in 1586, and it became an imperial city in the following year under Toyotomi Hideyoshi. Existent arrangements or treaties were therefore often of limited value to the Jesuits, who had to secure their status and even their existence with new ruling powers. The *sengoku jidai* and the political developments at its end consequently created problems for the Jesuits, regardless of their new and more accommodative strategies for their missionary approach toward possible Japanese converts. These political changes, nevertheless, initially did not interfere too much with the development of the city of Nagasaki, which continued to grow and counted 5,000 inhabitants in 1590 and around 15,000 in 1600 (Oliveira e Costa, 1993, 39-43).

The Jesuit efforts were at the same time not only based on Valignano's activities alone, as Jesuits like Luís Fróis also invested much of their energy in getting culturally closer to the Japanese with the aim of making them more receptive to Christianity. The rule of Cabral had not lessened their enthusiasm to learn the Japanese language and get familiar with the local customs and rules of etiquette (Loureiro, 2000, 161). In the early 1580s, Fróis finished his short *Tratado das contradições e diferenças de costumes entre a Europa e o Japão* (Treatise on the Contradictions and Differences of Customs between Europe and Japan) (Fróis, 2004; see also Jorissen, 1988). The *Treatise* makes it clear that Valignano was not the only one who had reflected on Japanese culture, and "Luís Fróis, in these writings, appears as an attentive and inquisitive observer, registering detailed information about politics, society, culture, and religion" (Loureiro, 2000, 159). In contrast to Valignano, Fróis had lived in Japan uninterrupted for a long time and also spoke Japanese quite well. His writings were supposed to help newly arrived Jesuits as well, as the "booklet would prepare them for the daily confrontation with a world so different from their own" and the "newly arrived Jesuits could steer clear of certain habits so common in Europe, but looked upon as unsocial in Japan, such as spitting on the ground, sneezing in public, hugging another man, or wearing shoes inside the houses" (Ibid., 162).

Fróis's later magnum opus, the already-mentioned *Historia de Japam*, which he began to work on in 1585 at the request of the Jesuit historian Giovanni Pietro Maffei (1536-1603), was to provide all known things about the island country in one work, and the Jesuit padre was considered the right man for this task because he had lived there for so long and had even managed to learn the Japanese language quite well. Valignano, who had claimed authorship of all writings about Japan that had been sent to Europe before, was challenged by Fróis's new task in a way, but the latter would serve as Valignano's secretary in Macao between 1592 and 1595 before he was allowed to return to Japan, where he died in Nagasaki in 1597. Although the work about Japan was finished before his death, Valignano did not send it to Europe and, in a way, prevented its publication (Ibid., 165). Whatever the reasons for this might have been – maybe Valignano wanted to prevent different views than his own about Japan circulating among the Jesuits –, Fróis had been criticized for his adaptation to Japanese habits, perhaps even going too far, as he enjoyed debating religious topics with Japanese non-converts (Feldmann, 1993; Sioris, 1997). His open mind was consequently probably too open for some, although the tensions with Valignano can hardly have been the consequences of this openness to Japan and its people. Fróis's life nevertheless remains emblematic of the experiences of the Jesuits in Japan and "exemplifies the existential paradox lived by some of the Jesuits of the Japan mission. The European fathers, while trying to immerse themselves deeply into Japanese life, were supposed to remain utterly faithful to their Christian and Western roots" (Loureiro, 2000, 166).

That they also had to be aware of these European roots becomes obvious when one takes a closer look at the diplomatic mission to Rome, which led four Japanese boys to the center of Christian power. Diogo de Mesquita (1551-1614), who would later be the responsible dean for the colleges in Amakusa and Nagasaki and also tried to cultivate Western plants in Japan (Correia, 2003), later traveled with the four Japanese – Itō Mancio, Chijiwa Miguel, Hara Martinho, and Nakaura Julião – who left Japan in 1582 and would return with the Visitor in 1590. Valignano described the Japanese as follows in a letter from Goa on 20 November 1587:

> They are now grown men, very satisfied with their experience, very full of the qualities and the greatness of His Holiness and of the other Christian princes, and very enthusiastic about our things [*muy afficionados a nuestras cosas*]. And they have made such progress in virtue and are so eager to explain our things to the Japanese and to help in the conversion of Japan that I assure Your Paternity that words cannot express the consolation they have brought me, And I have no doubt that when they arrive in Japan they will make every bit as great an impression there as they did in Europe. (Roman Archives of the Society of Jesus, Japonica-Sinica, 10 II, fl. 291, cited in Moran, 1993, 7-8)

Valignano wanted not only to prove the success of the mission in Japan but also to impress these four sons of Japanese noblemen with the great achievements of Christianity in Europe. In his instructions for the diplomatic mission, the Visitor described the purpose of the mission in very specific detail, as the following reflection shows:

In sending the boys to Portugal and Rome our intention is twofold. Firstly it is to seek the help, both temporal and spiritual, which we need in Japan. Secondly it is to make the Japanese aware of the glory and greatness of Christianity, and of the majesty of the princes and lords who profess it, and of the greatness and wealth of our kingdoms and cities, and of the honour in which our religion is held and the power it possesses in them. These Japanese boys will be witnesses who will have seen these things, and being persons of such quality they will be able to return to Japan and to say what they have seen. Since the Japanese have never seen our things they cannot believe us when we tell of them, but these witnesses will confer proper credit and authority on us, and thus they will come to understand the reason why the fathers come to Japan. At present many of them do not understand; they think we are poor people, of little consequence in our own countries, and that we come to Japan to seek our fortunes, with the preaching of heavenly things as a mere pretext. (Valignano, 1943, 395-398, cited in Moran, 1993, 8-9)

The four boys had studied at the college in Arima, and when the young men returned to the island country in 1590, they would provide new hope for Christianity in Japan, where the situation had become more dangerous for Japanese converts and European missionaries since 1587. The four Japanese ambassadors had become an essential part of the missionary work, as they had also entered the Jesuit Order (Pacheco, 1971, 437-438). In addition to them, Mesquita had brought back a printing press and the necessary "*letra rodonda*" for the Japanese language from Europe, which, in the future, would be used to print books in Japan that were supposed to help the missionaries with their work, especially with regard to the provision of textbooks that could help to improve the language capacities of the Jesuits (Schilling, 1940, 648; see also Schurhammer, 1928). The equipment, however, might have arrived too late, as the Jesuit Order now faced serious problems in Japan.

Anti-Christian Persecutions and Decline

Toyotomi Hideyoshi was able to expand his rule over most of Japan before also attempting to invade Korea and even China (Jacob, 2017). Once he had done this, he initiated anti-Christian measures (Elison, 1973, 109-141), which Tokugawa Ieyasu would later continue, and Christianity would be fully prohibited and all missionaries officially expelled in 1614 (Friedrich-Stegmann, 2018). This, however, was not only a religious issue; the anti-Christian decrees, as has been emphasized by several researchers, were related to political aspects and the prevention of resistance and social changes that might have threatened the newly established shogunate of the Tokugawa family (Ōhashi, 1996; Murai, 2002). The decree of 1587, according to which churches were to be closed and "recently-arrived Mendicant missionaries in Nagasaki" were to be executed, began a "decade of instability" (Tronu Montane, 2012b, 3). Although, after Toyotomi Hideyoshi's conquest of Kyūshū, half of the territory was held by Christian daimyōs (Laures, 1959/60, 384-385), the new ruler of Japan ordered a policy of persecution, which caused the Jesuits to give up some of their institutions, e.g., the college in Bungo (Cieslik, 1959, 40). The Christian rulers had to act carefully not to be too openly resistant against the new edicts, and the number of new conversions dropped, especially since many daimyōs feared the repercussions of such a step. When missionaries visited those leading families who remained faithful Christians, they were consequently quite busy caring for these communities, especially since all actions related to religious services had to be taken care of as secretly as possible to avoid any suspicion from forces that would have used knowledge about these Christian acts to make a case against the local rulers (Laures, 1959/60, 386-387).

The new situation was not easy to deal with, as the Jesuits could hardly establish permanent presences, even in the Christian parts of Kyūshū, and they were consequently driven back to strongholds like Nagasaki, although they tried to keep their service to the respective communities in Japan alive. When Valignano returned to the island country in 1590, he was able to meet Toyotomi Hideyoshi for an audience in Kyoto. On the way to the capital, Valignano visited the Christian nobility in Kurume and baptized around 150 people there. The situation was still flexible, it seemed, especially since "[o]bedience to these edicts had not so far been enforced," so Valignano felt that there was still room for debate and negotiation, although for many missionaries and converts, "uncertainty and anxiety remained" (Moran, 1993, 16). The Visitor was received as an ambassador, and the four Japanese who had been sent to Europe accompanied him, as well as João Rodrigues, who translated for Valignano when he met the new ruler of Japan in person. The Jesuit Visitor was quite annoyed by the political changes that had taken place since he had left the country because the efforts that had been undertaken to drive the missionary work forward seemed to have been in vain: "As soon as we begin to preach or make conversions anywhere, such strange events take place that it really seems as if Our Lord is undoing what we do, so that we not only gain nothing, but lose what had previously been gained with such effort" (Moran, 1993, 57).

Regardless of such feelings, Valignano, whose talent as a negotiator was obvious, successfully persuaded Toyotomi to relax his decree and obtained permission for the Jesuits to stay in the country as long as their work was undertaken rather discreetly. Although the order's missionary work had become more complicated, it could at least continue. Regardless of this success, the Jesuits could no longer hope to continue their previous strategy, related to the principle of *Cuius regio eius religio*, which concerned how they had usually converted the daimyōs, e.g., Arima Harunobu, whom Valignano had baptized in 1580, whose subjects – 70,000 in Arima – would have automatically followed this conversion that was perceived like an order (Ibid., 64). Now, with Hideyoshi's decrees, although softened, the previous missionary strategy, "convert the ruler, and his subjects would come flocking to the Church" (Ibid.), could no longer be pursued.

Due to this strategy, many Japanese Christians could not be considered to be devoted believers but often only accepted the foreign religion as a consequence of the conversion of their feudal lord. The latter, in addition, might only have converted due to political or economic considerations, as proximity to the Jesuits could have generated access to trade or military support. During the *sengoku jidai*, the success of the order in Japan was, therefore, at least to some extent, a consequence of the political necessities of the daimyōs, and the situation caused a serious setback for the missionaries, as those Christians who had only converted half-heartedly would now reverse their decision due to the demands of a more centralized Japan under Hideyoshi's rule. The relatively large number of converts in the early 1580s was also too much for the relatively small number of Jesuit missionaries, and, as Valignano described, "the great majority of Japanese converts do not have the right disposition for baptism, are inadequately instructed and tested, and are unimpressive or unedifying when they become Christians" (Ibid., 65). For practical reasons, the Jesuits had focused on converting the rulers in the first place, which would now, due to the new circumstances, cause tremendous problems, especially in the cases where daimyōs renounced their Christian faith so as not to cause conflict with the new ruling authorities. At this point, it might also have been rather unfortunate that none of the four Japanese ambassadors who had returned from Europe was willing to establish a link with Hideyoshi, who had requested their service, and, instead, that they all decided to continue their path toward the Jesuit novitiate. In the situation that was presented to them in 1590, with the anti-Christian decrees in place, it would have been wiser to establish close ties with Hideyoshi and persuade him of the advantages Christianity might have been able to offer for his rule (Ibid., 17-18). However, this chance was not taken, and further historical developments would cause more problems for the Jesuits.

Although the decrees had been softened, it was not possible for the Jesuits to visit Christian communities that were now ruled by anti-Christian daimyōs, as was the case in Hakata, where Kobayakawa Hideaki (1577-1602), a nephew of Hideyoshi, ruled (Laures, 1959/60, 392). This case emphasizes the dilemma of the Jesuits, who were not only no longer more than tolerated guests in Japan but also guests who had to remain silent and unseen. Regardless of this fact, there was a short revival at the end of the century when Toyotomi Hideyoshi died, and Tokugawa Ieyasu had not yet fully taken over the former's power. The

Jesuits experienced a short break from persecution at this time, and their capable leadership now tried to use this situation to strengthen Christianity in Japan again. The Christian daimyōs from Kyūshū, who had accompanied the Japanese army to Korea, where Hideyoshi had attempted to create an empire based on expansion (Lewis, 2015; Swope, 2016), now returned and offered the Jesuits another chance to strengthen their influence in southwest Japan. Mōri Hidekane (1567-1601), who had returned from Korea, allowed the Jesuits to return to his domain, Kurume, where a Jesuit father and a brother could soon resume their activities and would also prepare the baptism of the daimyō's vassals (Laures, 1959/60, 393). The events of 1587, therefore, clearly emphasize that the Jesuits had to pay special attention to the local politics in Japan to secure their position and even their existence as such. The revival of Christian activities was soon destroyed again during the war Tokugawa led against his enemies, as the latter wanted to take Hideyoshi's position and therefore needed to wage war against those who supported the son of the former ruler. The Jesuit missionaries' position consequently once again became dependent on the outcome of a local struggle for power (Ibid., 395).

Luis Cerqueira (1551/52-1614), the second bishop of Japan, would turn Nagasaki into a center of Christianity in Japan in the early 1600s, and regardless of the political changes, in the initial period of the 17th century, he seems to have been able to continue the successful work of the Visitor. However, Valignano, who in general had a positive view of Cerqueira, again stressed the problems faced in Japan in a report from 1601:

> The properties and qualities of this country are so strange, the mode of government of the state so different, and the customs and ways of living so extraordinary and so far removed from our own that they are difficult to comprehend even for those of us who have been living here and dealing with the people for many years. How much more difficult, then, to make them intelligible to people in Europe. (Valignano, 1601, Dedication, cited in Moran, 1993, 29)

Reports were consequently not always accurate and provided misleading images, which Valignano himself intended to correct: "In some cases the writer had only just arrived in Japan, and put down what he heard from others, without knowing anything of the language, or having any knowledge or experience of the country.... The consequence is that full and complete information is not yet available in Europe about this nation of Japan" (Ibid., 30). In a way, Valignano, who considered himself to be the "Japan expert" within the Jesuit Order, hereby expressed an indirect criticism of Cerqueira, who would nevertheless revive Christian life, although with a clear focus on Nagasaki (Kataoka, 1985; Oliveira e Costa, 1998).

The limitations regarding the visibility of the missionaries had obviously posed a problem since 1587:

> To introduce Christianity to Japanese society, missionaries constructed residences, churches, hospitals and schools in villages and towns, interacting with the Japanese. The prohibition of Christianity by the Japanese authorities involved not only the desacralization, dismantling, and appropriation of all Christian spaces, but also the production of Buddhist temples and civil authorities' buildings in their stead. (Tronu Montane, 2012b, 10)

In Nagasaki, this problem was not that serious, and Christianity continued to play an important and visible role there, especially since the city was also home to Portuguese and other European residents. In other parts of the country, however, more than 200 Christian churches were closed, and the religious care of the Jesuits was consequently restricted to the private spaces of converts. While other orders, like the Franciscans, continued to build new churches or hospitals, e.g., in Kyoto and Osaka, the Jesuits in Kyūshū had rather limited options to counter the prohibition measures that were in place from 1587 (Tronu Montane, 2012b, 11).

Bishop Cerqueira's success in the late sixteenth and early seventeenth centuries was consequently a locally limited one, and as Tronu Montane pointed out:

> Nagasaki presents three distinctive characteristics that make it richly suited for such a spatial analysis. First, its foundation and rapid growth as a town was intimately linked to the close collaboration between Jesuit missionaries and Portuguese merchants. Second, most of its population was Christian since its foundation: the Christian community of Nagasaki included not only missionaries and Japanese Christians, but also the Portuguese and Spanish merchants who resided in Japan temporarily or permanently. Finally, when the Bishop of Japan established his See in Nagasaki, it became the centre of Japanese Christianity. (Ibid.)

When he reported his successes, he did so in the context of "a rather atypical Christian community, unrepresentative of most early modern Japanese Christian communities" (Ibid.). Nevertheless, the "Christian town" continued to flourish until 1614, when Tokugawa Ieyasu eventually decided to ban the foreign religion and its representatives from the country completely until it was reintroduced to the country after the forced opening of Japan in 1873.

Due to Tokugawa Ieyasu's edict, most Jesuits had to leave for Macao or Manila, and only in hiding were some communities able to keep their Christian faith, while the missionaries who continued their work in the country were prosecuted by the authorities (Hagemann, 1942). It was possible to remain Christian, although contacts with foreign elements were totally cut off, so it was a surprise when "in 1865 a community of underground Christians revealed its faith to the French missionaries of the Société des Missions Étrangères de Paris in Nagasaki" (Tronu Montane, 2012b, 9). The already-mentioned Diogo de Mesquita had hoped that Tokugawa Ieyasu would revert the severe punishment for Christians like Toyotomi Hideyoshi had relaxed his own edicts before, but this did not happen, nor could the Jesuits and the converts they wanted to take care of be secured by the daimyōs who had so far supported the order's activities in Japan. In a letter from 6 October 1514, Mesquita describes his diplomatic efforts in this regard:

> I was sent to the Court because I know and am friendly with the governor who persecutes us. I went to see whether this persecution could be halted by our proving our innocence, because the principal reason, among many others, why they persecute us is that they look on all of us as conquerors of foreign kingdoms on behalf of our king under the guise of spreading Christianity. But on my arrival at a city called Osaka next to Miyako, I was prevented by its governor from continuing to the kingdom of Suruga where the king and his Court reside. This was probably because the priests expelled from Osaka and Miyako were there at that time, their churches had been pulled down and burned, and the persecution was at its height. (Roman Archives of the Society of Jesus, Japonica-Sinica, 36, fl. 37-37v, cited in Pacheco, 1971, 435)

Regardless of his attempts to find a diplomatic solution, Mesquita eventually had to give up, and a month before he died in Nagasaki on 4 November 1614, he wrote in a letter dated 6 October,

> I think that God is expelling us from Japan in punishment of our defects and sins. May it please His Divine Majesty that we make amendment for them so that we may once more return to the work of conversion and to preaching among such fine Christians. I can assure you from my long experience with them over many years and particularly during this persecution (as you will see in the Annual Letter that is being sent off) that there does not seem to be any church in the whole of Christendom which surpasses them. Indeed, I regard them as the best in the world. (Roman Archives of the Society of Jesus, Japonica-Sinica, 36, fl. 37, cited in ibid., 436).

Three days after Mesquita's death, the Jesuit missionaries who were leaving the country set sail for Macao and Manila. The hospitals run by the Jesuit Order could continue their work for a few more years, but by 1620, according to a report to Rome, "the few churches that had remained standing had been pulled down, the cemeteries had been desecrated, and the hospitals had been burnt down" (Ibid., 437).

The Jesuits who stayed behind would end up as martyrs of the Christian faith (Trigault, 1623; Imago, 1640; Omata Rappo, 2020a; 2023). In 1597, Toyotomi Hideyoshi had already ordered 26 Christians to be crucified in Nagasaki – six Franciscans, three Jesuits (two of them had just been ordained the day before), and 17 Japanese Christians (Moran, 1993, 2; Omata Rappo, 2020b) –, and martyrdom would become the general fate of the Jesuits in Japan after 1614 (Vitelleschi, 1632; Cieslik, 1959, 35-36; Kataoka, 1970; 1979), an experience often described as "Resolute. Glorious. Triumphant" (Heuts, 2015, 79).[2] Afterward, the letters of the remaining Jesuits were more accusing in tone, and "the Japanese are described in stark contrasts between the converted and the murders with little to no middle ground [and] the Japanese were portrayed either positively, purely on the basis of their Christian habits, or negatively based on their aggression towards Christianity" (Ibid., 98). By 1600, the Jesuits had been successful in converting around 300,000-500,000 Japanese to the Christian faith, but the Battle of Sekigahara, which cemented the rise and rule of Tokugawa Ieyasu, was a turning point and opened the century that would soon see the end of Jesuit activities in Japan (Ibid., 102; see also Yamamoto, 2012, 250). Regardless of the reforms of the 1580s and the Jesuit attempts to master the Japanese language to make their missionary work more effective, the Japanese case became a disaster, although it was ultimately not mistranslations that would play the decisive role. Like in Peru, the uncontrollable political circumstances were responsible for the end of the mission, although, unlike in Latin America, the missionary work in Japan could not be continued. The efforts by the missionaries to increase intercultural understanding through effective education with regard to the Japanese language therefore eventually proved unsuccessful, as the missionaries could not prevent the local authorities from burning down their churches and killing the Jesuits who resisted the newly established anti-Christian order.

The Jesuits and the Japanese Language

Boscariol divides the adaptation methodology with regard to Jesuit language education in Japanese into three periods, namely an experimental one during

---

[2] Cristóvão Ferreira (ca. 1580-1650) is the one known case in which a Jesuit, after being captured by the Japanese, committed apostasy (Cieslik, 1973). On the role of the Jesuit fate in Japan and its presentation within European popular culture see Watanabe (2023).

the entry period (2013, 56-85), a consolidation period under Valignano (Ibid., 85-124), and "one of [the] systematization and understanding of the language in grammars and dictionaries, which would assist the teaching and learning of Japanese," which was related to the activities of João Rodrigues (Tçuzu) (Ibid., 125-150). Like Fróis, Rodrigues had managed to learn Japanese quite well and provided essential instructions on the use and grammar of the language that future Jesuits needed to get familiar with. Consequently, "[t]he early-modern, Portuguese-sponsored Jesuit mission to Japan left behind a body of Christian literature in Japanese whose alphabetic texts have been a treasure trove for linguists, its existence a point of pride for Christian sectarians, and its content rich material for historians" (Schwemmer, 2014, 466; see also Doi, 1939; Farge, 2002). Manoel Barreto (ca. 1564-1620), for example, provided his fellow Jesuits with a "382-folio manuscript … containing a variety of basic Catholic texts – gospel readings for the entire church year, miracle stories, devotional meditations, and saints' lives" (Ibid.).[3] The text is significant as it provides an impression of the things the Japanese would have heard from the missionaries. In addition to such text collections, the dictionaries the Jesuits prepared prove that they spent time and effort in getting themselves familiar with the Japanese language (Rojo-Mejuto, 2018).

In contrast to the Jesuits in Peru, the knowledge about and the use of the Japanese language was much more important, as there were no colonial authorities in Japan who used the language of the missionaries. Consequently, the Japanese was not only a tool for evangelization as it was in Peru but also an essential means to survive. Without speaking it, the Jesuits in Japan would have been lost and unable to approach possible converts at all. They were not backed by an existent colonial structure but, to use a more business-oriented expression had to be able to penetrate their potential market first. Language education was consequently not a debatable topic, and the resistance of people like Cabral shows that the lack of a global mindset and resistance to accommodation would cause problems both for the missionaries' work and with regard to the overall aim of the Jesuits in Japan, i.e., successful proselytization.

Highlighting the necessity to train the Jesuit members in Japan particularly well with regard to the language, in 1601, Valignano argued that

> It has to be understood that the language and government of Japan are very different indeed from those which we have in Europe – there has never, after all, been any contact between them – and they also have different names for things. Now some of these names can in a sense be regarded as corresponding to our words, but they do not really match

---

[3] The manuscript is stored in the Vatican Library: *Reg. lat.* 459, ff. 78–82v.

> them very well, so that it cannot properly be said that they mean the same things. We use the titles emperor, king, duke, marquis, count, for certain ranks. In Japan they do not use these titles, and the titles which they do use do not correspond very well to the meaning which these words convey in Europe. But since in Europe the Japanese titles are not understood, the Portuguese and Ours, so as to be understood, use our words for these things when they speak or write to Europeans. In transferring titles in this way mistakes are frequently made, especially by those who do not really know the meaning of the words, and so it is essential to provide some explanation of this empire, and of the names and ranks of the Japanese lords. (Valignano, 1601, ch. 5, cited in Moran, 1993, 31)

Language must consequently have been understood as more than just a form of communication but also as something like a "cultural code" that needed to be learned first through language so that the Jesuits could instrumentalize it as a tool for successful proselytization in Japan. Valignano thus continues his evaluation:

> The only kind of learning known and respected in Japan was learning in the language and writings of Japan, but the seminary aimed eventually to produce priests, and this was impossible without Latin. In Japan knowledge of Latin and "the true sciences" conferred neither status nor esteem, and this in a society where status and esteem were everything. Those who know Latin, become priests, and also master Japanese language and letters will indeed command respect, but this is a very distant prospect, and in the meantime the boys apply themselves eagerly to the study of their own language and literature, but very reluctantly to Latin and "our other sciences." But it is essential that they study Latin first and Japanese only when they have completed the Latin course, for Latin is very new and very strange to them, and those who do not learn it young do not learn it at all. And they should be separated from those who study Japanese, for when they are together the students of Latin, sunk in melancholy, "dumb and deprived of language," watch the others going forward, able to preach and write, and are consumed with longing to study their own language. (Valignano, 1601, ch. 5, cited in Moran, 1993, 165-166)

While the Jesuits therefore initially had to rely heavily on Japanese translators and preachers, in later years, they successfully trained Western missionaries as well, although not all mastered the language at a similar level.

In contrast to the Jesuits who tried to learn Japanese and struggled with the language (Moran, 1993, 178-188), many Japanese struggled with Latin – causing an obstacle for possible aspirations of becoming a Jesuit and a priest – when they became novices of the Jesuit Order. Valignano recommended separating these student groups, and indeed, the problems for both groups with regard to studying the respective languages could thereby be diminished. However, the shortage of priests to take care of the numerically growing communities of Japanese Christians made the order rely on the work of *dōjuku*, Japanese lay leaders who supported the missionaries in their work (Fujita, 1991, 74-76; Moran, 1993, 167; Fujitani, 2016, 307). Regardless of these issues, the Jesuits had no choice but to make sure that the missionaries were educated in both languages, as they were needed to address Valignano's demands for a cultural accommodation policy deemed necessary to secure successful proselytization. In the *Sumario de las cosas de Japón* (1583), the Visitor stressed this necessity in particular when he emphasized that

> however much we learn of the language, and with however much effort, we still sound like children compared to them, and we never reach the stage of knowing all about their writing, and being able to write books ourselves, and yet this is something absolutely essential in Japan, for without it we shall never earn the reputation or be held in the esteem which we need, nor shall we be able to translate or write the books necessary for the fostering and the governing of Christianity. And this is perfectly clear from our experience up to the present, for all that has been done has been done by some Japanese brothers that we have in the Society. (Valignano, 1954, ch. 13, cited in Moran, 1993, 179)

At the same time, the Visitor highlighted

> the great difficulty of learning their language, which is so elegant and so copious, as we said above, that they speak in one way, write in another, and preach in a third, and there is one set of words to be employed in addressing the gentry, and another in addressing the lower classes, and there is the same sort of difference, in many cases, between the words used by children and women and the words used by men. And in their writing they have an infinite number of characters, so that none of Ours can learn to write or compose books that can be shown to anyone. Some of them get to the point where they can preach to the Christians, but when they do it is so different from what any Japanese brother, even an ignoramus, can do, that when there is a brother present the fathers are reduced to silence. (Valignano, 1954, ch. 16, cited in Moran, 1993, 179)

It is, in a way, tragic that the Jesuits followed Valignano's lead and invested so much effort to succeed with regard to their language-related education but, in the end, could not use it to resist the orders announced by the new political leadership of Japan. While the Japanese state had been unified again and brought under the strong central control of the Tokugawa family, the Jesuit Order had been turned into an obstacle to that unity that left no alternative for the new rulers of Japan but to get rid of those foreign elements within their ruled territory: "In any case, Hideyoshi Toyotomi and Ieyasu Tokugawa, who ended the Warring States period, refused to coexist with Christians, and this policy was maintained until the mid-nineteenth century when the Edo Shogunate collapsed" (Ōhashi, 2016, 126).

Jesuit Missionaries in Japan

The documented number of Jesuits in Japan grew steadily between 1553 and 1614, climaxing in 1606/7, when 136 Jesuits, 60 padres (fathers), and 76 irmãos (brothers) are documented. The number of padres reached its climax in 1614, with 62 serving in Japan at the same time, while the number of irmãos reached its all-time height in 1592/93 with 85, declining to 53 in 1614. It can also be argued that real growth in the numbers, and thereby the organization's ability to deal with larger numbers of converts efficiently, did not substantially increase before the 1570s when educational facilities were established to train new novices.

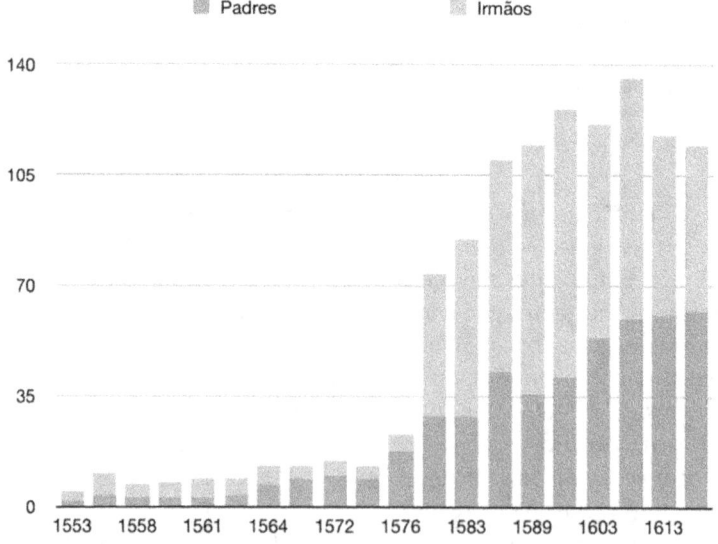

Fig. 4.3: Number of Jesuits in Japan between 1553 and 1614.

Tab. 4.3: Number of padres and irmãos serving in Japan between 1553 and 1614 (including available data for Japanese padres and irmãos).

Year	Padres	Irmãos	Japanese Padres	Japanese Irmãos
1553	2	3		
1555	4	7		
1558	3	4		
1559	3	5		
1561	3	6		
1562/3	4	5		
1564	7	6		
1571	9	4		
1572	10	5		
1575	9	4		
1576	18	5		1
1581	29	45		20
1583	29	56		26
1587	43	67		35
1589	36	79		60
1592/3	41	85	/	/
1603	54	67	/	/
1606/7	60	76	2	55
1613	61	57	5	44
1614	62	53	5	/

It is also worth noting here that the number of Japanese irmãos grew from one in 1576 to 60 in 1589, while in the same period, no Japanese was promoted to the rank of padre. The first Japanese padres are documented in 1606/7, but they only count for two out of a total of 60. Although their number rose to five in 1614, it must be argued that the Japanese Jesuit mission failed to fully and equally use the local potential for the management structures in place. This might have been responsible for the impression that the Jesuits were a purely foreign organization that only exploited the native irmãos, who were often reported to act as preachers. In the smaller Jesuit units, whose members were responsible for more peripheral regions, it would not have been surprising for a Europan padre to work with a native irmão to ensure that the native population could be addressed by someone who spoke Japanese as his native language.

Entry Period (1549-1563)

The entry period is demarcated by Francis Xavier's first visit to Japan in 1549 on the one side and the conversion of the first daimyō Ōmura Sumitada (1533-1587) to Christianity in 1563 on the other. The following 18 Jesuits[4] served during this time period in Japan (Tab. 4.4).

Tab. 4.4: Jesuits who served in Japan between 1549 and 1563.

Fathers (Pater/Padre) = Leading management	Brothers (Frater/Irmão)
Luis de Almeida	Pero de Alcáceva
Joannes Baptisla	António Díaz
Nunes Barreto	Melchior Díaz
Balthasar Gago	Joáo Fernández
Cosme de Torres	Luís Fróis
Gaspar Vilella	Estávan de Góis
	Guilherme
	Juan Hernandes
	Lourenço
	Fernán Méndez
	Ruy Pereyra
	Duarte da Silva

---

[4] A detailed list for all reported years is provided in Appendix 1 (10.1).

The Cases

During the entry period, only once, specifically in 1555, are more than 10 Jesuits reported to have served in Japan. While a few hundred Jesuits had been trained in Macao at the same time, Japan remained a rather peripheral province of the order in the first 15 years of its existence. Nevertheless, the leading Jesuits were quite active and could report the first major conversion of a local feudal lord in 1563.

Consolidation Period (1564-1587)

During the consolidation period between 1564 and 1587, when Toyotomi Hideyoshi, one of the three unifiers of Japan, issued a decree against the Jesuits, the number of their members in Japan increased to more than 100, among them 43 padres (Tab. 4.5).

Tab. 4.5: Jesuit padres who served in Japan in 1587.

Antoninus	Marcus Ferrarius	Alfonsus de Lucen	Gonçalus Rebellus
Joanes Baptista	Antonius Fernández	Theodoro Mantels	Franciscus Rodríguez
Franciscus Calderonus	Joseph Fornalelus	Damianus Marinus	Joanes Rodríguez [Giram]
Franciscus Carrionus	Aloicius Fróis	Gil de Mata	Aries Sanches
Georgius Carvalhal	Petrus Gómez	Melchior de Mora	Joannes Franciscus Stephanonius
Gregorius de Céspedes	Sebastianus Gonçales	Cristophorus de Morera	
Antonius Franciscus Chritana	Alfonsus González	Organtinus	
Gaspar Coelius	Fulvius Gregorius	Franciscus Passius	
Celsus Confalonerus	Franciscus Laguna	Petrus Paulus [Navarro]	
Petrus Crassus	Christophorus de Leone [de León]	Franciscus Pérez	
Joanes de Crasto	Antonius López	Julius Pianus	
Alvarus Diaz	Balthasar López	Petrus Ramonus	

The Jesuits successfully continued their missionary expansion after the entry period, established educational facilities (*collegios*), and began educating Japanese novices. Nevertheless, the leadership of the order in Japan remained in European hands. With regard to a global mindset, an internal conflict among the leading Jesuits had weakened the missionaries' efforts quite substantially, although the order's eventual decline was stimulated by external events. The steady unification process started a centralization process that would also lead to hostile governmental measures against the Jesuits. Toyotomi's decree of 1587 therefore marks the cesura between the consolidation period and the one of decline.

Period of Decline (1588-1614)

Regardless of the changed political climate, the official report for 1589 names 116 Jesuits in Japan – 37 padres, 19 European irmãos, and 60 Japanese irmãos. The number of padres had increased to 62 by 1614 (Tab. 4.6), although the overall number of reported Jesuits decreased by one to 115, and only four of the padres were Japanese. The management level of the Jesuit Order in its Japanese context was consequently still predominantly European, although a large number of the irmãos had been recruited within the country, and they played an important role in the missionary work as they were usually the ones to allow a broader level of communication with the Japanese converts.

The number of padres consequently steadily increased, while the number of novices and irmãos seem to have been negatively impacted since the mid-1580s when the Japanese authorities began to act against the Jesuits. With Tokugawa Ieyasu as the new shōgun (highest military leader of Japan) and his policies that were supposed to secure the Tokugawa family's power for the future (Jacob, 2014), the decline of the Jesuits, which had been initiated by Toyotomi Hideyoshi, the second of the three unifiers of Japan in the late 1580s, could ultimately no longer be countered. Ieyasu acted against all representatives of Christianity in Japan because he considered the Christian ideas spread by the Jesuit missionaries a danger to the internal security of the newly united country. The Jesuits had failed to realize these changes early on and to persuade Ieyasu of the values the Jesuits' missionary activities could have for Japan's spiritual unification. However, it might be added here that even a closer tie to the ruling elites might not have guaranteed further success, as Christianity as such challenged the new social order Tokugawa Ieyasu wanted to see applied to separate Japanese society into four social classes, namely warriors, artisans, peasants, and merchants. A religious belief that demanded the equality of all people would hardly have helped Ieyasu secure the warrior class' leading role.

The Cases 81

Tab. 4.6: Jesuit padres who served in Japan in 1614.

João Mateus Adami	Camillo Constanço	João Rodriguez Girão	Francisco Pacheco
António Álvarez	João da Costa	Ruy Gómez	Francisco Pírez
Jerónimo de Ángeles	Nicolao da Costa	Manuel Gonçalvez	João Pomério
João Vicente Antolhete	Mateus de Couros	António Ixida	João Bautista Porro
Jácome António	Gaspar de Crasto	Francisco Lobo	Sebastião Quimura (Japanese)
Nicolai de Ávila	António Francisco Critano	Afonso de Lucena	Vicente Ribeiro
Ambrosio de Barros	Álvaro Dias	Francisco Luis	Jerónimo Rodríguez
João Bautista	Carlo Espínola	Luiz (Japanese)	Manuel Rodríguez
João Bautista Bayeça	Francisco Eugénio	Pero Márquez	Bertholameu de Siqueira
Manuel Borges	Marcos Ferraro	Gabriel de Matos	Bertolameu Soares
Manuel Borralho	Christóvão Ferreira	Pero Martins	Thomé Tçuji (Japanese)
Francisco Calderón	António Fernández	Pero Morejón	Balthezar de Torres
Martinho Campo	Bento Fernández	Belchior de Moura	Sebastião Vieira
Diogo Carvalho	Máncio Firabayaxi (Japanese)	Julião Nacaura (Japanese)	Joãp Bautista Zola
Valentim Carvalho	João de Fonseca	Pero (Pietro) Paulo Navarro	
Celso Confalonero	Garcia Garcéz	João Nicolao	

Jesuit Managers in Japan: Some Examples

The following section will provide some short "manager portfolios" for the Jesuit leadership during the three periods of the order's missionary work in Japan. It will provide more detail on the leading individuals to the extent that sufficient data could be collected about them and their individual cases allow some evaluation of general issues in their respective time periods.

Francis Xavier

Francis Xavier is probably the most important Jesuit with regard to the history of the Jesuit mission in Japan (Bartoli, 1858; Venn, 1862; Bodkin, 1952; Rodrick, 1952; Pacheko, 1974; Takahashi, 2001; Ellis, 2003; Rubiés, 2012), as he was the first of the order to visit the island country in 1549 (Katorikku Bunka Kyo⁻kai, 1949). In a later letter, Xavier (1552) described the landing at Kagoshima as follows:

> By the favor of God we all arrived at Japan in perfect health on the 15th of August, 1549. We landed at Cagoxima, the native place of our companions. We were received in the most friendly way by all the people of the city, especially the relations of Paul, the Japanese convert, all of whom had the blessing to receive the light of truth from heaven, and by Paul's persuasion became Christians.

In reality, the Jesuits were lucky that Japan was not united at the time, and the local feudal rulers, the daimyōs, were interested in ties with foreigners, who could act not only as a representative for a new religion but also as a link to foreign trade networks. Furthermore, it was not the first time that an alternative religion had been imported from abroad, as Shōtoku Taishi (574-622) had declared Buddhism to be the state religion and therefore initiated a transition from Shintōism, the seminal pantheist religion of Japan, toward a state-oriented Buddhism, whose representatives would remain quite privileged until the end of the Tokugawa period in the 1860s, when a state Shintō was revitalized instead (Como, 2008; Ketelaar, 1990). With regard to Xavier's initial contact, the "market entry" of the Jesuits in Japan met advantageous conditions, namely the lack of a central government and an interest from the local rulers in Japan's southwest to combine a religious mission with trade-related aspects. The Jesuits were consequently considered to act not only as missionaries but also, through their "religious mobility" (Coello de la Rosa, 2022, 174-175), as agents of early modern globalization, from whom the daimyōs in some Japanese provinces intended to gain.

Xavier had left Lisbon in 1541, and before reaching Japan eight years later, he initially served in Goa (India) after spending some months in Mozambique. Between 1545 and 1547, he would spend time in Southeast Asia, especially the Maluku Islands, e.g., Ambon Island (Bouhours, 1743, 130-159). Xavier consequently had some experience with missionary work in culturally different contexts before he eventually landed in Japan and could assess the possibilities

The Cases 83

for future missionary work there as well. In a letter to his colleagues in Europe, he emphasized

> Japan is a very large empire entirely composed of islands. One language is spoken throughout, *not very difficult to learn.* This country was discovered by the Portuguese eight or nine years ago. The Japanese are very ambitious of honors and distinctions, and think themselves superior to all nations in military glory and valor. They prize and honor all that has to do with war, and all such things, and here is nothing of which they are so proud as of weapons adorned with gold and silver. They always wear swords and daggers both in and out of the house, and when they go to sleep they hang them at the bed's head. In short, they value arms more than any people I have ever seen. They are excellent archers, and usually fight on foot, though there is no lack of horses in the country. They are very polite to each other, but not to foreigners, whom they utterly despise. They spend their means on arms, bodily adornment, and on a number of attendants, and do not in the least care to save money. They are, in short, a very warlike people, and engaged in continual wars among themselves; the most powerful in arms bearing the most extensive sway. They have all one sovereign, *although for one hundred and fifty years past the princes have ceased to obey him,* and this is the cause of their perpetual feuds. (Xavier, 1552; my emphasis)

Xavier's "market evaluation" was consequently quite realistic, and he realized that while Japan was officially under the rule of an emperor, the tennō, it was ruled in quite a decentralized way. That there was only one supposedly easy language was also considered an advantage for a possible missionary venture in the island country. In addition, Xavier highlighted the lack of a similar religious belief (App, 1997; see also Rubiés, 2012), which is why he emphasized the niche the Christian missionaries could probably address in the years to come:

> The Japanese doctrines teach absolutely nothing concerning the creation of the world, of the sun, the moon, the stars, the heavens, the earth, sea, and the rest, and do not believe that they have any origin but themselves. The people were greatly astonished on hearing it said that there is one sole Author and common Father of souls, by whom they were created. This astonishment was caused by the fact that in their religious traditions there is nowhere any mention of a Creator of the universe. (Xavier, 1552)

Like modern-day managers, Xavier had provided a "market analysis" and some insight (Ellis, 2003), which should have been considered during the later "market entry" when the Jesuits began their missionary work in Japan. The Jesuit missionaries who followed his lead would gain from this analysis, as they had at least some information relevant to their work in a culturally quite different context. Xavier himself did not speak Japanese, which made preaching during his visit complicated (App, 1997a), but he was accompanied by a Japanese named Anjirō, who had informed the Jesuit about the circumstances in his home country beforehand. As such, Xavier was not "flying blind" but could already rely on information he used quite successfully for his first trip to the new region for possible missionary work. Xavier eventually started the journey with Anjirō and three other Jesuits, and they were received quite amicably by the daimyō Shimazu Takahisa (1514-1571) (Niina, 2017), who ruled the province of Satsuma on Kyūshū. Xavier traveled to other parts of the country as well and received permission for Jesuits to preach in some provinces. The "market entry" was consequently successful under Xavier's leadership, although he had no relevant language skills. Nevertheless, he had used the resources at hand, especially the knowledge of his intercultural mediator Anjirō, and he was dogmatically flexible enough to look for an initial niche for the missionary work rather than follow an aggressive replacement policy, although conflicts with Buddhist leaders could not be fully avoided during the early years of the work of the Jesuits in Japan (Tōkyō Daigaku Shiryō Hensanjo, 1990).

Cosme de Torres

Cosme de Torres was a Spanish Jesuit, born in Valencia, who would be essential for the early history, i.e., the "market entry" of the Jesuits in Japan. He joined the order in 1535 and subsequently served as a grammar teacher at the Mons Rrendinus University in Mallorca, which provided him with valuable language skills he could use during his later missions. After a return to Spain, he served in Santo Domingo and Mexico (Schurhammer, 1929, 11-12). Eventually, he accompanied Francis Xavier on his first journey to Japan, where Torres would, as mission superior between 1551 and 1570, be the leading Jesuit authority in Japan until his death in 1570 on the island of Amakusa, nowadays in Kumamoto Prefecture. While Xavier tried to get an audience with the Japanese emperor during his trip, Torres stayed in Yamaguchi, where the Jesuits had received permission to begin their missionary work. Regardless of conflicts with Buddhist monks (Fujita, 1991, 39), with whom Torres also had some intellectual dialogues (Schurhammer, 1929, 29-36), Torres was able to increase the number of converts steadily, and he reported to Jesuits in Valencia in 1551 that "[t]he Japanese are more than ready than any other country in the world for that our belief is planted in their country. They are mature for it beyond measure. They are led by reason, as much or even more than the Spanish people. They are more eager for knowledge than any other people I have met before" (cited in Schurhammer, 1929, 47).

Torres stayed in Yamaguchi until the mid-1550s when the Mori clan began to act in a hostile way against the missionaries. He was able to receive protection from the daimyō of the Bungo Province (northeastern Kyūshū), Ōtomo Sorin, who was a famous convert to Christianity in sixteenth-century Japan (Matsuda, 1947). Nevertheless, Sorin was only interested in the Jesuits as a political tool to achieve his aims with regard to his own position during the period of the warring states (*sengoku jidai*, 1467-1615). The Jesuits had arrived at a time when several feudal lords were trying to expand their positions due to the decline of the central rule of the shōgun, namely the Ashikaga shogunate (1336-5173), which did not end officially before 1573, but which was weak and opened room for ambitious daimyōs to contest the centralized rule of the highest military leader of Japan.

In the early 1560s, Torres moved to the harbor town of Yokoseura, where the local daimyō Ōmura Sumitada (1533-1587), the first of the Japanese feudal lords who had actually converted to Christianity in 1563 and was baptized as Bartolomeu, had opened the harbor for trade with the Portuguese. In later years, he would also grant the Jesuits and the Portuguese access to the port of Nagasaki in 1580 (Pacheco, 1973). Torres was successful in his missionary work not only because he was able to secure their support, which was often only related to political considerations, but also because he was able to gain the trust of the local converts, whom he addressed as valuable members of the Christian community (Fujita, 1991, 49). Furthermore, he secured education for the community, which included Latin for the converts as well as Japanese for the Jesuits. This twofold educational approach eventually secured the successful growth of the order's province in Japan. Torres consequently successfully continued the spread of Christianity during the period of the Jesuits' "market entry" in Japan.

Balthasar Gago

Balthasar Gago was a Portuguese Jesuit who initially served in Goa and was among the Jesuits who established a branch of the order in Cochin as well (Cieslik, 1954; Dehergne, 1973). In 1552, he accompanied Francis Xavier to Malacca and would later join the mission in Japan, where he arrived in 1555 to serve under Cosme de Torres' leadership. Consequently, Gago was part of the group that worked in the direct environment of daimyō Ōtomo Sorin and was able to establish a community of around 500 converts in Hirado. In addition to his missionary work, he provided the first Western account of the Japanese Shintō religion. Gago also provided a catechism for Japanese converts that was quite popular, and, therefore, his work was important for the development of the first Catholic nomenclature in the Japanese language (Zavala & Tamiyo, 2012). This made a more active missionary approach to Japanese women and men possible in the first place, which is why Gago's role in the early success of the Jesuit mission during its early existence must be considered quite important. In the early 1560s, Gago left Japan for Macao, where he helped to prepare further missionaries. His knowledge of Japan and the Japanese language was used as an asset for future missionaries who were supposed to be trained and sent to the island country in the years to come.

Gaspar Vilella

Gaspar Vilella (1526-1572) arrived in Bungo in 1556 after he had become a Jesuit in Goa some years before. He studied Japanese and was able to convert several hundred people to the Christian faith, especially on the island of Tokushima. Regardless of his willingness to adapt to the local circumstances in Japan, especially during the entry period, his presence and acts – he threw Buddhist artifacts into the sea and made converts destroy Buddhist temples in order to replace them with Christian churches – created conflict with the local Buddhist authorities. The conversion of Ōmura Sumitada in 1563 eventually stimulated anti-Christian violence led by Buddhist monks, which was also directed against Vilella as a prominent Jesuit. Before Vilella returned to India in the early 1570s, where he would later die, he introduced Luís Fróis, among others, to the Japanese mission. His case proves that the missionary activities of the Jesuit Order in Japan during the entry period met fierce resistance from existent competitors, i.e., the Buddhists.

Alessandro Valignano

As described above, probably the most important Jesuit in Japan was Alessandro Valignano, who defined the method of accommodation for the order's missionaries in Japan. Although he did not speak Japanese and although, as the Visitor, he was concerned with broader events and developments in the island country, his global mindset allowed Valignano not only to convert important daimyōs during the consolidation period but also to soften the anti-Christian edicts by Toyotomi Hideyoshi to allow the Jesuits to remain in Japan after 1587.

Valignano, after he was accused of wounding a man in Venice and sent to jail, joined the Jesuits in Rome in late 1566 (Moran, 1993, 1) and afterward studied philosophy and physics at the Collegio Romano. Via Lisbon, he reached Goa and later Macao. As Visitor, he later visited Japan three times and always had a decisive impact on the missionary work there. Valignano demanded the Jesuits to apply and even extend their global mindset and to study the Japanese language, although this was not only to provide communicative means but also to achieve a better understanding of the cultural otherness that existed in

Japan. Although Valignano was a visionary, his personality might have been responsible for strife as well, as his orders were not always well-perceived, and the Jesuit Visitor met with resistance from those he gave orders.

Francisco Cabral

Valignano's ideas were contested by Francisco Cabral. The latter was one of the leading figures as provincial in Japan, but he did not speak Japanese, nor was he flexible with regard to dogmatics, and often looked down on the Japanese, whom he did not accept as equal members of the Jesuit Order. Nevertheless, Cabral had been successful in the early consolidation period in converting some leading daimyōs in southwest Japan. Cabral acted according to European ideas and experiences, where the conversion of the ruling elites was the main aim. The provincial of Japan therefore did not care too much for the ordinary believers and possible converts in Japan. He was not really interested in any form of cultural accommodation. Cabral's case consequently proves that short-term missionary success was possible without language skills and a global mindset, but as a person, he was not liked a lot, especially as far as the ordinary Japanese were concerned. His anti-Japanese attitude eventually made him clash with Valignano, who eventually released him from his duties in Japan.

Luís Fróis

Luís Fróis spent most of his life in Japan (Rocha, 2014, 41-56) and can be considered one of the most important witnesses of the Jesuit mission there (Fróis, 1976-1984). Raised in the court circles of Portugal (Loureiro, 2000, 155), Fróis was a well-experienced accountant and administrator whose talents would not go unrecognized during his early years within the Society of Jesus (DI 4, 1948, 403, 458). The young Portuguese entered the order at the age of 16 in 1548 and, in the same year, traveled to India, where he would begin his service (Loureiro, 2000, 156). In Asia, Fróis would see different places before he reached his final destination.

> [He] first served in Bassein, a Portuguese fortress and town in the northwestern coast of India. Then, after a short period in Goa, he settled in Malacca between 1555 and 1557, where the Portuguese held a most strategic fortress. Back in India, Fróis completed his religious education and formation in Goa, where in 1561 he pronounced his vows and entered the priesthood. And in the following year, at the age of thirty, he set sail for the Land of the Rising Sun, where, but for a short stay in Macau, he was to live for the rest of his days. The first part of his life had been spent in Portugal, the second part, in sundry Asian territories, but always within a Portuguese institutional and cultural framework, not

especially favorable to deep crosscultural practices. In Japan things would be different. (Ibid., 156)

He arrived in the East Asian country in 1562 and would later only leave it for a short time with Valignano to serve as the Visitor's secretary. Fróis was not only an important chronicler of the Japanese mission (Schauwecker, 2015, 4) but also an important missionary who served in different parts of Japan "sometimes because of specific Jesuit needs or strategies, other times because local or regional circumstances were favorable or adverse to the missionaries" (Loureiro, 2000, 158). Due to the fact that he often served in regions where no Portuguese lived, he had to study Japanese to be able to communicate with the local communities and converted Japanese. All in all, his case resembles those of rather unknown Jesuits who, due to their missionary work in the peripheral regions – similar to the Peruvian Jesuits who will be discussed later – were forced to become familiar with the language and customs in the regions in which they were active. When Fróis later served in more leading roles, he was criticized for sometimes being too close to the Japanese, as his experiences were not always shared by Jesuits who had served in other parts of Japan, e.g., in a more "Portuguese city" like Nagasaki.

Diogo de Mesquita

Diogo de Mesquita was a Portuguese who became a member of the Society of Jesus in 1574 and arrived on the shores of Japan three years later. He would later accompany the four Japanese ambassadors to Rome and return to Japan in 1590 (Pacheco, 1971, 431-432). Afterward, Mesquita served at the college of Nagasaki, which he led as rector until 1614, when the Jesuits were expelled from the country due to Tokugawa Ieyasu's anti-Christian decrees. Mesquita was an open-minded Jesuit who not only supported publication projects that would help further strengthen the Japanese understanding of the Christian religion but was also interested in a genuine exchange of ideas between Jesuit missionaries and Japanese converts due to his global mindset. He died in 1614, knowing that his efforts had not been sufficient to secure the existence of Christianity in Japan, which must have been quite a tragic moment in the life of this relatively progressive Jesuit.

Human Capital, Global Mindset, and Proselytization

The Japanese case shows how important a combination of language skills and a global mindset is for successful intercultural management in a culturally different context. The Jesuits who arrived during the entry period got into conflicts with Buddhist monks but were able to convert the first feudal lords.

The said conflicts were, in addition, not really severe, as they did not threaten the existence of the Japanese mission.

Alessandro Valignano, during the consolidation period, emphasized the importance of language education for the Jesuits and proved that a global mindset was essential, even if it could not be backed by language proficiency. Valignano had successfully negotiated with Japanese daimyōs and even Toyotomi Hideyoshi after 1587, although he did not speak the language but needed to rely on translators. However, during the consolidation period, besides a conflict between Valignano and Francisco Cabral over the mission's long-term strategy, more and more Jesuits would learn the language and therefore secure a growing number of converts.

Consequently, the Jesuit proselytization was successful because it relied on language skills as an important human capital as well as a global mindset among the Jesuits, who, according to Valignano's and Fróis's experiences, had to accommodate their European self to a foreign Japanese other. Successful intercultural management in the Japanese case heavily relied on both aspects, although the years after 1587 show that the existence of both of these factors would not secure the Jesuits' missionary work in Japan against a rapid and abrupt change to the country's political context.

The External Factor

When Toyotomi Hideyoshi decided to sign an anti-Christian decree in 1587, it marked the beginning of the end for the Jesuits in Japan. Although Valignano could negotiate with the ruler of the country so that the order and its missionaries were allowed to continue their work, albeit preferably unseen and unheard, he could only postpone the final clash between what the Jesuits represented, i.e., Christianity, and the new rulers of Japan. Tokugawa Ieyasu would continue Toyotomi Hideyoshi's anti-Christian policies, especially since he wanted to establish an order – later referred to as the Pax Tokugawa – that would secure his rule against any popular resistance. Christianity was seen as a factor that particularly fueled the latter, and therefore, all Christian elements, including the Jesuit missionaries, needed to disappear for good. Regardless of their language skills and global mindset, the Jesuits were forced out of the country and could not avoid this final conflict after all.

4.3. Peru

The 16th century was not only an "age of discovery" for the secular empires but also for the Church, whose representatives often acted as agents for this expansion. Columbus had not only discovered new land of a "hitherto unsuspected size" but also "numbers of people in urgent need of conversion," a raison d'être for clerical activities in the so-called "New World" (Fraser, 1992, 19).

Religious orders, and not only the Jesuits, took this opportunity and followed the conquistadors to the Americas, supporting the Spanish expansion in this region by their words about a new god and an afterlife that promised salvation after the misery and sorrow experienced under the new colonial rule. In this context, the Jesuits "constituted a new intermediate category between the secular priesthood and the older religious orders, above all subject to the Pope rather than to the Spanish Crown. They perceived themselves as Christ's militia, soldiers on an educational crusade" (Ibid.). As the Jesuit Order grew during the sixteenth century (O'Malley, 1994, 18), it became "clearly a major force in the church" (Forrestal & Smith, 2016, 6). The Jesuits often followed the colonial expansion[5] and were not only active in South America but also in North America (Ekberg, 2000; Li, 2001) and within trans-Pacific networks (Buschmann et al. 2014, 64; Coello de la Rosa, 2022, 175). They thereby, in a way, combined Christian salvation – often in an adjusted form or with a locally suitable narrative (Forrestal & Smith, 2016, 9) – and early globalization (Clossey, 2008).

The conquest of Peru and the missionary work of the different Christian orders consequently represent a violent history, and Peru, as Basadre remarked, was "born of blood and tears in an abyss of history, with a loud crash that shook the world" (1947, 105, cited in Thurner, 2009, 44). The name "Peru" itself "came to mark the abyss of conquest [that] was in part a 'projection' of colonial desire" (Thurner, 2009, 47), a desire also shared by the Jesuit fathers (padres) and brothers (hermanos) who would be active in this particular colonial sphere. Regardless of the ambivalent nature of the Christian proselytization, the Jesuits would have "a profound effect on cultural and intellectual life in Latin America" (Newson, 2020, 1) that still can be felt in several regards even today. The missionary process in this region, within which the Jesuit Order held a prominent and influential position, led to "the crystallization of a process that would define an 'Andean Christianity' by which a standardized language would be developed at the same time as Christian beliefs were assimilated. This language was appropriated and often adopted by indigenous people in their endeavor to gain access to colonial power" (Dejo, 2023, 239). Until the order was expelled from the Spanish territories in the Americas in 1767 (Friederich-Stegmann, 2018), its members had administered more than a quarter-million indigenous conversions (Newson, 2020, 1) and acquired large amounts of money and worth in real estate (Brown, 1987, 27). The Jesuits had therefore been successful managers in a twofold way, firstly as active Christian missionaries and secondly, as a result, in being able to generate a substantial economic surplus.

---

[5] For a broader analysis of the colonial role of the church in Peru in the sixteenth and seventeenth centuries, see Acosta Rodríguez (2014).

That the Jesuits have attracted the interest of many historians is not surprising at all. The order was not the only Christian one in the Latin American context, but the system of detailed reports and communication with the order's European centers allowed a better insight into the organization's structures and activities (Depuy, 1921, 62). The amount of sources, something Gehl referred to as a "publishing empire" (2003, 436), provides an enormous corpus of knowledge in all kinds of fields, as the Jesuits did not only report on their own activities but also wrote chronicles about current events and descriptions of the flora, fauna, and geography of the newly conquered regions under Spanish rule (More, 2020). In addition, "[a]s highly educated men who considered science and education to be an important part of their missionary program, some Jesuits became significant researchers in several fields" (Anagnostou, 2005, 3). They also provided important maps of the newly explored territories that would have a tremendous impact on future explorations and exploitations alike (Saladin, 2020). In addition,

> the missionaries reported on the momentous political and military events of their lands, giving the first historical accounts of Asia and Africa to readers back in Europe. These writings, in many European languages, are subjective texts that reflect how Catholic missionaries saw the non-Christian world even while they recorded the acts and thoughts of those very missionaries. (Hsia, 2015, 224)

Although there were similar forms of religious syncretism to be observed that were somehow similar to the Japanese case (Marzal, 1985; Millones, 2007; Gutiérrez Estévez, 2013; Mujica, 2016), the presented sources are often problematic, as they only provide the perspective of the missionaries, for whom we can also refer to other existent sources, while the stories of the converts often remain in the dark. Like many other colonial historiographies, the one related to the Jesuits in Latin America leaves many questions unanswered. An evaluation that goes beyond a data-oriented reading of the sources consequently needs to be cautious not to replicate the Eurocentric biases and stereotypes that can be found in the Jesuit reports.

Early chronists of the newly acquired Spanish colonies, like Pedro de Cieza de León (ca. 1520-1554), Cristóbal de Molina el Chileno (1494-1580), Pedro Sarmiento de Gamboa (ca. 1532-1592), and Juan Diez de Betanzos (1510-1576), wrote the first important works about the history of the conquest of the "New World" and thereby also established a tradition of narratives the Jesuit works would refer to in later years as well (de Cieza de León, 1554; Fernández Duro, 1896; Romero, 1943; Landin Carrasco, 1946; de Bezanzos, 1996). When the Jesuits started their journey to serve in the colonial world and remote regions of the world that colonial authorities had begun to integrate into larger transnational empires, they could consequently already rely on reports that had reached Europe and therefore were probably influenced by existent stereotypes long before their actual mission began (Huiyi, 2017, 54). Regardless of such preconditioning, the Jesuits played an essential role in gathering new knowledge and insights about the indigenous people they intended to convert to Christianity. The Jesuit missionaries in Spanish America consequently

> pioneered interest in indigenous languages and cultures, compiling dictionaries and writing some of the earliest ethnographies of the region. They also explored the region's natural history and made significant contributions to the development of science and medicine. On their estates and in their missions the Jesuits introduced new plants, livestock and agricultural techniques, while they left a lasting legacy on the region's architecture, art and music. (Newson, 2020, 1)

The Jesuit missionaries were interested in many things beyond fulfilling their main task, i.e., proselytization. They were also "linguists, ethnologists, ... historians, ... geographers, naturalists, pharmacists, and physicians," sometimes all of these at the same time, and therefore their impact in Latin America and the history of its future nations was quite intense (Anagnostou, 2005, 3). In particular, their "vocabularies and grammars [e.g., de Anchieta, 1595; Ruiz de Montoya, 1640] of native languages ... are not merely linguistic studies but also demonstrate the Jesuits' efforts to save the natives' languages as an important element of their cultural identity" (Anagnostou, 2005, 3; see also Segovia Gordillo, 2020, 454-455). The Jesuits, due to their personal encounters with the native populations within their respective colonial contexts, also helped, at least partly and sometimes in a less biased way than official reports by the colonial governments, to preserve something of the native history of Spanish America (Acosta, 1590; de Acuña, 1641; Porras Barrenechea, 1962; Pérez Tudela y Bueso, 1998; Coello de la Rosa, 2005). What makes such works and sources particularly interesting is the fact that they do not follow a specific categorization of colonial or Christian literature but instead offer a variety of perspectives that are as diverse as the context and the sphere in which they were active (Dürr, 2017, 487-488). A booming global history that expresses quite a vivid interest in such diversity will therefore almost naturally have to include the broad source corpus that has been left by the Jesuits (Ibid., 488).

Dürr pointed out that it was the accommodation method of the Jesuits, i.e., their strategy to adjust their missionary work to the locally existent conditions, that is of particular interest, as it showed the extent to which the Jesuits were successful in applying new Christianization strategies and, at the same time, in what ways these were limited by the existent context and even contested by Jesuits who did not share such a strong global mindset (2017, 489; on the accommodation method, see Sievernich, 2002; 2005). Regardless of the latter, "the Jesuits were divided between their intention to see the presence of God in nature and their concern that the indigenous population could use this presence as the basis for their 'idolatries'" (Dejo, 2023, 241; see also Dejo, 2021).

The Jesuits' knowledge, however, was not only used in the colonial sphere but also had a strong impact in Europe, where the new knowledge, e.g., with regard to medicine, would be applied and cash crops and new consumer goods introduced to European people (Anagnostou, 2005, 4; Kaller & Jacob, 2019). In the historical works about Latin America's colonial period, it has been emphasized that the Catholic Church in general and the Jesuit Order in particular were big landowners (Chevalier, 1970, 239; Brown, 1987, 23). Although their "widespread economic holdings" gave the Jesuits some economic weight too, this was not enough to dominate the region (Brown, 1987, 25). Nevertheless, the Jesuits did help to create and determine the Spanish colonial world as a whole and Peru as one specific zone, where the order's representatives very much connected global perspectives with local ones and vice versa (Hosne, 2013, 7). They modified the space they were active in, shaping it to be part of a "modern" colonial world (Mignolo 2000, 13-50; Mignolo & Ennis, 2001).

When the first Jesuits arrived in Peru in 1568, their missionary engagements spanned most of the globe, as the order had already been active in Africa (Angola, Congo, Mozambique), Asia (China, India, Japan), and in other parts of Portuguese and Spanish America (Brazil, Mexico, Peru) (Ambrogio & Newson, 2020, 149). As the Spanish conquest in the latter regions was limited by geographical factors, so were the missionary attempts of the Jesuit mission, which "was severely tested by the encounter with the semi-sedentary and non-sedentary populations of southern Chile, the Chaco and north-western Mexico, where groups scattered across rugged valleys, mighty rivers and arid deserts strongly resisted Spanish conquest" (Ibid.). The mission of proselytizing decentralized and non-settled indigenous people obviously caused severe problems for the Jesuits, who had not encountered similar issues before. This eventually caused the missionaries to be as flexible as possible and to adjust the Catholic liturgic and other religious practices, e.g., baptism, to a local context, in which people needed to be carefully introduced to the new religious belief that had been brought from Europe to the peripheral Latin American regions (Ambrogio & Newson, 2020, 150; Catto, 2010).

In contrast to these peripheral regions, the politically centralized metropolitan spaces of colonial Peru were also Hispanicized, and the Jesuit effort to spread and strengthen Christianity there was promoted by the colonial state (Hosne, 2013, 9; see also Cushner, 1980). In general, there were two different spheres within the Peruvian context, and this division would sooner or later cause problems, especially since it also divided the Jesuits into different kinds of missionaries.

Of course, one of the essential vows of the Jesuits, made to the Pope himself, would allow them to be sent anywhere, but to be sent to a colonial context as such did not yet mean that the Jesuit in question was provided with a global mindset. In the Peruvian context, some might have been interested in replicating the European structures of the order within the colonial cities, while others were more oriented toward spreading the word of the Lord among the indigenous people. As will become clear later, this general division would cause trouble, especially when both groups were unwilling to accept the diversity of the Jesuit tasks and approaches toward them in the Peruvian colony.

Alongside theological questions, however, the Jesuits also had to act as managers in a more business-oriented way. Considering the massive rural properties the order would eventually own in Peru, it is not wrong to argue that the Jesuits were quite good managers in this Spanish colony. All in all, however, the story is not so easy, as Clarence-Smith emphasized:

> Initially, many fathers opposed money-making activities, but the order urgently needed funds to finance its urban colleges, for which tuition was free. Money was also required for other charitable activities, mission stations and general administration. Moreover, the order gradually accumulated large estates, either through direct donations of land, or through gifts of cash and valuables which could be invested in property. (2020, 209)

On their property, the Jesuits were often successful as farmers and improved the existent soils and crops (Colmenares, 1969, 99-100). The missionaries consequently represented all kinds of advantages, and it was not surprising that the Jesuits were soon summoned by European rulers to support their colonial ambitions in the new colonial spheres. Spain and Portugal had divided the world for their conquests as well as for their missionary attempts, expressed by the "responsibility for missionary work, which was called the right of royal patronage, i.e., the Spanish Patronato and the Portuguese Padroado" (Hosne, 2013, 2). As the Jesuit missionaries would follow these official preconditions, "from the outset, the Jesuits were dependent upon the whims of secular authorities and compelled to rely upon the support and protection of the rulers of those lands in which their Order served and to yield to the constraints they imposed" (Ibid.). The meaning of their mission was consequently also challenged and changed by decisions and experiences that were shared or contested by all forces involved in the process characterized by expansion and proselytization.

After their long journey that would mark the first phase of the Jesuit mission (Brockey, 2000, 64-70; Hosne, 2013, 2), it was their eventual experiences in their new environment and its impact on their missionary work that determined the final and often flexible as well as very individual interpretation the Jesuits had about themselves and their final goal. Although, ideally, the "where" should not determine the work of Jesuits too much – "Jerome Nadal, one of the first Jesuits, did not leave room for doubt: totus mundus nostra fit habitatio (our place is the world)" (Hosne, 2013, 3) –, the performance of the Jesuit "managers" in their respective order provinces can hardly be fully separated from these external factors. Nevertheless, Ignatius of Loyola, the order's founder, left no doubt about his order's global mission and availability when he argued that Jesuits "must be indifferent and do what we are told, without being more inclined to one part than another. And if I were, like you are, more inclined to go to the Indies, I would try to incline myself to the opposite side, to reach that perfect indifference, which is necessary to reach the perfection of obedience" (Loyola, 1553, cited in Hosne, 2013, 3-4). Initially coming from Portugal (Telles, 1645) and later from Spain, the Jesuits would thereby reach all parts of the world, and in 1568, the first Jesuits arrived in Peru, although other religious orders had been active there before. The Jesuits consequently entered an already colonized space, a market, so to speak, which other contesters had had their first shot at already.

It was the famous conquistador Francisco Pizarro who delivered the final blow to the Incan Empire and was the first European to lay his eyes on the northern coastal regions and settlements of Peru in 1528 (Scott, 2009, 1). His conquest would be the basis for the establishment of the later Spanish colonial order there, and the first report, the "Relación Samano-Xerez, a brief report of uncertain authorship" (Ibid.), would make other Europeans dream about this new land:

> [T]here are many sheep and pigs and cats and dogs and other animals and geese, and there [in the coastal towns] the blankets of cotton and wool that I mentioned above are made, and [also] the needlework and the beads and objects of silver and gold, and the people are very rational; they appear to have many tools made of copper and other metals with which they work their fields, and they mine gold and practice all kinds of farming; the streets of their settlements are very well laid out; they have many types of fortresses and they live in a state of order and justice; the women are white and well-dressed and almost all of them are embroiderers; there is an island in the sea near the settlements where they have a temple built in the style of a rustic shelter, hung with very fine embroidered cloth, and where they have an image of a woman with a child in her arms and who is called María Mexía. (Cited in Ibid., 1-2)

Although the text must be understood "as an exceptionally vivid fantasy of familiarity and, by extension, of possession" (Ibid., 2), it would not take long until the first adventurers and missionaries of all sorts made their way to the shores of this recently explored and conquered region of the world.

Therefore, "early modern Europeans who ventured to Peru and other parts of the New World did not occupy merely linguistic and cultural spaces, exclusively shared with their companions and compatriots in distant Europe. Rather, they also traveled through real geographical spaces, traversed physical terrain, and interacted in diverse ways with indigenous peoples" (Scott, 2009, 2). For the Jesuits, who intended not simply to rule but to reach people spiritually within this culturally different context, the transition from European Christianity to a Christian mission in a non-European colonial space caused serious issues (Nebgen, 2007). In addition, this new setting was not only determined by the foreignness of the place but also related to the identities the new arrivals had themselves, ranging from conquistador to traveler to Jesuit missionary (Ibid., 3). The images of Peru were also different, and each of the new arrivals had started their journey with a different conception of what their goal would actually be like. Some might have started looking for El Dorado in the Andes, others were hoping for a social advance, and still others to become rich in the colonial economy to return to Europe with the financial capacity for social advancement (Thurner, 2011, 8).

Regardless of the different motives, the space these new arrivals would soon occupy, control, and transform was not empty but inhabited by a large number of indigenous people, who were exploited early on as a workforce in the mines, on the larger land estates, the *haciendas* (Mörner, 1973), or in other production facilities of the colonial society (Arrelucea-Barrantes, 2012, 274). In the larger cities, like Lima, the indigenous population was exploited as slaves, who "were used in production, trade and services." Later on, "[s]lave possession extended in both the elite class and the middle and lower class sectors, including indigenous people and freedmen" (Ibid., 275). The evangelization or proselytization of a large number of indigenous people had begun with the eventual conquest of Peru in the early 1530s and, early on, was "supported by a blossoming-yet-fragile pastoral and ecclesiastical jurisdiction" (Hosne, 2013, 4). In these early years of missionary work among the native people, Augustinians, Dominicans, Franciscans, and Mercedarians played their role. "By and large, they were receptive to local pre-Hispanic religions and believed that the Indians had to embrace Christianity gradually, saving complex dogma like the mysteries of faith for later" (Ibid.), so the early contact of the natives with Christianity was determined as relatively pragmatic. The Dominicans, like Domingo de Santo Tomás, had also begun to use doctrinal texts in local languages, like Quechua, to reach the native population and to provide them with some essential readings (Ibid.). The first missionaries would consequently not challenge indigenous religious beliefs but rather blend them, especially since similarities between the native goddess Viracocha and Jesus Christ almost predetermined their use in a relatively open missionary attempt during this early phase (Hoyt, 2015).

This should, however, not conceal that "proselytizing cultures believed that it was their right and duty to change the existing fabric of societies" (Cushner, 2006: 3). This naturally led to conflicts in some regions where the missionaries intended to convert people to Christianity, although people in certain regions – Mexico, Paraguay, and Julí – seemed to be easier to convert. The character of the relationship between the Jesuits and the converts, what Cushner called the "partnership-loyalty connector" (2006, 4), decided the conversions' success or failure. When such "a new relationship was formed [by the Jesuits with the native population], the loyalty became deeper, and their religion became more acceptable" (Ibid.), and the conversions would eventually be "truer" than those forced upon the indigenous population in the colonial world. The first Jesuits had begun their missionary work in Brazil in 1559, experiencing and performing the initial contacts between the expanding Portuguese Christian power and the soon-to-be-converted natives in South America, and thereby bridged the two worlds of Europe and Latin America (Ibid., 4-5). The approach of the Church toward proselytization nevertheless went hand in hand with secular forms of rule, and when new political and legal control mechanisms were installed, the Christian orders played an important role when such a transformation needed to be secured.

This transformation, however, was not always as easy as the European intruders anticipated, and beyond the establishment of colonial rule, the "Native American groups were able to shield, protect, and interject key aspects of their cultural systems into the new culture presented to them. The overwhelming preponderance of European symbols proclaiming the destruction of the old affected segments of the native population in various ways" (Ibid., 8). Initially, "an almost catatonic effect on the native populations" (Ibid., 9) was created by the conquest and establishment of this foreign rule, as the people considered this a sign that their gods had abandoned them and, in a way, had been defeated by the Christian one. On the other hand, the European missionaries claimed that it was the devil who made the natives resist the former's missionary approaches. However, in later years, the missionaries realized that successful proselytization depended on other aspects and

> in general [they] were convinced that social stability and village life were essential for effective evangelization. Control and indoctrination were

keys to success. Besides the reductions of Paraguay, the town of Julí near Lake Titicaca and the reservations near Montreal were considered ideal places for religious indoctrination. Separation from the pagan masses and corrupting influences of traders and merchants was considered essential for producing European-like Native Americans. (Ibid., 12)

At the same time, many missionaries realized that the native religious beliefs were often very different from their own values or interpretations related to religion, although such realizations also took time and were based on experience. When the Jesuits began their work in Florida in 1560, they did not waste a thought on possible differences and "thought that they were sufficiently equipped both intellectually and spiritually for the task that lay ahead" (Ibid., 15). This kind of cultural arrogance would later lead to failure and stimulated a change of thought with regard to the Jesuit missionary approach toward indigenous people, especially in the peripheral regions of Peru.

Successful evangelization was consequently the result of a long process of learning and adaptation, and the Jesuits in particular seem to have possessed a global mindset, i.e., a kind of dogmatic flexibility, to adjust their strategies toward the local necessities, so that the "writing of grammar texts, historical treatises, and the recording and critique of native religion became part of the modus operandi of the Jesuits in America" (Ibid., 16). This also was related to the Council of Trent (1545-1563) and the "almost new spirit of Catholicism" (Ibid., 17) it had achieved by a discussion of Christian doctrine and related ideas (Mullet, 1999, 29-68). The changes determined by the Council of Trent would eventually also allow the Jesuits to agree that there were good natives who simply needed to be baptized to achieve true salvation, as "[a]lthough removed from divine favor, man retained a nature, which made him a creature of dignity, worth, and potential virtue" (Cushner, 2006, 17). The Council of Trent therefore stimulated a rather positivistic view of human beings and their seminal nature, which allowed the Jesuits to adapt their missionary approaches successfully to a large number of indigenous people who had not yet been in contact with God but who also did not need to be condemned.

The semiotic system of signs (Barthes, 1977, 2; Eco, 1979, 3-7) needed to be transplanted from its European to its Latin American context and was consequently reshaped by integrating parts of the sign systems that existed in the indigenous religious world. The Jesuits therefore had to manage a "translation" of their own system to be understood by the native people they wanted to convert (Bauer & Marroquín Arredondo, 2019). This almost naturally led to a synthesis of elements of both semiotic sign systems and created a specific interpretation of Christian beliefs that matched those of the people who were to be addressed and encouraged by these new religious explanations of the world (Mills, 2007). Religious rites and symbols were consequently important, but also only functional if they were to be understood by the native converts, a fact that made it necessary for the Jesuits to explain them in a language that would be better understood by the addressed as well. Baptism was particularly important within this cultural translation process, as it would be the most important religious act for the indigenous person who could thereby become Christian and secure their salvation, at least according to the Christian belief taught by the Jesuits and other missionaries.

Due to the existence of multiple relevant factors during the missionary process, the Jesuits themselves had to undergo an intellectual and spiritual transformation:

> The European missionary brought with him to America a complex configuration of values and ideas about what the world was and what it should be. These values and ideas had been shaped and refined by his family, society, and the religious order to which he belonged. What he absorbed in his seminary training and Jesuit life was more often than not surrounded by the values that were operative in the Western world around him. Before the final acceptance of a Jesuit value core, many values had been rejected, some replaced, and others revised by the prospective missionary to accompany the new order of values that the Society of Jesus expected to operate in the individual. (Cushner, 2006, 20)

Considering this, it is hardly surprising that the Jesuits would not preach a purely European-Catholic version of Christianity but often mixed the message with local elements to reach a broader audience, whose members could identify parts of their religious semiotic system in the message of the Jesuit missionary. The "immediate goal," in contrast to heaven as the "ultimate" one (Ibid.), was to establish a sense of community that would include the Christian values preached about by the Jesuit fathers and brothers.

As mentioned before, the Jesuits were dogmatically flexible enough to do that, in particular, because they considered the indigenous people as spiritually capable of such a transformative act: "On their part the Indians had to be willing to listen to, accept, and carry out what they heard. These three elements, goal, givens, and methods to achieve the goal, were encased in cultural assumptions and attitudes that the Jesuit had learned over his own lifetime from his culture. Indians, on the other hand, were caught between competing and rival rituals, one that they had practiced from childhood, the other brought by the invaders" (Ibid.). In the case of many Jesuits, the necessary flexibility and experience were also at hand, regardless of the fact that they had all been trained in larger cities when they visited the Jesuit colleges in Europe and the metropolis of the new colonial world, because many of them had grown up in rather peripheral and rural regions of Europe or other parts of the world and were therefore quite familiar with all kinds of rituals and popular beliefs that they would later encounter again in their role as missionaries. In contrast to the riches of the "New World," the missionaries were relatively uncontested at first when it came to converting the indigenous people, as other individuals who traveled across the Atlantic (Heid et al., 1997) were looking for material wealth, social progress, or purely adventure instead. Soon after the explorational period, the state would nevertheless begin to interfere with the work of the missionaries, so their activities became limited by "the parameters set by sixteenth-century church-state relations" (Ibid., 28).

The Church was almost naturally a part of the process of establishing imperial domination in the newly occupied territory and was aiming to secure foreign control over the indigenous people, who were supposed to be exploited for the greater good of the Spanish Empire:

> The missionary thus played a key role in the Spanish plan of conquest and colonization. Exploration and conquest was the task of the conquistador. Evangelization was considered a joint effort that obligated civil as well as religious authority. Both stood to gain. The crown could count on new resources in the form of gold and silver, mined by or collected from the inhabitants of its new kingdoms, and the church could satisfy its zeal to enroll new members. (Ibid., 29)

The Jesuit missionaries were not only acting in the name of God but also in the name of the colonial authorities, and although they did not always agree with the latter's policies, the order's servants supported colonial domination, while they also acted directly or indirectly as colonial agents.

Jesuits as Colonial Agents

When the Jesuits arrived in Peru, they reached a region of the world that was contested, to say the least, as "[e]arly modern Ibero-America was a quite unique set of new societies, with people coming – either freely or under coercion – at least from three continents, going through uprooting experiences and demographic collapse, interacting together within new kinds of hierarchic patterns and colonial forms of domination and labor pressure" (Maldavsky, 2018, 41). As colonial agents, the Jesuits played as much of an important part as the other groups that helped to extend the influence of the Spanish Crown in the newly conquered regions of Central and South America. The conversion of indigenous people must consequently also be understood as a colonial act, performed by the Jesuits and other religious orders, although these men might have intended their work to serve a more spiritual purpose (Armas Medina, 1953; Vargas Urgate, 1963-65; Balandier, 2001). This rather negative impact of the Christian missionary history in Latin America often remained undisputed in older or sometimes hagiographic histories about the Jesuits in colonial Peru, as the authors tended to highlight the work of the Jesuit Order as successful Christianization and the men themselves as defenders of the indigenous people against the new political order that had been established by the conquest of Peru by the Spanish state (Lopetegui, 1942; Marzal, 1988; Perez Fernandez, 1988).

In fact, the religious history of Peru is quite a lot more complicated, and indeed contested, with the Jesuits as one of the players who, on the one hand, must be understood as political agents of Spanish domination and, on the other, as religious mediators as well, all in all presenting a much more complex and indeed ambivalent history of proselytization (MacCormack, 1991; Griffiths, 1996; Mills, 1997; Ramada Curto, 2005; Maldavsky, 2012). This should also cause some hesitation when reading the relevant sources, as they were not only, as mentioned before, biased and one-sided but also addressed to a European readership (Maldavsky, 2018, 43). Since the evangelization and proselytization processes had begun immediately after the Spanish conquest, there were other Christian influences at work before the Jesuits arrived as well, which in a way also created a kind of competitive situation during the entry period of the Jesuit Order's work in the Peruvian context (Estenssoro Fuchs, 2003).

The Spanish colonial system in Latin America in general, and Peru in particular, was an exploitative one, in which indigenous people were exploited as a workforce in the mines or as laborers within the *encomienda* system, which allowed landowners the right to extract a form of tribute from the natives who lived on their property (Hampe, 1982; Cole, 1985). This right was not granted free of any exchange, and so "the encomenderos were responsible for their people's evangelization and compelled to provide them a priest. By delegating the right to extract goods and work from the indigenous peoples, the King delegated part of his evangelization duty" (Maldavsky, 2018, 45). It was therefore in the *encomienda* system that the interrelationship between colonial rule and evangelization became quite visible. Viceroy Francisco de Toledo (1515-1582) used this system in Peru during the 1570s as a form of reward that would consequently establish the base for the colonial social system (Ibid.). The religious orders that arrived before the Jesuits had already encountered such structures and established themselves within them, which made the entry period for the Jesuits particularly challenging, as some of their competitors had been active in the region since the 1530s. The Dominican order had founded a province in Peru in 1540 under the leadership of Vicente Valverde, who had come to Peru with Pizarro in 1532 and later served as the first bishop of Cuzco (Torres, 1932; Hehrlein, 1992). The Dominicans were followed by the Augustinian order in 1551, the Franciscans in 1552, and the Mercedarians in 1560. The Jesuits were consequently relatively late when they entered the colony of Peru in 1568 (Maldavsky, 2018, 46).

All of the orders had begun to convert the Andean people, but even if the latter considered their gods to have been defeated by the European intruders, this did not mean that they immediately fully converted to Christianity, even if they had been baptized by the different missionaries who were actively trying to engage them to believe in the Christian God and Jesus Christ. The "conversion should [rather] be interpreted as a negotiated process undertaken by a diversity of European religious agents, who did not deliver a unified message in the first decades. Andean people absorbed and selected what they could of the new faith" (Ibid., 47). The missionaries' efforts were, in addition, not taking place in a political vacuum, as the Spanish Crown was also trying to instrumentalize proselytization and therefore needed to provide some conformity for all conversion attempts undertaken within the territory it controlled. In 1551, 1567, 1574, and 1582/83, the Crown formulated and "published the Ordenanzas de Patronato to clarify its own prerogatives in religious affairs" (Ibid., 47). These would regulate the missionaries' work according to the central power's necessities, as "[f]our European actors, with contradictory motivations but compelled to a certain degree of compromise, were on the scene. The friars, the Crown, the encomenderos and the secular clergy, handling spiritual as well as political argumentation, were to some extent competing for the control of indigenous souls and bodies" (Ibid.). This already highlights that the missionary strategies in colonial Peru were not uniform and that the Jesuits would encounter different interests there, which needed to be carefully taken into consideration so as not to arouse any trouble with existent structures and "missionary players" or competitors.

That the role of the indigenous people and their conversion was not a purely spiritual or religious one also becomes obvious in the attempt to gather them, for better fiscal control, in newly established villages, which resembled Spanish cities, but which 1) destroyed the natural ways of life in the region and 2) demanded the missionaries, and in particular the Jesuits, to settle in these villages as well (Echanove, 1955). An often mobile form of missionary work was consequently forced to be located in a single settlement, where only a limited number of conversions could be undertaken before the Jesuits' work there turned into permanent spiritual service or supervision (Málaga Medina, 1974; Saito et al., 2014; Saito & Rosas Lauro, 2017). Along with the different problems with regard to the practical organization of missionary work, there were issues with the dogmatic chaos in Peru, as many different views on how evangelization was supposed to work were applied. In 1551, Jerónimo de Loaysa, Archbishop of Lima, "started the effort of unification of doctrine from the 1540's on, producing instructions for the clergy on teaching the indigenous population and combatting ancient Andean beliefs," and he therefore called in the first Provincial Council which was supposed "to put an end to what was understood as a doctrinal disorder, which certainly existed until the end of the century" (Maldavsky, 2018, 50). The problems, however, could not be fully solved, so further councils had to take place in 1567 and 1582/83, and in the 1580s in particular, Jesuits would be active discussants there, too (Hyland, 2003). These debates were, however, not only representing religious struggles but also expressed the necessity of the colonial authorities to centralize the missionary efforts within their own territory. The councils also documented the struggle between religious and civil authorities, who, in a way, competed for access to the indigenous population in the region as well. The work of the Jesuits in Peru after 1568 was, from its start, influenced by struggles that were already taking place before the order's representatives arrived in this particular space of the new Spanish colonial empire in South America (Stern, 1982). There, "[s]tate and state-free societies (with endless variations) faced European newcomers who imagined 'conquests' and rights to rule, pursued gain in tribute and trade, and believed they could force 'conversions' to Christianity. While learning that all these presumptive impositions came laden with challenges" (Tutino, 2021, 13), and the Jesuits had to overcome the latter.

The Jesuits' Entry Period in Peru

The Jesuits in Peru did not start completely from scratch, as the order had been active in Brazil before and could rely on previous experiences when beginning its involvement in Peru (Ribadeneira, 1592: 144-145; Chakravarti, 2018). King John III of Portugal had actually requested the support of the Jesuits in his colonial possessions, and Pope Paul III answered this request by referring it to Ignatius, whose order was supposed to help (Roemer, 1946, 2; Kriegbaum, 2006). In Portugal itself, the Jesuit Simon Rodrigues had opened the Colegio de Jesus of the University of Coimbra in June 1542, where Jesuits who would later serve in the Americas were trained. Initially counting 17 students – among them two from Castile, two from France, three from Italy, and three from Portugal –, their number would grow to 70 in 1544 (Roemer, 1946, 2). Nine years later, there were already more than 300 students who would soon spread across the globe to serve the Almighty as well as the Jesuit Order. It took until 1547 before Philip II of Spain allowed the establishment of a Jesuit Order province in Castile, but this one would be particularly important for his own colonial consolidation in the Americas in the decades that followed, and it was not until 1568 that the Spanish king gave permission for the Jesuits to become active in his American colonies. Nevertheless, as "part of the colonial enterprise" (Ibid.,

4), the Jesuits were now at least able to play an active role in Peru as well. Like modern-day companies, the Jesuit Order was forced to gain ground fast to survive, as all other Christian orders had been able to establish basic organizational structures already. The entry period for the Jesuits was marked by several problems. They not only had to begin converting indigenous people but also had to struggle with serious and better-established competition (Hosne, 2013, 15). Therefore, they could not simply focus on their missionary work but also had to address local politics to secure the order's standing with the colonial society of Peru.

There were different players involved. Along with the indigenous people, the Jesuits needed to deal with the Inquisition, which had also been exported to the "New World," and the local civil authorities, represented by Viceroy Toledo, who initially supported the newly arrived missionaries but also tried to keep them close under his own control (Ibid.). The Jesuits began to establish schools where the sons of the colonial elites, including creole and indigenous ones, were trained, thereby linking the order to influential groups in the region (Fraser, 1992, 19). As the Jesuits had not participated in the previous period of discovery and the establishment of the colonial order, they were able to set up an extremely important support network that would also help them to secure their own standing within their new environment. Initially, Toledo backed these efforts and took some Jesuits with him, including Jeronimo Ruiz de Portillo, the Jesuit Order's provincial at that time, when he toured the Peruvian highlands in 1570. The Jesuits were allowed to expand their activities to Cuzco the following year (Ibid., 20), but a conflict between the indigenous people and the Viceroy would soon lead to problems for the missionaries.

In 1572, the Inca Tupac Amaru was captured by Captain Martin Garcia de Loyola, and Toledo sentenced him to death. The Jesuits, who supposedly had been able to successfully convert the indigenous ruler to Christianity, opposed his execution, which "earned them the trust of some powerful branches of the Inca nobility" (Fraser, 1992, 21). Toledo, however, changed his attitude toward the order, and the situation became more complicated. In addition, the Inquisition had started a trial against Francisco de la Cruz, a Dominican missionary who had argued that the native population could hope for God's salvation without believing in the Trinity and the Incarnation. He was burned at the stake in 1578, and his death marked an intensification of the doctrinal and dogmatic struggle over what was supposed to be taught about the Christian God to the indigenous converts (Maldavsky, 2018, 52). When the Jesuits tried to establish themselves in La Paz in 1574, another foundation of the order was denied by Toledo. The same happened in Arequipa in 1578 (Brown, 1987, 26), but there it "was promptly denied by the civil authorities on Toledo's orders and the Jesuits were 'violently' thrown out and their belongings confiscated. An almost identical pattern of events unfolds in Potosi, where in July 1577 they had received permission to settle from the regional administrative body, the Audiencia, but a few months later were expelled, again on the orders of the Viceroy" (Fraser, 1992, 23).

The Jesuits adjusted their own missionary strategies to the local conditions as well. While traditionally, looking back to the medieval missions, one would have to move around to spread the Christian message (Kriegbaum, 2006), the colonial Latin American context demanded different strategies. In the main cities, like Lima or Cuzco, the Jesuits established a strong presence, which was especially visible through the important colleges they founded (Tutino, 2021, 12), and in the countryside, the Jesuits replicated existent missionary structures, like the *reducciones*. In the Spanish as well as Portuguese colonies, early forms of these later organizational structures were known by the names *aldeias*, *misiones*, or *doctrinas* (Ibid.). The concept was simple: in exchange for protection and security, the indigenous people would convert to Christianity. The *reducciones*, however, demanded the permanent presence of the missionaries and, therefore, transformed the traditional idea of continually moving around to spread the Christian belief. The protection that was granted was a dichotomic opposite to the violence of the conquistadors, which is why the native population responded relatively positively toward such settling possibilities, especially since baptized indios were still being harassed by colonial authorities and therefore considered the Jesuits' protection essential for their own well-being. As said before, this does not mean that the work of the Jesuit Order should be seen as positive, as their work also supported the further existence of a colonial order of exploitation, although individual Jesuits might have opposed such an order per se.

The harsh reality was even more limiting for the Jesuits, who could only act according to a privilege they had received from the Spanish king (Kriegbaum, 2006). They had to follow the patronats (*patronato real* by the Spanish king) that had been published in Peru before the order's representatives arrived and, therefore, had to adjust their own goals to the limitations of the "market" they had to deal with after 1568. The fact that the Spanish Crown had accepted the order at all was probably related to the necessity to evangelize a large number of indigenous people and to build new churches, colleges, and other institutions that would not only help to strengthen Christianity in the colonial space but also support the centralization and organizational penetration of the colony. The missionaries were consequently solely invited to support the authorities, and if this support was no longer needed or accepted, the orders could be expelled again, as the Jesuits eventually were from the Spanish colonies in 1767. On the other hand, the Jesuit Order also needed the protection of the Spanish Crown and its representatives in colonial Peru, as its members could not rely on any military or political power to act on their own. The symbiotic relationship between the Jesuits and the civil authorities was nevertheless fragile, and therefore, the Jesuit managers had to be quite careful not to destroy bonds that were important. While they needed to be dogmatically flexible to convert the indigenous people of Peru, they also needed to comply with the demands of the local authorities not to risk affecting their influence at all. In many ways, this dilemma is still encountered by expanding SMEs today, whether they are born global or traditional.

The entry period between 1568 and 1575 was therefore marked by a stronger focus on the European colonists, and only after 1576 did the missionaries' work with regard to the Peruvian native population increase. Considering the relatively small number of Jesuits during the years of the entry period, this was probably the most the men could do, especially since they needed to build up a stronghold first, which could then be used as a base for further expansion. This began in the 1570s with new foundations and more intense proselytization efforts in the rather peripheral regions of colonial Peru as well. Furthermore, during these early years, "the Society of Jesus was required to impose Tridentine Catholicism by Philip II, independently of Rome, a task that entailed compliance with the colonial authorities' demands, and specifically those of Viceroy Toledo" (Hosne, 2013, 8). In contrast to Japan, where the Jesuits needed to pay more attention to the power of a foreign authority, i.e., the daimyō, in Peru, they had to observe the laws and limitations created by a European government, although the latter acted in a culturally different space. It was not only this specific colonial space that caused problems for the Jesuits, who, as mentioned above, had been in trouble with the Inquisition in Europe before and whose schools were also "hindered by a plethora of difficulties" (Carlsmith, 2002, 216) in Italy, to name just one example. The Jesuits might often have been too modern, innovative, and flexible for their own times, and regardless of the distance between them and Rome, the order's provinces were also regularly controlled by superior Jesuits. The pressure on the missionaries must have been quite immense. The conflict between the Christian mission and colonial exploitation on the one hand and the order's goals and the civil authorities on the other must have caused quite a lot of tension that was felt by the organization as a whole as well as by the individual fathers and brothers alike.

Independence was naturally important in such a situation, which is why the Jesuits might have tried to remain as self-sufficient as possible. In contrast to other orders, who lived off the financial interest they made from loans to third parties, the Jesuits farmed their own lands to generate the needed crops or a financial surplus that was needed to finance the educational structures of the order. However, dependency was prevented whenever possible, which is understandable, considering the status of the order in colonial Peru. The college in Arequipa, for example, also owned vineyards and larger farms, among other kinds of real estate (Brown, 1987, 27). With regard to its main rules and activities, the order also remained a hybrid, as it "preached an outgoing, activist, and highly affective personal piety for the laity. It also embodied military ideas of discipline, obedience, and centralization, this last based on obedience to the General of the Order and through him, to the pope" (Gehl, 2003, 437).

Looking at the entry period, the Jesuits began to establish their first colleges in Peru and thereby continued the order's education-based strategy of expansion as had been followed since the Jesuits' foundation. They thereby replicated their educational efforts in Europe (Schöndorf & Funiok, 2017), where they had already opened 33 colleges by 1556, a number that would grow to 300 by the end of the sixteenth century, including similar colleges in Asia and Latin America (Ibid.). The colleges allowed the Jesuits to combine their educational and missionary efforts and firmly establish themselves as an important provider of the possibility of social advancement as well as training for the next generation of Jesuit padres. Furthermore, these facilities represented an aspect that made the Jesuit Order particularly appealing for young novices, as membership in the order offered an insight into knowledge that could not be accessed so broadly and systematically anywhere else at that time.

Considering their religious approach to their missionary task, "the experiences of the Jesuits were certainly the most original" (Imbruglia, 2014, 21) when it comes to their actual interaction with the indigenous people, who were approached with much more dogmatic flexibility than by other orders or clerics and offered not only salvation but a religious utopia that attracted many women and men in the colonial world of Spanish America (Rieter, 1995). In contrast to violent experiences of evangelization and missionaries who literally combined the cross and the sword, at the local level, the Jesuits often "paid great attention to the different social and cultural situations in which they were intervening" (Imbruglia, 2014, 23). The religious strategy of the Jesuits as a whole in Peru had three dimensions: "the religious, the anthropological, and the political, and that it was through the construction of their 'empire' that these three facets were brought together" (Ibid.). In Japan, these dimensions were also existent, but the parameters they had been determined by were, especially with regard to the political one, quite different.

The Spanish Crown demanded that the Jesuits help to turn the indigenous people into Christian subordinates who served a foreign empire (Egido, Burrieza Sanchez, & Revuelta Gonzalez, 2004), while the missionaries themselves, of course, wanted to convert the native people as well, but also care for their souls at the same time. Their initial ambition for proselytization, at least in theory, was consequently not related to an exploitative agenda

(Imbruglia, 2014, 25-27). The military conquest had not provided the expected results, and it was the Jesuits who "realized that to fulfil their new charge, they would have to change the strategies that had served them so well in other locations" (Ibid., 28). They also realized that their original idea of high mobility had to be abandoned in the new environment because

> temporary missions were proving useful within Europe as instruments for improving the Christian life of communities already familiar with the gospel; they helped to ensure that the Tridentine standards of religious life were being respected, or uncovered heresy. But among people who had never heard Christ's word they were useless. Thus, because they were addressing different conditions, Jesuits thought that in their missions in the Americas they had to develop new forms and practices tailored to the sorts of human beings and cultures that were their targets. Jesuits recognized that the task of bringing such peoples to Christianity and transforming their societies into Christian worlds would require time, as well as continuous control over and direction of local missions. (Ibid.)

José de Acosta (1539/40-1600), who would determine the policy of the order in Peru during its consolidation period, made it clear in his later work that new methods were needed to convert people who had not been encountered before – "novo generi hominum novam evangelizandi rationem" (1670, 1, 16, cited in Ibid.). For the successful missionary, it was essential that

> the gospel had to be preached *non evangelice*, in a non-evangelizing fashion; "culture" was to provide the means through which "men from the forest" or "savage men" ("homines sylvestres") were to be transformed into rational individuals. Acosta added another identifiably "Jesuit" element to this strategy: if the indigenous populations were willing to be civilized, they were to be treated with gentleness; otherwise, for "their own salvation" ("pro sua salute"), they were to be entrusted "legitimately" ("non illiberaliter") to wise men who, with violence if necessary, would persuade them to live "as human beings and not as beasts" ("humane et non bestialiter"). (Imbruglia, 2014, 31)

Although dogmatic flexibility and a global mindset are visible within such considerations, these also show that violence as an ultima ratio was not off the table for Acosta. However, violent methods were not supposed to lead the way to a successful conversion. It instead seemed necessary to use existent local religious beliefs in combination with the Christian narrative, which is why, to name just one example, miracles seem to have been an aspect that could easily be translated to match the spiritual space of the experience (*Erfahrungsraum*) and horizon of expectations (*Erwartungshorizont*) (Koselleck, 2010, 349-375) of the natives as well. To be able to successfully translate the religious elements of Christianity to make them understandable for the indigenous people of colonial Peru, as well as other regions of the world, the Jesuits had to embrace the local traditions and gain the trust of the future converts (Nobili, 1971, 82, cited in Imbruglia, 2014, 32).

The Jesuits were ultimately so successful because the order's members "could adapt [themselves] to the world into which [they were] sent to live, not because he expected to find there elements of continuity with his original cultural world, but for exactly the opposite reason: because he had been taught to forget his origins." Eventually, "the Jesuit missionary was no longer a European priest; he was but a Christian" (Imbruglia, 2014, 32) with the aim to spread Christianity to every human being. To achieve this goal, dogmatic flexibility was necessary, a fact the Jesuits had accepted early on, and they began to include it in their educational preparation for future missions (Imbruglia, 1992). The Jesuits were consequently successful during the entry period in Peru, although some conflicts had existed with the civil authorities, first and foremost Viceroy Toledo. However, the Jesuit Order was successful in adapting to the local situation and would expand its missionary work and influence during the consolidation period, a success that was particularly related to Acosta's role as the new provincial.

Jesuit Consolidation in Colonial Peru

It has already been mentioned that the expansion of Jesuit colleges and missionary structures was initially hindered by Viceroy Toledo's hostile attitude toward the order. The Jesuits, namely Father Antonio Lopez and Brother Marco Antonio, secretly founded a college in Cuzco in August 1578 (Fraser, 1992, 23), and the authorities tried to revert such acts based on legal interpretations. The Spanish king supported the Jesuits eventually, which is why the attempts to sabotage the order's expansion in Peru could be circumvented without too much heat. By 1576, the Jesuits had already moved into Julí, "a sizeable indigenous township situated beside Lake Titicaca on the road between Cusco to the north and La Paz and Potosi to the south" (Ibid., 24), a move that had been made possible under José de Acosta's new leadership, who, as the second provincial of the Jesuit Order in Peru, had intelligently countered Toledo's resistance that the Jesuits had experienced in 1574 when they were expelled from La Paz. In the following years, the new provincial and his fellow Jesuits succeeded in further expanding the Jesuits' sphere of influence in Peru, namely to Potosi in 1580, Arequipa in 1581, and La Paz in 1582 (Ibid., 25). In the latter three cases, the Jesuits had tried to establish their own sites before, but Toledo's resistance had prevented them from openly claiming rights there; however, the alliances with people in high places in Peru and with the Spanish Empire eventually made it possible for them to show their presence openly. The Jesuits consequently had links to powerful circles, which supported their activities, especially in the larger cities, where the existence of a Jesuit college, without any doubt, also meant an increase in prestige. Considering these developments, the managerial activities of the Jesuits must be deemed successful, as they "found benefactors across a wide spectrum of society, rich and powerful, old, sick and lonely, Indian and Spaniard, men and (at least as often) women. Unsurprisingly, these benefactors were usually childless, but – equally unsurprisingly – the donations were often disputed by people claiming to be the legitimate heirs" (Ibid., 26).

In this regard, the Jesuits also gained from the wishes of many wealthy people in the colonial space who had an interest in acting as a supporter for a foundation that would be named after them. One could argue that

> the Jesuits probably exploited the insecurities of the nouveaux riches, of those whose families had not yet been named the founders of anything, whose fathers or grandfathers had played bit-parts in the events of the Conquest or, worse still, those who could not claim descent from one of the original conquistadors at all, but although they certainly did attract such people as donors, there is little evidence that they sought out a specific social group. (Ibid., 27)

Such people, however, only represented one of the interest groups to whom the Jesuits had to pay attention. In general, they were not supposed to spend their energies solely on groups that were already Christian before the Jesuits' arrival but to convert the indigenous people. However, as a precondition for economic self-sufficiency, the order and its managerial staff had to find ways that provided the pecuniary means for missionary work in the periphery. The approach toward the colonial space and, thereby, the role of the Jesuits themselves was, from the beginning, dual and ambivalent. The financial backbone of the order was the colonial metropolis, like Lima or Cuzco, while the missionary field of operation was located on the outer rim of Peru. In the east, the Jesuits had begun their mission at Lake Titicaca, where experiences with the native population would help them to further shape their strategies for the evangelization of the indigenous people in the following years and decades (Kriegbaum, 2006).

The *reducciones* were eventually applied as a way to reach those indios who had still been living in hunter-gatherer societies and had resisted proselytization in the past. What initially was used to exploit the native population as a cheap workforce was thereby transformed into a successful way to transform the indigenous societies and attract them to Christianity. The unification of nomadic and semi-nomadic people in these *reducciones* was not only done by the Jesuits but, in several regions, became a successful representation of the latter's work as well (Ibid.). Toledo intended to use these forms of social organization and living to exploit the native people as laborers in the mines and just considered proselytization as a useful side effect, while the Jesuits, in some cases, increasingly became agents of the indigenous cause rather than of the Spanish colonial authorities (Hosne, 2013, 16). The first *reducciones* had served the interests of the colonial power but would nevertheless play an important role in the missionary activities in Latin America as well, highlighting that the mission as such can hardly be separated from the history of colonialism in this particular region of the world (Kriegbaum, 2006). The messengers of the Christian faith, therefore, had to manage their dual identity as Christian missionaries and colonial agents.[6] Although all Jesuits were confronted with this problem, some had to face it on a more regular basis, especially when they served in the higher management ranks and needed to position themselves between colonial and Christian interests.

Some, like Bartolomé Hernández, were more critical. He reported that the indigenous people were forced into Christianity rather than having been persuaded of the ultimate salvation it would grant (Ibid.). He emphasized that it would be wiser to provide these people with a better life and thereby almost naturally guide them to the Christian faith. Others opposed such an opinion, and the divide between those who were dogmatically flexible and those who were rather more interested in pragmatic *realpolitik* that addressed the existent necessities of the colonial space became wider. The Jesuits who actually lived with the native people in the *reducciones* would often act as their protectors against aggressive forms of white settler colonialism, while some of the Jesuits, and this should not be omitted here, also ruled in a paternalistic way as intermediaries between the indigenous population and the colonial viceroy (Ibid.).

However, next to the organizational aspect of the Jesuits' missionary work, it is also worth keeping in mind the diversity of approaches chosen to achieve the proselytization of the people in peripheral Peru. One example will show that the establishment of a semiotic system related to the Christian message the Jesuits wanted to explain in various ways for their indigenous recipients involved the Italian Jesuit and painter Bernardo Bitti (1548-1610), who traveled

---

[6] Such an identity conflict also exists for SME managers who have to find a balance between their commitment to customers and the demands from their company's leadership or shareholders.

through the viceroyalty and created important altarpieces that bridged the European religion and the regional indigenous beliefs in a way that increased the local converts' intrigue: "Bitti's contribution at Juli can serve as but one example of how the Jesuits used art as part of their methodology of conversion" (Irwin, 2019, 270). The missionaries also learned from early failures and changed their own tactics and approaches accordingly, a fact that emphasizes the dogmatic flexibility of the Jesuits as well, and Blas Valera (1545-1597), a mestizo Jesuit, who had previously positioned himself against the execution of Tupac Amaru in 1572, would emphasize the necessity to react better instead of force a dogmatic message upon the native people (Ibid., 271).

Some Jesuit missionaries like Valera would rely on the local pantheist concept of *huaca* (or *waka*) (Brosseder, 2014; Itier, 2021), which later caused a conflict with Acosta (Hyland, 2003). Valera tried to use the pantheist considerations of the natives to create a link between the natives and the Christian God:

> The natural places were heavens, elements, sea, earth, mountains, creeks, mighty rivers, fountains or springs, deep lakes or lagoons, caves, sliced living rocks, mountain tops; all of which things were revered by them, not because they understood that there was some divinity or virtue of heaven, or that it was a living being, but because they believed that the great God Illa Tecce had created and placed it there and marked it with a particular and unique object, different from what commonly other places of that genre have, to serve as a sacred place and as a sanctuary where he and the other gods were worshipped. (Jesuita Anónimo, 1968, 157, cited in Dejo, 2023, 248)

With regard to the eventual Christian semiotic system of the Andes, the Jesuits represented a softer approach than the colonial authorities in other regions of the world. They must have "c[o]me to realize the complexities of transmitting the Christian narrative among indigenous populations, and it must also have strengthened their eagerness to arrive at a more appropriate understanding of the Andeans' spiritual background" (Dejo, 2023, 250). Consequently "the Jesuits did not force the complete destruction of Andean culture, but instead utilized their knowledge of local life to aid in their own efforts to teach Christianity. There was, simultaneously, a campaign to introduce European, Christian culture" (Ibid.). Especially the visual arts helped in this regard, as paintings helped to present the stories related to European Christian beliefs, and the evangelization effort of the Jesuits was often a visually stimulated one, as "painting and sculpture had the potential to break through the language barriers that inhibited the communication of the Christian faith's tenets and beliefs" (Ibid., 272). Besides the actual measures chosen to achieve proselytization in Peru, the role of the managers who led and decided on these processes seems quite essential, as is made obvious by the case of José de Acosta, whose provincial rule dominated the consolidation period.

Acosta arrived in Peru in 1571 and was sent by provincial Jerónimo Ruiz de Portillo to the colony's interior, where he was able to collect diverse impressions related to the Jesuit mission (Acosta, 1670):

> His travels took him to regions inhabited solely by natives and a few Spanish settlements in the burgeoning cities of this widespread territory. Acosta made this trip in the company of the Jesuit Antonio González de Ocampo, but mostly he travelled with the Jesuit Luis López and with Brother Gonzalo Ruiz, a mestizo – mixed-race – with "sound knowledge of the Indian language." (Hosne, 2013, 15)

Acosta was thereby able to gather impressions about the actual situation within the colony to prepare a strategy he would later follow as the order's provincial between 1576 and 1581 (Ibid., 16-20). This case also shows that the Jesuits in Peru initially relied on the language capacity of locally recruited brothers (hermanos), whose language capacities were well-appreciated and used not only in the entry period but during the consolidation period as well. Acosta also "acquired the rudiments of the Quechua language" (Ibid., 15), which he deemed substantially significant to his further work in Peru. Acosta would, in addition, become the most important theologian in the colonial Peruvian context, authoring the *Doctrina Christiana y Catecismo para Instrucción de Indios* (1584/85), a work that was supposed to

> erase, on the one hand, the first evangelization receptive to pre-Hispanic elements based on minimal content for salvation and, on the other hand, to establish Tridentine orthodoxy as a final direction, incompatible with the indigenous 'idolatrous' religions. The DCC reflects the purposes, intentions and goals of the Jesuits in Peru, all of whom found in Acosta a spokesman who, more than once, overshadowed other Jesuits who had envisioned things differently in that mission. (Ibid., 5)

Acosta, as provincial, tried to centralize the order's province and to create a homogenous space with a universal dogmatic interpretation of Christianity and how it should be applied within the Peruvian context. These interpretations, formulated in the *Doctrina Christiana y Catecismo para Instrucción de Indios*, were, according to the Third Lima Council (1582/83), also supposed to be translated into Quechua and Aymara in order to provide texts and instructions in the native languages as well. However, Acosta's rule as provincial was ultimately not that easy, although his influence and dogmatic flexibility seem to have been able to secure at least some stability and a period of growth in which the expansion of the order within the colonial sphere continued while the number of Jesuits steadily increased to new heights. The consolidation period shall consequently be taken into closer consideration here before the actual debates related to native languages as they began to be more heatedly expressed during the Third Lima Council are discussed.

Acosta was appointed provincial at the age of 35 and held this position from 1576 until 1581 (Hosne, 2013, 16-20). In his primal year, the Jesuit Order held congregations in Lima and Cuzco, and Acosta prepared a draft proposal on what the missionary work of the Jesuits was supposed to look like in the following years. Especially in Cuzco, Acosta could rely on Jesuits who spoke the indigenous languages and could support the developed approach toward the indigenous people, e.g., Alonso de Barzana (Soto Antuñedo, 2016a; 2016b; 2018), Bartolomé de Santiago, and Blas Valera. Therefore, early on, Acosta relied upon those who held the knowledge needed to continue the evangelization of the native population in Peru. Although Acosta showed that he had the needed dogmatic flexibility to orchestrate the further work of the order in its Peruvian context successfully, he also had to make some pragmatic decisions that were not fully supported by all Jesuits or that at least aroused suspicion among them.

Before becoming provincial, Acosta had been appointed to serve the Inquisition during the trial against Francisco de la Cruz, a Dominican who had been active in Peru since 1561. As a qualifier of the Inquisition, Acosta served an institution that in the past had been relatively hostile toward Ignatius and the order itself, and when the accused was eventually burned in 1578, it was because the new provincial had accused him of Lutheran heresy. De la Cruz had argued that faith alone would be sufficient to secure an indigenous person's salvation, which challenged the Catholic method of evangelization in general. Beyond this process, which was not only a clerical but also a political event, Acosta forged closer ties with Viceroy Toledo, a fact that drew a wedge between him and some of his Jesuit colleagues, who wondered if he was still acting on behalf of the order's best interests. However, Acosta was politically successful and, despite the internal disputes, secured "a pre-eminent role by the royal authorities regarding the evangelization and indoctrination of the Indians in Peru, while the Dominicans were pushed into the background" (Ibid., 16). While the provincial secured the political position of the order in colonial Peru, men like Barzana provided the know-how for the missionary approach toward the natives, who needed to be addressed in Quechua and Aymara. He composed one of the first lexica for the Quechua language, which was supposed to further enable the education of Jesuit fathers and brothers for their later service in the respective regions of Peru. These preliminary works would be collected during the Third Lima Council in the *Doctrina y Catecismo para*

Instrucción de Indios to set centralized standards for the Jesuit service that encountered these native languages.

Barzana had previously been in support of Father Luis López, who had openly challenged Toledo during the entry period and, with the former's help, had founded colleges in Cuzco, Potosí, and Arequipa. What made López's case particularly problematic for the internal Jesuit debates was the fact that he had also been tried by the Inquisition between 1573 and 1576, together with Francisco de la Cruz. In view of this issue, Acosta adopted a flexible posture, as he needed the civil authorities and their support to consolidate the work of the order and secure its economic income and thereby its organizational stability (Cushner, 1983), but also the dogmatically more open Jesuit fathers and brothers, who were supposed to do the groundwork for the order in the future. The fact that Acosta navigated these different interest groups and kept the Jesuit Order in a rather influential position speaks for his skills as a manager. He also allowed Barzana to continue his important work, regardless of his former support for López, which means that Acosta was flexible enough with regard to the existence of a global mindset to avoid accusations where the argument seemed unnecessary and solely based on theological aspects. This was probably a pragmatic decision since Acosta needed Barzana's skills during the consolidation period, rather than him being interested in dogmatic puritanism, especially since Barzana, next to the lexica, also wrote confession manuals for his Jesuit colleagues that they could use in their daily work among the indigenous people.

In 1578, Acosta oversaw the foundation of new Indian parishes (*doctrina de indios*), e.g., in Julí, and new colleges in Potosí, Arequipa, and La Paz. Indian parishes were controlled by the respective Jesuit fathers there, who not only had to oversee the organizational duties related to those places but were also responsible for the religious questions and missionary development. These *doctrinas* counted around 400 indigenous people in Acosta's time and also represented a fulfillment of Toledo's demands with regard to settled missionary work. However, "this represented a harsh attack on the Jesuit vocation of mobility," and the "doctrinas de indios required a commitment to spiritual care – cura de almas – in the long term, so Jesuits had to settle there. Moreover, in the doctrinas the parish priests received a stipend, which was also against the Formula of the Institute – the fundamental rules of the Society" (Hosne, 2013, 18). Acosta obviously had no choice but to comply if he was unwilling to take a chance on resisting for the sake of custom. The choice was easy: succeed with the mission by bending the rules or fail without trying. Therefore, Acosta seemed to have made the right call concerning the situation that presented itself to him, but his decision also divided the order.

Acosta's ties to Viceroy Toledo and the Inquisition created resistance from a group of Jesuits that was led by Luis López and the Visitor Juan de la Plaza, who tried to counter the course of the Jesuit Order in the provincial's early years. As the Visitor and provincial both claimed to possess uncontested authority, a conflict, as happened in Japan due to Valignano's involvement, seemed inevitable until de la Plaza left for Mexico in 1580. The fact that the Inquisition had turned against López also stimulated distrust toward Acosta, who was considered a traitor by the anti-inquisitional forces within the Jesuit Order in Peru. The leading Jesuit consequently had to navigate through dangerous waters but ultimately remained in his position: "In a world of manifest and horrific injustice, the Jesuit ascetic ideal that Acosta adapted to the contingencies of Spanish America legitimated action by posing both the corrupt colonial and the recalcitrant Amerindian as obstacles to overcome in a trial of the will that would ultimately reaffirm the providential order realized through the Spanish occupation of the New World" (Green, 2016, 117). Acosta was a pragmatic man who realized the problems that surrounded him and, in his later works, "explicitly links the workings of the devil in the New World with the moral evil of his fellow Spaniards" (Ibid., 119). Nevertheless, he also realized that he could not act against everyone's interest at the same time and thus accepted suitable solutions. As a manager, he succeeded in fulfilling the demanded tasks as far as possible.

It is therefore not surprising that the consolidation period "started with great promise and triggered the optimism of Crown and Church authorities, whose success in evangelizing native Andeans had been limited in the turbulent postconquest period of civil war and Inca revolt" (Charles, 2014, 60). Early on, even with limited numbers during the entry period, the Jesuits had begun to travel to "the highland communities of the interior to teach native Andeans about the errors of the ancestral divinities and the rewards of Christianity" (Ibid.; for more details, see Vargas Ugarte, 1963, 1, 43-54). Alongside the missionary successes, the colonial authorities were naturally also interested in the schools and colleges the Jesuits had established in the urban centers of Lima and Cuzco, as they were considered important facilities "to transform the manners and customs of colonial society" (Charles, 2014, 60).

The Jesuits also acted strategically with regard to their spiritual approach toward the indigenous people, which they tried to achieve in a top-down way by first attracting the Andean chiefs to the new religion. A successful evangelization of the local elites, almost like the European saying "cuius regio, eius religio" documented, provided the Jesuits with a clear advantage, as such conversions came with an increase in authority over the former Incan territories. The Jesuit colleges, in particular, like the Colegio del Príncipe that was established in 1618 by the Spanish king, would fulfill such important missionary duties:

> It was here that adolescent notables of the Pacific coast and central Andean highlands undertook schooling in Castilian literacy and Christian doctrine, on the condition that upon completion of the course of study, they would return to their home villages and serve at the behest of Spanish provincial governors (*corregidores*) and the clergy in temporal and spiritual administration. The Jesuits at the colegio planned to mold a select cadre of hereditary chiefs (*curacas*) who would teach and personify orthodox Christian values and practices in local native communities that were seen as politically resistant and prone to religious error. (Ibid., 61)

It was Acosta and de la Plaza who had agreed on the role the educational facilities should play to strengthen the Jesuit influence in Peru. The order's congregation in 1576 made it clear that Jesuit colleges would accept "only the eldest sons of hereditary elites (caciques principales and segundas personas) … entering between the ages of nine and sixteen, and remaining cloistered for a period of six years" (Ibid., 63). They would read and study the major works of Castilian literature and only use Spanish as an educational lingua franca, although the Christian doctrines were supposed to be studied in both Spanish and their native language, Quechua. In addition, the students had to become familiar with "Catholic liturgy, devotional readings, and spiritual exercises" (Ibid.) so that the young men would be well prepared for missionary voyages in the Spanish American colonies once their education had finished. The students' indigenous identity was not, however, to be replaced but rather complemented: "The [Indian boys] should not be deprived of the laws and customs and way of governing of their lands, provided they are not contrary to natural and Christian law. Nor is it wise to transform them completely into Spaniards, which not only would be difficult and [a] cause of discouragement for the students but also a great obstacle to their government" (MP 2, 460, translation cited in Charles, 2014, 63). The Jesuits' educational aims were therefore directed early on toward the achievement of cultural symbiosis, as native Jesuits would probably become much more successful missionaries. Accosta, and probably de la Plaza as well, had realized that "there was no quick fix for transforming barbarous habits into Christian ones; they believed that to create an Andean Catholic society, the future caciques should impose the new laws and customs gradually upon the conquered groups with patience and flexibility" (Charles, 2014, 63).

Accepting indigenous men as novices and students at their colleges allowed the Jesuits to gain knowledge of the regional language and culture, knowledge that was considered important and essential to guarantee the success of the order's missionary work in the future. This not only helped to collect useful information, but the work of the indigenous Jesuits would also allow the order to prepare the first dictionaries and text corpora that could be used in the following missions. The indigenous students were consequently seen as replicators of knowledge, and their synergetic effect cannot be overemphasized. The idea was also to educate these young men to become Jesuit priests, and Father Diego de Torres (1551-1638) would present this Jesuit intention to the Spanish Crown and the Curia in Rome. The plan, however, did not succeed, as the local church authorities, as well as the ones in the Vatican, resisted it and prohibited the advance of indigenous novices to the "supremas facultades" (highest faculties) (Charles, 2014, 64). Due to the different opinions and positions toward the character of the missionary work, the new provincial Baltasar Piñas (1528-1611) and the rector of the Jesuit college in Lima, Juan de Atienza (1546-1592), tried to use their influence during the Third Lima Council in 1582/83 to achieve a more homogenous approach toward it (Hosne, 2013, 20). The Council would also debate the most suitable practices for the proselytization of the indigenous people, as the previous experiences were somehow ambivalent:

> The spread of saint worship among assimilated indigenous Andean people in colonial Peru was seen by contemporary Catholics as one of the greatest successes in their colonial evangelization efforts. Several other methods, such as the extirpation of idolatries, and the use of baptisms, confessions, and the incarceration of indigenous religious specialists, proved of little success when employed in isolation. (Brosseder, 2012, 383)[7]

The Third Lima Council was supposed to provide clearer instructions for the missionaries, and it "produced three major texts that shaped encounters between Catholic priests and indigenous people throughout the seventeenth century" (Ibid., 384). Acosta used the opportunity to shape the further Jesuit efforts as well and later emphasized his commitment in a letter he wrote in April 1584:

> During all these years I have dedicated my efforts to the provincial Council here celebrated, and which entailed many difficulties and hard work, and it was done in God's best service and was fruitful. Because, even if it were no more than the Christian doctrine and catechism written and translated into the language of these Indies by the work of

---

[7] For a more detailed analysis, see MacCormack (1991, 2004).

the Society and now printed in our house, it has been very useful. (MP, 3, 401, translation cited in Hosne, 2013, 20-21)

Acosta was aware of the necessity for strategies that took account of the heterogeneity of the diverse local contexts, but it was the missionaries themselves who needed to set the example of a good life for the indigenous converts. He also pointed out that the exploitative control of the Spanish colonial authorities and non-Jesuit clericals would often leave no time or space for the converts to actually *be* Christians. These later statements of Acosta seem to indicate that he was quite interested in a successful mission that would, however, treat the native population as a valuable part of the Christian community of the future. He consequently also critically reflected upon the exploitative measures, like the continuation of the *mita* (a labor quota already used during the time of the Incan Empire), used by the Spanish authorities, especially with regard to mining work (del Valle, More, & O'Toole, 2020, 3) Regardless of these reflections, however, "it was always clear to him that, in Peru, he would collaborate with the Spanish crown and its representatives in his capacity as [a] theologian, even if this caused frictions inside the Society in the Peru province. Right from the beginning, Acosta sharply detected where the power was and never fought against it, nor resisted it; he was actually a collaborator" (Hosne, 2013: 42).

The catechism and rituals applied during the missionary approach toward the native people were eventually centralized by the Third Lima Council, and the *Doctrina Cristiana* was published in Spanish, Quechua, and Aymara a year later. It was supposed to function as a handbook for those who would be on missionary duty in every part of the colony and, therefore "contained both sermons and a confession manual and stressed preaching, confession, and communion, whereas individual faith and salvation were highlighted and a specific pedagogy was promoted" (Maldavsky, 2018, 52). Regardless of such official decisions, the realities would remain different in the decades that followed. Baptism, to name just one example, was considered to be associated with sickness or human death, as it was initially applied by missionaries in such contexts and was therefore often not accepted by indigenous people (Ibid., 56). What had been formulated on the theoretical level in Lima could consequently not always be applied to the practical one (Giudicelli, 2011).

> Within th[e] marginal territories, where the Jesuits were becoming the most important Christian force in the 17th century, they tried to produce detailed classifications of the peoples they were seeking to convert and evangelize. An effective strategy required a classification of 'nations,' with languages, territories, political organizations and cultural features. Missionaries thought in terms of culturally and linguistically

homogenous populations. Their classifications did not always fit the complex reality. (Ibid.)

The struggle between the dogmatic demands and the missionary realities, which had caused problems in the past, would eventually also cause the end of the Jesuit Order's province of Peru, which would be divided in the early 1600s.

Dogmatic Struggles and Decline

The Jesuits represented a "utopian Christian-social project" (Carrasco, 2018, 207) in the Spanish colonies of Latin America, but at the same time also took part in the exploitation of the indigenous and enslaved African people that had been sold to the "New World," a fact that is proven by the more than 17,000 slaves in Spanish America and almost 6,000 slaves in Brazil that the Society of Jesus owned when its members were expelled from there in 1767 (Weaver, 2018, 119). The work of the Jesuits in the colonial world in general, and in Peru in particular, was consequently twofold from its beginning. The division between Christian utopia-oriented missionary work and hard facts-based pragmatic *realpolitik* had been problematic since the order's initial arrival in 1568, and it became a major issue again in the early 1600s. The different spatial and cultural geographies also determined the identities of the Jesuits, as

> the frontier between the Andes and Amazonia was real enough under Spanish rule. It is possible to trace the eastern border of effective Spanish occupation and control in Peru with some precision, since for the main, it followed the line of the upper *montaña* – the easternmost slopes of the Andes, steep, wet and heavily forested. That is to say, Spain's writ ran as far as the upper montaña, with the highlands and coast to the west considered the colonial heartlands. Beyond, the European presence was often either limited, or indeed negligible, in lowland territories that were in no sense regarded as core to the colony. (Pearce, 2020, 314)

The languages differed (Adelaar, 2020), as did the aims of the Jesuits. The agenda of those who trained the elites in the Jesuit colleges was obviously different from that of those who lived with the native people in the peripheral regions of the colony, defending them against exploitation and suppression (Maldavsky, 2012, 162-183).

Acosta, like many others, in a way, looked down on the natives (Acosta, 1605, 32-33), and the first missionaries were not actually sent out before 1585, as the Jesuits were more interested in securing their fragile position before marching out to expand Christianity. However, some were not interested in a life in the metropolis but instead lived up to their missionary vocation, such as Father Diego de Samaniego (1542-1627), to name just one example here (Coello de la Rosa, 2007, 155). It was the "Jesuit missions on the eastern frontiers of Charcas that constituted the beginning of the expansion of the Ignatian Order in the south and east of Upper Peru. This was also due to the need to occupy new spaces in the Amazon foothills to evangelize the Indians not subjected by the civil powers, such as the chiriguanes, the mojos and the chiquitos" (Ibid., 152). Those who actually went out to preach the Christian belief had to be able to adapt their messages to match their audiences (O'Malley, 2013, 91). While "[e]ven at its founding moment, the Society of Jesus had features, specified in the Formula, that set it apart with regard to certain long-established patterns for religious orders" (Ibid., 225), the colonial realities would demand that the Jesuits further intensify such differences and abandon dogmatic considerations to achieve missionary success.

Therefore, the mission had no other choice but to adjust itself to meet the demands of the local religious beliefs, and the missionaries needed to adapt their approach to match the particular context of their work (Hosne, 2013, 1). It is consequently not surprising that

> [r]egulating translation was a prevalent concern among Jesuits in late sixteenth- and early seventeenth-century Spanish America, especially due to the translator's simultaneous importance to evangelical projects and the diversity of subject positions he or she could occupy. The variety of names employed to describe translating figures in Jesuit texts from this period characterizes the indeterminacy of their role in facilitating inter-linguistic communications for the order: lengua, traductor, intérprete, chalona, loro, asistente, apóstol, doku, mestizo, simiyachac, catequista, indio ladino, negro ladino, and perito de lenguas are just some examples. (Brewer-Garcia, 2012, 365)

In the late sixteenth century, such questions dominated the Jesuit disputes, as can be observed during the Third Lima Council, and they became even more heated in the early 1600s (Mannheim, 1991, Charles, 2003, 2004, 2007; Durston, 2007). While the Jesuits had initially used mestizos as translators to bridge the language gap between them and the soon-to-be-converts, they soon made it an essential aspect of their missionary agenda to train the fathers and brothers of the order to achieve the best possible outreach in all parts of Peru, an inclusive strategy that initially provided an advantage when compared with the missionary work of the other Christian orders (Brewer-García, 2012, 365-366).

The favorable position toward these mestizos was nevertheless not shared by all Jesuits early on (MP, 1, 327, 332-333). Actually, the skepticism about equality between Spanish and indigenous Jesuits increased (MP, 2, 183), and in 1582, it was not only the pressure from the Spanish Crown and the Curia in Rome but a unanimous vote of the Jesuit leadership that prevented the ordination of native Jesuits and thereby their chance to advance through the order's ranks (MP, 3, 205-206). Three reasons were named as to why the mestizos should be excluded:

1) the "proof" that mestizos (as a general type) were unfit for Jesuit membership,
2) the exclusionary precedents set by other religious orders, and
3) pressure from the Crown to refrain from ordaining mestizos (Brewer-García, 2012, 368).

While the Third Lima Council debated the role of language, the order had already decided that it would not allow the representatives for these languages and the cultures they expressed to be part of the higher leadership, a fact that further separated the different groups within the Jesuit province of Peru: "In the period that followed, the Jesuits would tenaciously combat heterodoxy. However, it is easy to overlook the fact that in the midst of this process of intercultural encounter, a great deal of discernment – of similarities and differences – continued to operate in their minds and hearts" (Dejo, 2023, 241).

While Acosta "chose mestizo Jesuit priests as key translators for the Third Lima Council translation project" (Brewer-García, 2012, 366) and thereby emphasized their important role, it was obvious that this was just yet another form of exploitation. Acosta was strictly against forms of syncretism and "firmly against using the relationship with nature to anchor the Andean people's faith in the Christian God" (Dejo, 2023, 241). He argued that superstitions

> are so widespread among our barbarians that the kinds of sacrifices and *guacas* cannot be counted: it does not matter if it is mountains, slopes, prominent rocks, springs that flow gently, rivers that run quickly, high peaks of rocks, huge mounds of sand, the dark whirlwind of an abyss, the gigantic carving of a thousand-year-old tree, indicating the vein of a metal deposit, a less usual or a little more elegant form of any stone. In short, and to say it all at once, as soon as the barbarians discover that something stands out among the other beings of their species, they instantly recognize a divinity there and worship it without a moment's hesitation. The mountains are full of this most hateful plague of idolatry, the valleys, the towns, the houses, the roads are full, and there is no piece of Peruvian land that is free from this kind of sacrifice. (Acosta, 1987, lib. 5, 9, 11, 257, cited in Dejo, 2023, 247).

The Cases

One might get the impression that the further debate about the role of language (Estenssoro Fuchs, 2003, 94-114) was a proxy debate about the standing of indigenous Jesuits within the province as well. All in all, the language debate presented a dilemma:

> Although few Church leaders ever completely denied the importance of teaching Christian Doctrine in indigenous languages (at least for a time), there were opposing positions regarding how this linguistic question should be addressed: some believed that the ultimate goal should be to teach the Doctrine in Spanish to native Andeans to ensure orthodox comprehension, while others saw that a better and more practical goal would be to train European priests to master indigenous languages in order to preach in the tongues of their catechumens. The Jesuits, who arrived in Peru toward the end of the first evangelization period, firmly believed in the value of teaching the Doctrine in native languages, and thus at first their ideal solution was to train and ordain mestizo priests who had a strong command of Spanish and native languages to be the leaders of indigenous missions. (Brewer-García, 2012, 367)

The centralization of language use and instructional texts had already marked the consolidation period and limited the existent flexibility that had marked the dogmatically relatively unchallenged entry period (Estenssoro Fuchs, 2003, 241-310). Since Acosta had agreed to follow the colonial authorities' demands, resisting the necessary changes was out of the question, even if that meant sacrificing the order's dogmatic flexibility, at least to a certain degree (MP, 2, 477-478).

This did not mean, however, that the order did not further engage in its educational policy regarding the native languages: "Colonial common languages such as Quechua (Andes), Nahuatl (Mesoamerica), and Tupi (Brazil) were not only vernacular languages adopted within linguistically fragmented spaces. They were colonial because they were cultural and political instruments used to create a unified context for heterogeneous indigenous populations for the purpose of evangelization and labor" (Maldavsky, 2018, 58). Furthermore, the order's competition was also quite active. A large percentage of the secular priests who had been appointed in the diocese of Lima actually also spoke a native language, so it must be highlighted here that the Jesuits did not possess an edge in having a solid command of the indigenous tongues (Ibid., 61).

In December 1600, the Jesuits met for another provincial congregation in Lima, where the debate about the use of native languages and its implications was renewed. This turned into a more general struggle about questions related to the evangelization of indigenous people. Nicolas Mastrili Duran, who had been active in Peru since 1592 and who acted as superior in Julí, "an important *doctrina de indios* (community of native converts) ... [spoke] passionately on behalf of missions to native Americans" and "argued that every Jesuit was obliged to learn the indigenous languages. Opposing this statement was Diego Álvarez de Paz, rector of the Jesuit college in Cuzco, the ancient Inca capital in the highlands" (Hsia, 2014, 51). The two men represented the different factions within the Peruvian Jesuit province. The latter, "[a] professor of theology in Cuzco, ... undertook no missionary activities among the native Americans because he did not speak their languages. While supporting indigenous missions, Álvarez disagreed with Duran's linguistic and missionary imperatives, arguing that the Jesuits in Peru could choose their specialization and not everyone was obliged to learn Quechua or Amara" (Ibid.). The order had consequently been divided into the "college Jesuits" of the metropolis and the "preachers" on the periphery, and it seemed this split could not be bridged anymore. Eventually, the internal struggle and the geographical scope of colonial Peru, which had become too broad, led to a restructuring of the provincial map between 1605 and 1607: "the northern part of the viceroyalty of Peru became the new Jesuit province of New Granada, comprising today's Ecuador and Colombia; the southern part split off and became the vice-province of Chile; and the Paraguay mission was conceded to Portuguese Jesuits from Brazil" (Ibid., 53).

Although the Jesuits were the first to have claimed the term "missionary" for themselves (Strasser, 2020, 20), they failed to defend missionary ideals against a colonial government, an incapacity that drove a wedge into their own ranks and eventually led to a divide that could not be overcome. The order's work nevertheless continued until 1767, when the Jesuits were expelled from Spanish America, but the Peruvian case had already shown that dogmatic flexibility and colonial pragmatism would hardly go hand in hand. The Peruvian case held better preconditions for the Jesuits than they faced in China or Japan, where the ruling powers were independent and considered themselves to be superior (Reinhard, 1976, 530), but it was, as in some decades in Japan, the order's internal debates that weakened its performance and ultimately prevented its success.

Jesuit Missionaries in Peru

The Jesuits arrived relatively late in Peru, specifically in 1568, by which time other religious orders had already been active there. Regardless of this situation and the relatively small numbers of padres (there were not more than 15 in the order's province until 1573), the Jesuit impact in Peru would be felt, especially from the 1580s, which saw an increase in their numbers and the foundation of

The Cases

Jesuit colleges in the new colonial centers of Spanish Peru in particular. Consequently, the number of Jesuit fathers (padres) and brothers (hermanos) exceeded 100 in 1583 and 240 in 1595.

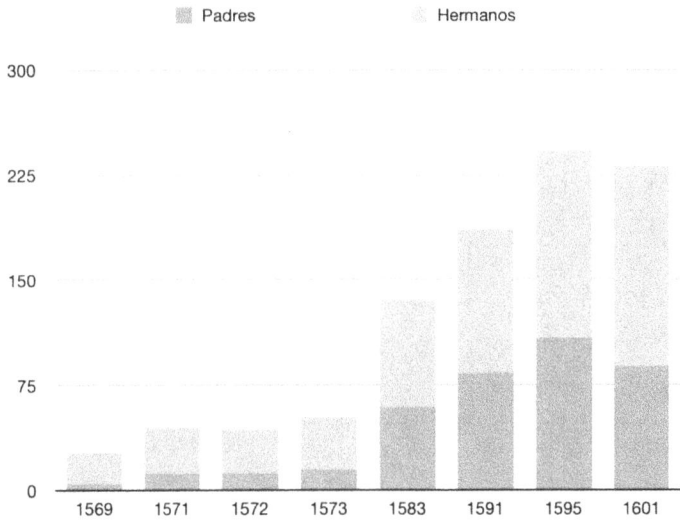

Fig. 4.4: Number of Jesuits in Peru between 1569 and 1601.

Tab. 4.7: Number of padres and hermanos serving in Peru between 1569 and 1601 (including available data for Peruvian padres and hermanos).[8]

Year	Padres	Hermanos	Peruvian Padres	Peruvian Hermanos
1569	5	22		
1571	12	33		
1572	12	31		
1573	15	37		
1583	59	77	6	11
1591	84	102	/	/
1595	108	134	11	13
1601	88	143	6	14

---

[8] The catalogues for 1591 are unfortunately not as detailed as for other years.

Entry Period (1568-1575)

Tab. 4.8: Jesuits who served in Peru between 1568 and 1575.

Fathers (Padres) = Leading management	Brothers (Hermanos)
Joseph de Acosta	Alonso del Aguila
Sebastián Amador	Juan Pérez de Aguilar
Alonso de Barzana	Pedro de Añasco
Didacus (Diego) de Bracamonte	Joán de Anaya
Joán de Çúñiga	Marco Antonio
Pedro Miguel de Fuentes	Diego González Carasco
Juán (Jóan) Gomez	Francisco de Carrión
Bartolomé Hernandez	Joán de Casasola
Andrés López	Martín de Contreras
Luis López	Hernando Despinar (Hernando de Espinar)
Antonio Martínez	Francisco de Espinosa (Francisco Despinosa)
Mesía (Pedro Mexía or Mezia)	Leandro Felipe
Diego Ortún (Hortún)	Diego Flores
Leandro Philipe	Juan Garcia
Jherónimo Ruiz de Portillo	Antonio González
Cristóval Sanches	Joán Gutiérrez
Joán de Zúñiga	Francisco de Heredia
	Estevan Izquierdo
	Pedro Lopez
	Francisco López
	Antonio Martínez
	Diego Martínez

	Francisco de Medina
	Juan de Mendoça
	Pedro Mexía
	Joán Miguel
	Martin Miguel
	Juan Pérez de la Milla
	Andrés de Montalvo
	Blas Morán
	Antonio González de Ocampo
	Alonso Pérez
	Santiago Pérez
	Martin Piçarro
	Joseph de Ribera
	Pedro de Rojas
	Juan Rodriguez
	Francisco Romero
	Baltazar Ruiz
	Gonzálo Ruiz
	Juan Ruiz
	Juan Ruiz
	Joán Sanchez
	Blas Valera
	Antonio Vázquez
	Vicente Yáñez

In contrast to Japan, the number of Jesuits in Peru grew faster during the entry period as the order worked hand in hand with the Spanish colonial authorities and did not need to get permission for its work from foreign rulers, as was the case with the Japanese daimyōs. However, there were conflicts with the Inquisition, which was exported to colonial Latin America by the Spanish Crown. These were related to dogmatic questions and, therefore, already pointed to a conflict that would intensify in later years. Regardless of these early problems, the overall missionary work of the Jesuits in Peru remained uncontested by the authorities, and the dogmatic flexibility of the order allowed the padres and hermanos to reach an increasingly wide number of indigenous people for conversion, although this act was often not solely voluntary but also stimulated by force which, in contrast to Japan, could be applied by the Jesuits in the colonial environment.

Consolidation Period (1576-1599)

Tab. 4.9: Number of Jesuits in Peru in 1591 according to location (MP 4, 1966, 674).

Place	Number of Jesuits
Lima	77
Cuzco	23
La Paz	10
Ariquipa	16
Potosí	15
Quito	16
Julí	12
Panamá	7
Santa Cruz	5
Tucumán	5

During the consolidation period in Peru, the number of Jesuits grew rapidly, rising to 186 in 1591, although their numbers were particularly high in the larger cities. Although "Peruvian" Jesuit padres are listed as well, these were mestizos and, as children of European settlers and indigenous elites, they represented the new colonial ruling class. From 1582, it was officially forbidden for indigenous people to be granted such a position. The Jesuits consequently remained an element of colonial rule in Peru, which must have been considered "foreign" as a consequence. In addition, the split between those who intended to replicate European educational structures in the colonial environment and those who were rather more interested in the mission and the indigenous population as the one the Jesuit efforts should be centered around intensified and would eventually lead to a struggle that accompanied, if not stimulated, the end of the existent provincial structure in the early 1600s.

In the more peripheral regions of the order's province, contacts with and perceptions of the indigenous people and their necessities were obviously different. With a growing number of Jesuits, who were most numerous in the newly established colleges, the divide between these two different colonial spaces intensified. Language education and its use had become a central element of internal debates since the early 1580s, but this was even more the case in the early 1600s when the province was restructured. Similarly to the numerical development of the Jesuits in Japan, the order's province was really witnessing an increase in interest, and therefore, a growing number of Jesuits arrived from the early 1580s.

Tab. 4.10: Jesuit padres who served in Peru between 1576 and 1599.

Joseph de Acosta	Joán Díaz	Francisco de Medina	Joán Baptista Rufo
Joán de Aguilar	Joán Frías Errán	Hernando de Mendoça	Alonso Ruiz
Joán Alonso	Bartholomé de Escobar	Alonso Messía	Joán Ruiz
Joán de Alva	Luis de Estella	Antonio Messía	Hierónimo Ruiz de Portillo
Diego Alvarez de Paz	Onofre Estevan	Alonso de Miranda	Diego de Samaniego
Pedro de Añasco	Diego Flores	Angelo Monitola	Agustín Sánchez
Joán de Anaya	Joán Fonte	Herónimo de Montesinos	Bartholomé de Santiago
Hierónimo de Andión	Pedro Miguel de Fuentes	Joán de Montoya	Luis de Santillán
Francisco Angulo	Lucio Garcete	Hernando Morillo	Joán Sebastián (Joán Sebastián-Daraco)
Ruperto Arnono	Juán (Jóan) Gomez	Miguel Muñoz	Gonçalo Suárez
Joán de Atiença	Antonio González	Christóval Narváez	Juan Suárez de Lara

Joán de Avellaneda	Diego González	Antonio Núñez	Joseph Tiruel
Estevan de Avila	Joán de Güémez	Estevan de Ochoa	Diego de Torres
Herónimo de Avila	Andrés Hernández	Joán de Olivares	Diego de Torres (2nd entry)
Antonio de Ayanz	Joán Herrán	Pedro de Oñate	Joán de Truxillo
Lorenço Barriales	Francisco de Herrera	Andrez Ortiz Orruño	Miguel de Urrea
Alonso de Barzana	Hernando de Herrera	Diego Ortún (Hortún)	Diego de Vaena
Joán Beltran	Andrés Hortiz	Christóval de Ovan	Luis de Valdivia
Ludovico Bertonio	Christóval Hortiz	Bernardino Papiol	Alonso de Valdivieso
Didacus (Diego) de Bracamonte	Ignaco Iñiguez	Antonio Pardo	Blas Valera
Francisco Camorano	Ignacio Jaymes	Diego Paz	Antonio Vallejo
Valentín de Caravantes	Paulo Joseph	Hernán Pérez	Joán Vásquez
Pedro de Cartagena	Luis de Leiute	Joán Pérez de Aguilar	Manuel Vásquez
Pedro de Castillo	Joán de León	Joán Pérez Menacho	Antonio de Vega
Gerónimo de Castro	Andrés López	Francisco Perlín	Gabirel de Vega
Ignacio Cataño	Antonio López	Leandro Philippe	Herónimo de Vega
Estevan Cavello	Joán López de Almansa	Balthasar Piñas	Dionisso Velazquez
Gabriel de Chaves	Joán López Viana	Martín Pizzaro	Pedro Vicente
Gregorio de Cisneros	Marciel de Lorençana	Francisco de Portillo	Alonso de Villalobos
Diego de Cuenca	Gonçalo de Lyra	Diego Ramírez	Antonio de Vivar
Hernando de la Cueva	Rodrigo Manrique	Pedro Rodríguez	Vicente Yáñez
Diego de Çúñiga	Antonio Martínez	Joán Romero	Francisco Zamorano
Lope Delgado	Diego Martínez	Pedro de Rojas	

The Cases

In the consolidation period, the number of Peruvian Jesuits did not really increase, especially since their ordination as a priest was prohibited. The majority of the Jesuit missionaries in Peru during this period were recruited from Spain, where the order had established a strong presence and educational facilities to fuel the flow of well-trained missionary staff.

Period of Decline (1600-1605)

During the final period, the number of Peruvian Jesuits did not increase. However, a change was documented regarding some Jesuits' language proficiency, as in 1601, some were listed as members who could preach or take confession in one or more indigenous languages. The necessity to communicate with the indigenous population was consequently addressed, particularly in the peripheral regions of colonial Peru, although a dogmatic dispute with regard to the necessity to address the latter in their native languages also arose.

Tab. 4.11: Jesuit padres who served in Peru in 1601.

Hernando de Aguilera	Julián Delgado	Alonso Messía	Pedro Rodríguez
Juan de Aldana	Sebastián Delgado	Alonso de Miranda	Joán Baptista Rufo
Joán Alonso	Juan Domínguez	Angelo Monitola	Hernando de Salinas
Diego Alvarez de Paz	Niculás Durán	Gaspar de Montalvo	Diego de Samaniego
Hierónimo de Andión	Bartholomé de Escobar	Juan Muñoz	Agustín Sanches
Francisco de Aramburu (Arambulo)	Francisco de Espinosa	Joán de Olivares	Joán Sebastián (Joán Sebastián-Daraco)
Juan de Arcos	Luis de Estella	Christóval de Ovan(do)	Joseph Tiruel
Joán de Avellaneda	Christóval García	Estevan Páez	Diego de Torres
Estevan de Avila	Juán (Jóan) Gomez	Diego Paz	Diego de Torres Rubio
Juan Baptista Chiqueti	Antonio González	Joán Pérez de Aguilar	Joán (Juan López) de Truxillo
Joán Beltran	Diego González	Joán Pérez Menacho	Joán Vásquez
Ludovico Bertonio (Vertonio)	Joán de Güémez	Herónimo de Montesinos	Martín Vázquez

Antonio Bivar	Andrés Hernández	Pedro de Oñate	Pedro de Vedoya
Rodrigo de Cabredo	Hernando de Herrera	Andrez Ortiz Urño	Antonio de Vega
Valentín de Caravantes	Philippo Leandro	Antonio Pardo	Dionisso Velazquez
Pedro de Castillo	Luis de Leiute (Leyva)	Miguel Pastor	Pedro Vicente
Gerónimo (Hierónimo) de Castro	Joán López de Almansa	Julio Pesce	Francisco de Victoria
Gregorio de Cisneros	Gonçalo de Lyra	Francisco Perlín	Ignacio Xaimez
Philipe Claver	Rodrigo Manr(r)ique	Juan Perlin	Andrés Ximenes
Diego de Cuenca	Diego Martínez	Balthasar Piñas	Juan de Ybarra
Francisco Daza	Francisco de Medina	Diego Ramírez	Francisco Zamorano

Jesuit Managers in Peru: Some Examples

The following section will provide some short "manager portfolios" for leading members of the Jesuit mission during the three different periods to highlight some of the important individuals about whom more is known with regard to their role and work as part of the Jesuit missionary endeavor in Peru.

Jerónimo Ruiz de Portillo

Jerónimo Ruiz de Portillo (1532-1590) was the first provincial of the Jesuit Order in Peru (Torres Saldamando, 1906; Zubillaga, 1943; Medina, 2001). He became a Jesuit in 1551 in Salamanca, Spain, and belonged to the first generation of Spanish Jesuits. Later, he acted as a provincial in Peru and founded, among other institutions, the Jesuit college in Cuzco. Although he traveled with Viceroy Toledo during the latter's trip through colonial Peru, there were issues related to the Jesuit's global mindset, as he did not want to accept all the missionary doctrines of which Toledo and the Dominican archbishop Jerónimo de Loayza were so fond.[9] A conflict with the local authorities was inevitable, and this would not be solved until José de Acosta replaced Ruiz de Portillo as provincial in Peru.

---

[9] Conflicts between the Jesuits and the Dominicans were not uncommon (Steinkerchner, 2020).

José (Joseph) de Acosta

José de Acosta was born in Medina del Campo, Spain, and he entered the Society of Jesus in 1552, having been educated at the Jesuit college of his hometown during his early years. He later studied philosophy and theology at the University of Alcalá de Henares (Caraccioli, 2021, 110) and was sent to Peru in 1571 after he had personally requested to be sent abroad (Hosne, 2013, 14). On his way there, he spent time in Santo Domingo, Puerto Rico, South Cuba, and Jamaica, arriving in Lima in 1572 (Ibid., 15). There, he would establish close ties with Viceroy Toledo, whose reforms in the colony he supported. Acosta traveled through the country, gained experiences in a *reducción* in Julí, and became provincial in 1576, holding this position until 1581. Acosta had a major influence on the Jesuit mission, and his often pragmatic and close ties with Toledo secured the Jesuits' missionary work, which was less interrupted by the local authorities and the Inquisition, with whose representatives Acosta also had good relations. At the Third Council of Lima (1582/83), Acosta was quite influential, authoring the acts of this council before he moved to Mexico and then back to Europe in 1587. His later works, like the *De procuranda Indorum salute* (1589) and *Historia natural y moral de las Indias* (1590) (on this work, see Anagnostou, 2005, 5), made him quite well-known as an authority on matters related to the "New World" (Lopetegui, 1942; Burgaleta, 1999; Hosne, 2013; Green, 2016; on the influence of his works, see Caraccioli, 2021, 105-110). Acosta traveled widely in Peru and studied, at least rudimentarily, the Quechua language (Hosne, 2013, 15), which means that he at least partially tried to acclimatize himself culturally in the region before he became provincial. His very pragmatic position in the latter role made other Jesuits quite suspicious of him, as they were particularly worried about his close ties to the Inquisition and the Viceroy. Nevertheless, Acosta's leadership secured a prosperous period for the order with regard to the Jesuits' history in Peru.

Blas Valera

Blas Valera (1545-1597) was a mestizo born in northern Peru, and he joined the Society of Jesus as an important person as he spoke Quechua and could be sent to different parts of the colony in the following years. He was one of the first mestizos who were allowed to join the ranks of the Jesuits, but he was not uncritical of the exploitation of the indigenous people. He participated in the Third Lima Council and left some important works, e.g., a lexicon of the Quechua language as well as a historical work on the Incas (Hyland, 2003).

Human Capital, Global Mindset, and Proselytization

In the Peruvian case, in contrast to the Japanese one, language proficiency was not so important. Since Peru was a Spanish colony, the Jesuits there represented the ruling order and could therefore rely on the backing of the colonial authorities to begin their missionary work in this context. This meant that the entry period was much easier than in Japan, where local competitors could rely on the political support of the ruling power. The Jesuits in Peru only had to consider the competition of other Christian orders or the local authorities, including the Inquisition, which had been transplanted to the "New World."

The only conflicts during the entry period were related to the colonial government under Viceroy Toledo and the Inquisition that attacked Jesuits who were too open-minded. Their global mindset went too far for the conservative elements in the colonial order. Once the new provincial Acosta had addressed these problems, the order could act relatively uninterrupted by the local authorities and would, during the consolidation period, focus on other issues related to missionary work. While a global mindset, usually shared by all Jesuits, was necessary to adapt to the local context, in Peru, it could also lead to a struggle with elements that did not share such a mindset. Nevertheless, considering the whole period, it supported the establishment of a strong Jesuit presence in the Peruvian context.

The actual experience, however, shows that language became more important when addressing the indigenous population away from the colonial metropolis, as they needed to be addressed in their native language to have the elements of the Christian religion explained to them. It was especially the Jesuits who were active in these contexts who began to study the respective languages and provided instructions to further develop this necessary human capital, which was deemed essential for a successful evangelization of the indigenous population. As the data has shown, a global mindset was the necessary base for the Jesuits' missionary work in Peru, but if the fathers there wanted to reach beyond the Spanish-speaking communities and the new colonial elites, they needed to engage with the indigenous people, using the latter's language. It becomes obvious that language is more than a practical form of communication here but a tool that supports cultural adaptation processes through a form of "cultural translation."

However, such a process also increased the awareness of some Jesuits about the situation of the indigenous people, who were exploited and physically threatened within the colonial order. The missionaries who witnessed these cruelties and had managed to learn indigenous languages and were thereby directly informed by possible converts about their mistreatment also began to criticize the existent order. A successful Jesuit proselytization also developed a form of Jesuit agency for the native people in the Peruvian context.

The External Factor

Aside from the struggle with Viceroy Toledo and the Inquisition during the entry period, the Jesuits were relatively independent of external factors. As mentioned before, the Jesuits in Peru represented the colonial order, and as long as they were an accepted element within it – this was the case until 1767, when the Society of Jesus was expelled by the King of Spain – they would not have to fear any problems with regard to their existence and missionary work in the region. That the province was divided in 1605 in a way reflects the internal struggle some Jesuits found with regard to language training and use, but in reality, the decision was rather unrelated to the Jesuits' missionary work. The authorities had simply realized that the Peruvian space was too diverse and too large to remain undivided. This, in contrast to Japan, means that the Jesuits in the analyzed time period did not suffer from any external factors. The success of their missionary work was based on human capital and a global mindset, although the pressure to develop the former was much less than in Japan.

Chapter 5

Successful Intercultural Management and Early Modern Proselytization[1]

Findings for Japan

The presented case study for Japan proves that language is an important precondition to overcoming cultural differences. Language proficiency not only serves as a tool for communication but is also essential to identify and address cultural diversity, which means intercultural management in culturally distant environments can be positively stimulated by managers who succeed in learning the local language. Even more important, however, is the existence of a global mindset. As has been shown with regard to Japan, managers who did not speak the language but showed a global mindset, first and foremost Visitor Valignano, were able to achieve much when dealing with the local authorities. If a global mindset and language proficiency were not existent, as in the case of Cabral, severe problems could be faced due to the fact that the managers in question are considered and identified as particularly foreign.

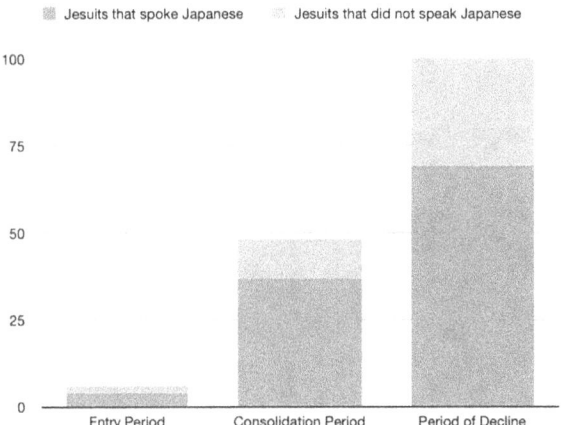

Fig. 5.1: Jesuits in Japan who spoke Japanese.[2]

---

[1] All numbers presented in the findings are based on the analysis of the data provided in MHJ for Japan and MP for Peru.

[2] Jesuits who spoke the language only "mediocrely" or "a little" were not counted as Japanese-speaking members of the order's higher management.

The percentage of Jesuits who spoke Japanese increased during the consolidation period, but not only because Valignano's accommodation policy demanded it. In contrast to Peru, where the missionaries acted in a space that was ruled by a colonial power, i.e., Spain, the necessity to study the indigenous languages was not pressing; however, it was one that was related to the Jesuit wish to convert the indigenous people in the more peripheral regions of the colonial space as well. In Japan, language proficiency was a critical aspect to address from the start, which is why the Jesuits who served there simply had to study it if they wanted to keep the Jesuit mission in Japan in existence and reach a larger number of possible converts.

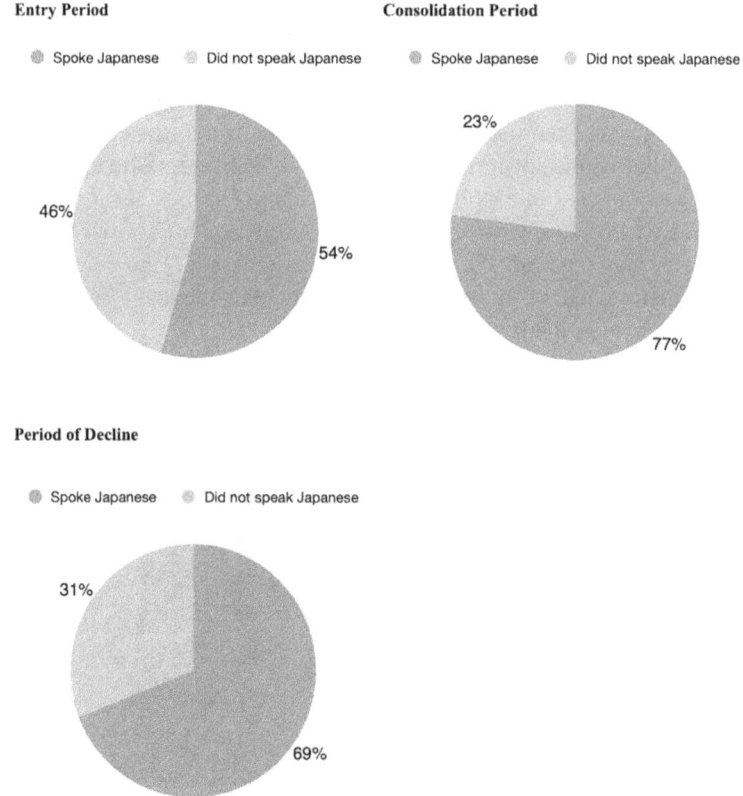

Fig. 5.2: The percentage of Jesuits who spoke Japanese in the respective periods.

A global mindset can be constated for most of the Jesuits who served in Japan. They had either served in India, Macao, or other parts of Southeast Asia before and, through their wish to enter the Society of Jesus, already emphasized their acceptance of a duty that would lead them to so far unknown and culturally different parts of the world. The fact that a lack of a global mindset could only be identified in a few cases – and all these cases caused some kind of trouble, either with the local Japanese authorities or with the order's leadership – makes it crucial to highlight that a global mindset is a vital precondition for successful intercultural management.

Considering the case of Japan, it must also be emphasized that a global mindset will not be able to prevent problems related to political circumstances. Consequently, the management of an expanding SME should also pay close attention to the political context of the market of interest. The Japanese case shows that a global mindset, even if combined with a high percentage of language proficiency among the company's managers, cannot secure the company's interest against a political leadership that does not have an interest in it.

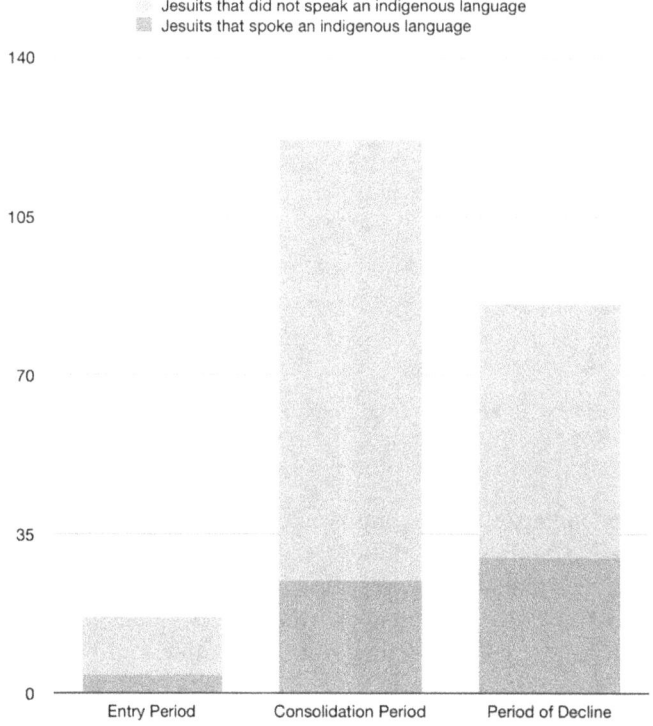

Fig. 5.3: Jesuits in Peru who spoke an indigenous language.[3]

---

[3] Jesuits who spoke the language only "mediocrely" or "a little" were not counted as Quechua- or Aymara-speaking members of the order's higher management.

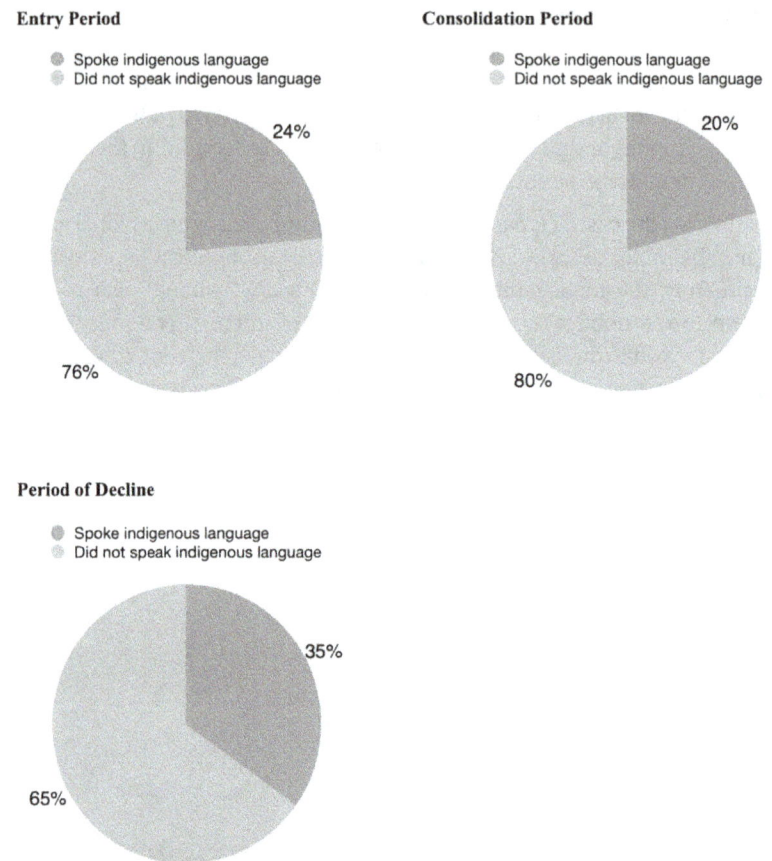

Fig. 5.4: The percentage of Jesuits who spoke an indigenous language in the respective periods.

In the Peruvian context, the global mindset of some missionaries that made them criticize the exploitation of the indigenous people was dangerous. Missionary practices that were too progressive could initially cause persecution by the Inquisition and its representatives in the "New World," and in the longer run, it could lead to a division of the Jesuits according to their support or repudiation of missionary work that addressed the indigenous people in their own native languages. The global mindset of the Jesuits, which was a necessary precondition for their work abroad, could, if developed further in the local context of Peru, become a hindrance for successful missionary work there if the local authorities considered it to "go too far." It is thus the local context that dictates how much language proficiency is necessary and the extent to which a global mindset is deemed acceptable.

Comparison of Results

When one considers the combined data for Japan and Peru (Tab. 5.1), it is more than obvious that the Jesuits in Japan, due to the existent political differences, must have had a bigger interest in studying the local language. The percentage of those who managed to speak Japanese (69%) in the period of decline was more than twice as high as the Jesuits in Peru (30%) who had managed to learn an indigenous language.

Tab. 5.1: Combined Data for Japan and Peru

Period	Total Number of Jesuits in Japan	Total Number of Jesuits in Peru	Jesuits in Japan who spoke Japanese	Jesuits in Peru who spoke an indigenous language	Percentage of Jesuits in Japan who spoke Japanese	Percentage of Jesuits in Peru who spoke an indigenous language
Entry Period	6	17	4	4	54	24
Consolidation Period	48	122	37	25	77	20
Period of Decline	100	86	69	30	69	35

This is not surprising, as the Jesuits in Peru acted in a colonial environment, and the Spanish authorities did not force the missionaries to learn the indigenous language, which was only considered essential by those Jesuit missionaries who actually had to approach indigenous people in the rather peripheral parts of the colony. The combined data, however, also shows that regardless of Valignano's approach and the quite massive increase of Jesuits who were able to communicate in Japanese, a conflict with the authorities during the period of decline could not have been prevented.

While the Jesuits in Japan and Peru faced conflicts with the local authorities during the entry period, when the missionaries and their work were perceived as competitors, either by Japanese religious groups and authorities or by the Spanish colonial government, both order provinces stabilized during the period of consolidation when the number of Jesuits who were acting as successful intercultural managers increased. These successes, however, were eventually threatened by a conflict with the local authorities in Japan or an internal conflict about the nature of the mission per se in Peru. These facts point out that human capital, especially language skills and a global mindset, are vital aspects to consider for successful intercultural management. However, political developments, from regional as well as global perspectives, must also be taken into consideration for a successful management strategy. While language skills could be determined to be an essential factor, they alone will hardly suffice to secure survival in an actual crisis.

The longitudinal qualitative analysis of the two case studies of Japan and Peru confirms theoretical reflections in recent studies that emphasize the necessity of expanding SMEs to pay attention to cultural differences when new markets are entered. The demand for constructive intercultural management that considers interculturality as a precondition for business efficiency and points toward possible synergetic effects can be proven by a closer look at the Jesuit missionaries in Japan and Peru. While some of the Jesuits especially tried to use such synergetic effects, their missions eventually failed, not because they did not invest enough effort to acquire human capital, i.e., language skills, but because they failed in using local synergies by including indigenous people in the higher ranks of the Jesuit Order's management. The Jesuits had to rely on the available human capital to build what Liebowitz (2000) called "organizational intelligence." Due to the fact that the missionaries provided regular reports due to the Jesuit tradition of letter writing (Boswell, 2003), this process of organization can be identified in their missionary activities in Japan and Peru as well. Mione's claim that the modern "intangible economy" is challenging the "traditional vision of management" (2015, 49) is therefore only partly correct (see also Teece, 2010; Zott & Amit, 2010), especially concerning human capital, which is important for modern companies in many ways (Adler, 2002; Cricelli et al., 2013). Polo et al. are correct in their evaluation that the "importance and significance of the intangibles in recent years seems unquestionable" (2014, 126; see also Grimaldi et al., 2017), but this study shows that intangibles in general, as well as human capital in particular, was already important to the success of religious intercultural management in the sixteenth and seventeenth centuries.

The present study could also emphasize the assumption that language education is a crucial intercultural skill that will positively stimulate business performance in a culturally different spatial context. While the Jesuits in Japan and Peru struggled with religious competitors or local authorities during the entry period, the missionaries in both regional contexts were able to increase their performance due to a more intensified study of indigenous languages. The Jesuits' internationalization attempts were consequently language-related in the first place and were not only based on but further stimulated their global mindset as well. Their language skills, which can be seen as "indicators of multicultural experience" (Thomas et al., 2015, 1107), allowed the Jesuits to establish lines for intercultural communication, addressing the local contexts of their respective religious management activities (Sanchez Salgado, 2017).

Like contemporary managers, the Jesuits faced challenges that demanded global management competencies (Bücker & Poutsma, 2010), first and foremost, the capacity to communicate in an 'interculturally' acceptable way. Of course, Latin was the word of the Bible, so to preach about it and explain its content, the Jesuits needed to rely on the local languages. Otherwise, the danger of being just perceived as a minor 'cult,' especially in the Asian, i.e., Buddhist, context with its myriads of gods was too great.

Furuya et al. (2009, 202) defined four factors for a "successful transfer of global management competencies," namely:

1. beneficial organizational support,
2. positive intercultural personality characteristics,
3. positive self-adjustment, and
4. the firm's constructive repatriation policies and practices.

The first three, in particular, can be identified with regard to the Jesuits as well, who trained their missionaries and prepared them as well as possible for their tasks in the order's provinces and also provided them with the basis for a global mindset, i.e., positive intercultural personality characteristics. They were also encouraged to exchange their opinions with peers for the purposes of self-evaluation and self-adjustment.

The exposure of the Jesuits to other cultures stimulated the necessity to study the languages of the respective provinces, and those who did lay the foundation for successful missionary work and, at the same time, further increased not only their individual human capital but their global mindset as well as that of the institution – the Jesuit Order – as a whole. They consequently turned into multilingual and "effective boundary spanners" (Jaeger, Kim, & Butt, 2016, 248), who would further increase the success rate of new Jesuit missions. In Japan, Alessandro Valignano realized the importance of language skills and instructed the local Jesuits to study Japanese, though not only as a measure to improve communication, but to improve the cultural understanding of the Japanese. Similar requests failed in the Peruvian context, where those missionaries who supported a further strengthening of interculturality and the study of indigenous languages were unable to lobby for their demand successfully. The Peruvian Jesuits were divided, and the majority considered themselves to serve the colonial elite and, instead of dealing with the indigenous people in the colony's periphery, intended to replicate the educational structures the Jesuits were so well-known for in the European context.

Considering the combination of human capital and the global mindset, the present study shows that the latter seems to be more important, as Jesuits who did not speak the language in Japan or Peru could act as successful managers as long as they were willing to accept the existent interculturality and to address it properly, e.g. by relying on the support by indigenous people who acted as translators and thereby as support for Jesuit approaches toward the proselytization within their respective context of missionary work. It is, therefore, possible to argue that a global mindset without language skills can be sufficient to generate successful intercultural management, while language skills alone will not suffice if language is only understood as a tool to communicate instead of one to bring culturally different people closer together to secure synergetic effects of such a cooperation. In the case of the Jesuits in Japan and Peru, as well as in other missionary provinces of the order, the global mindset can nevertheless be described in a twofold way. As all Jesuits agreed with their initiation to the order to be willing to follow any assignment, no matter where it may lead them, the global mindset as a basic attitude was technically already a prerequisite before they started their missions. The precondition of "cultural exposure" with regard to their mission would have consequently increased or improved the missionaries' "intercultural competence" (Dias, Zhou & Samaratunge, 2017). In the specific cases of Japan and Peru, however, one can use two additional aspects to make a decision about individual Jesuits when determining the existence or absence of a strong global mindset.

1. If the Jesuits had been able to collect experiences in culturally different environments, i.e., if they had served in India, China, Mexico, or other parts of Latin America, the chances that their mission to Japan or Peru would not have been as challenging as for somebody who was sent to these provinces as their first missionary assignment would have been much higher. To make a conclusive decision about the existence or absence of a global mindset with regard to the Jesuit missionaries in question, it is vital to include data about previous missions.

2. Even more important to identifying a global mindset, in addition to previous experience in culturally different environments or contexts, is the dogmatic flexibility of the Jesuit missionaries. Were they able and willing to adjust their 'religious message' to reach the people they wanted to convert, or were they reluctant to adjust it to a culturally different context? This question must be answered for the individual Jesuits, the upper management of the provinces the present study focuses on, to include information about the existence or absence of a global mindset in the evaluation of the Jesuits' successful global expansion, i.e., the success of their intercultural management in Japan and Peru.

The analysis of the Jesuit managers' human capital, i.e., language skills, combined with an evaluation of their global mindset – theoretically considered to add to a company's human capital through "intercultural education" (Burford et al., 2012; Ng, Tan, & Ang, 2011) – allows the present book, considering external elements like the political context in the order's provinces as well, to evaluate the Jesuits' intercultural management and the relevant factors for its success or failure.

Like the missionary expansion of the Jesuits (Coello de la Rosa, 2022, 175), the "internationalization in SMEs is a complex phenomenon" (Zhou, Wu & Luo, 2007, 674) that relies early on networks and the exchange of knowledge as well (Ellis, 2000). Zhou, Wu, and Luo (2007) also recommend considering the role of social networks for the successful internationalization of SMEs (see also Adler & Kwon, 2002). It is also important not to forget the role of local foreign intermediaries (Ellis, 2000; Ellis & Pecotich, 2001), e.g., translators, who play key roles in the successful market entry of an expanding SME. The Jesuits knew this and used such intermediaries during their expansion in the sixteenth century and had to manage issues that are still pressing for modern-day SMEs. The present study has consequently addressed questions related to human capital and the global mindset that can offer a better insight into historical business expansion processes, from which managers currently active in SMEs that expand globally can gain.

Nevertheless, more constructive intercultural management could have helped the Jesuits to use their language skills and global mindsets in a more efficient way to strengthen their position in Japan and Peru, and the lack of proactive synergy from the Jesuit Order in Japan and Peru makes it necessary to recommend a culturally more aware management training for globally expanding companies in general and modern-day SMEs that attempt to perform a successful market entry into a culturally "foreign" context in particular. While studies related to constructive intercultural management have emphasized the positive effects of these synergies and tend to see interculturality as an opportunity rather than a burden, the present study was able to prove this, though only to a point where decisions are based on culturally motivated decisions. When political decisions are taken against the expanding SME, like against the Jesuits in Japan and Peru in the early 1600s, intercultural aspects no longer play a role. The Jesuits' language skills and global mindset could do nothing against either the decision of the Spanish Crown to reallocate the provincial order or Tokugawa Ieyasu's order to expel all Christians from Japan.

Chapter 6

Management-Related Recommendations

Despite the fact that the Jesuit missionary attempts in Japan and Peru failed, although the latter continued to exist in different structures and forms until the 1760s when the Spanish Crown expelled the Jesuits from Spanish America, one can condense some management-related recommendations from both cases that can be applied by modern-day SMEs who plan their further internationalization and expansion to foreign and culturally different markets. These recommendations will be presented in this section in relation to five central aspects: first and foremost, language skills and a global mindset, but also structural hierarchies, the indigenous element, and external factors that have an impact on a company's performance. While the data was collected in relation to historical cases, it can, as has been stated before, be used to provide recommendations for current SMEs that struggle with similar problems to the Jesuits when they enter culturally different markets today.

The Role of Language

As was shown by a close reading of the available data for the Jesuits who were active in Japan and Peru in the sixteenth and seventeenth centuries, language alone will seldom suffice or guarantee successful performance if it is not combined with a global mindset. However, a global mindset that cannot be combined with the work of a reliable intermediary who ensures the translation process is also quite limited. Globalizing SMEs that intend to expand to international and culturally different markets would gain from managers who actually possess language proficiency and are able to combine this proficiency with a global mindset. Language, furthermore, must not only be understood as a tool for communication but as a possibility to bridge cultural differences through experience. On the one hand, only if a language is actively spoken will it be helpful to fill gaps about the culturally different context. In addition, an attempt to engage with the local language makes the actual approach to the foreign market more credible. The Jesuits in Peru, who wanted to strengthen their training with regard to the indigenous languages, like Valignano attempted through his accommodation program in Japan, wanted to make sure that the people addressed in these foreign markets could be reached properly. At the same time, the "foreignness" of the organization would be decreased, making the company more credible and less foreign for those who were supposed to engage with it.

On the other hand, it is the local context that determines how important managerial language proficiency is. If the market the SME intends to enter is already very internationalized, i.e., integrated into the global economy, the less critical training for managers concerning the local language might be. Considering the Peruvian case, the Jesuits there were less in need of language capacities with regard to the indigenous languages than the Jesuits in Japan. In Peru, not only could the missionaries rely on Spanish as the lingua franca, which was also represented and enforced by the local authorities, but they also only needed language proficiency if they actually intended to address the specific group of possible converts who only understood an indigenous language. It is consequently the local context, the necessity for the company, and the group that is to be approached that determine the demand for managers to make themselves familiar with the local language. Without any doubt, however, for the credibility of a company within a culturally different context, it makes sense to show that its managers, as representatives of the SME, do not intend only to exploit the foreign market for financial gain but are willing to invest time and effort to properly address the people and the culture attached to this foreign market.

In short, language education for managers is never a bad idea but only really necessary if the local context dictates it is needed to overcome possible obstacles within the markets that are supposed to be penetrated by a globalizing SME.

The Role of a Global Mindset

Based on the two cases that have been analyzed in the present study, it is possible to say that a global mindset is even more important than language proficiency or language skills for managers who have to perform in a culturally different environment or context. Some cases, e.g., Valignano in Japan or Acosta in Peru, document that it is sometimes unnecessary to be an advanced speaker of a foreign language as long as the manager in question is willing to accept the existence and impact of cultural differences and the necessity to act appropriately.

One can consequently recommend to SMEs that intend to expand to global markets that are culturally different to look for managers with a global mindset to lead such an expansion. It would be ideal if these managers were also capable of showing language proficiency. If this is not possible, managers with a global mindset would usually realize this as an insufficiency and find proper solutions. At the same time, managers with language proficiency who do not possess a global mindset might be inadequate candidates for such a task, as they might not be able to address the situation in the proper way, especially when cultural flexibility is needed.

The case of Peru, however, also made it obvious that a global mindset can be problematic if the context of the market is not ready for progressive values. A manager who, for example, wants to immediately replicate company structures that are accepted in a different cultural context might clash with the local authorities. Although it is important for SMEs to provide progress for the market they intend to expand to, the managers in question have to be aware of the existent situation to prevent any confrontation. This fact presents a dilemma for all Western liberal SMEs that want to expand to markets dominated politically by anti-liberal forces, e.g., China. A successful manager will try to avoid a direct clash of interests and, by her or his work, try to positively impact the local context. To sum up the findings with regard to the global mindset, it is more important than language capacities and should, at best, be combined with them, although, again, the local context of the market determines the extent to which a global mindset can be turned into action. Progressive missionaries were limited by their own colonial authorities in Peru and, in Japan, by the social order that had been in place for centuries. A global mindset was consequently only possible if it was acceptable for those who held political power. Similar considerations, as sobering as this conclusion might be, must be taken into account when a modern-day SME decides to expand to a culturally different market. Based on these considerations, it will then be able to nominate or recruit the most suitable managers.

Clear Hierarchies

A problem that became obvious during the analysis of the case studies was that of conflicting or unclear hierarchies. The struggles between Valignano and Cabral and between Duran and Álvarez were consequences of unclear hierarchies and the lack of a clear agenda for the respective local context. For SMEs that intend to expand today, it is strongly recommended that they avoid local conflicts through the following measures:

1. Avoidance of the assignment of managers who do not share the same basic attitude toward the task;
2. Official outlines of tasks and acceptable strategies for managers who are assigned to foreign and culturally different markets;
3. Clear descriptions of measures that can be taken by the respective managers, i.e., the provision of some kind of managerial code; and
4. Clear hierarchies, although checks and balances, e.g., possibilities for complaints at the next level up, should be provided.

If these measures are fully considered, their implementation will most likely prevent local conflicts and thereby, problems for the company while it is active in foreign and culturally different markets. An SME that intends to expand globally must be aware of possible struggles over strategies and methods implemented in the new environment, and only clear guidelines seem to be able to prevent managerial disputes that could act as a hindrance to successful intercultural management in the local context.

The Indigenous Element

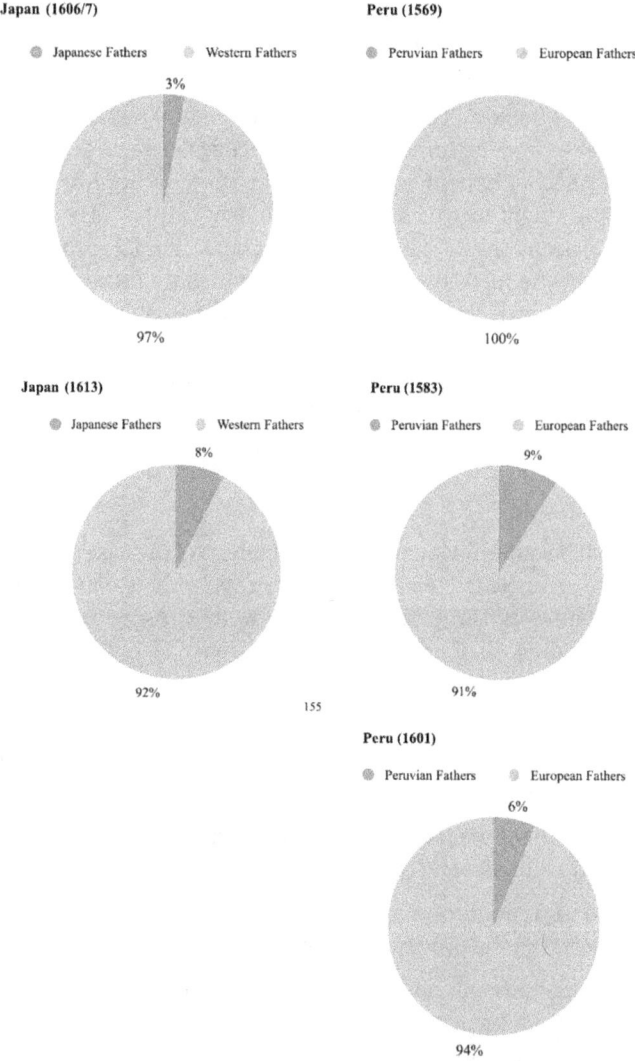

Fig. 6.1: The percentage of indigenous Jesuit fathers in Japan and Peru according to available data.

Both analyzed cases show that the Jesuits failed to include indigenous managers when developing their respective missionary activities.

In Japan and Peru alike, the Jesuits failed to integrate the indigenous people into managerial positions, ultimately making the organization appear foreign. This made any defense against a changed political order impossible, as the Society of Jesus and their representatives were simply considered agents of a foreign interest. In Japan, they were expelled, while in Peru, the indigenous people might not have trusted the approach of a missionary order whose structures merely replicated the ones of the colonial elites.

For an expanding SME interested in performing successfully in a culturally different market, it is recommended to consider addressing this issue. First and foremost, the integration of local managers will help to develop the language capacity of the overall company further, while their integration will, without any doubt, also provide further positive stimulation with regard to the global mindset in the organizational structure.

The External Factor

The case analyses for Japan and Peru have shown that the external factor is the most important one. The Japanese case study, in particular, emphasizes that language capacity and a global mindset will not count at all if the political circumstances change and a rather unfavorable situation is thereby presented to the expanding organization. In early Tokugawa Japan, the Jesuits could only react, and some leading ones who focused on the Christian community in Nagasaki rather than proactive approaches toward Tokugawa Ieyasu must have missed opportunities to secure the further existence of the Society of Jesus in Japan. The same can be emphasized in the Peruvian case, as the authorities eventually restructured the colonial environment. Of course, the Jesuit missionaries could continue their activities in the newly formed colonial spaces (e.g., in Paraguay: see Lozano, 1754; Caraman, 1975; Nonnemann, 2009), but they could not have prevented any other changes made by the colonial authorities at that time either.

Modern-day SMEs must, therefore, also pay close attention to the political developments related to their market of interest. Not only do they have to pay close attention to the political situation and stability when they enter the market, but they must also monitor developments all the time. In addition, they should try to use language proficiency and a global mindset to proactively generate positive cooperation with the foreign government to ensure good ties in moments of crisis. The Jesuits in Japan and Peru ultimately had no possibility to interfere with the politically enforced changes but could only leave the country or try to adjust their missionary work to the new possibilities, respectively. Since a globally active SME does not want to be forced to face a similar set of options, it is highly recommended not to act without a long-term analysis of the political developments that might take place in the context of the most interesting international markets.

Summary

An SME interested in successful intercultural management, according to the results of the two case studies presented in this book, must:

1. Take care of appropriate and context-related language education for its managerial staff before the market entry if this has been evaluated as necessary, especially when local intermediaries are not available.
2. Secure a managerial staff for the market expansion that is most likely to act according to a global mindset.
3. Provide a clear description of the task and, at the same time, outline the hierarchies that should be followed in the context of the foreign market expansion.
4. Encourage the management to include indigenous personnel and provide sufficient possibilities for their advancement within the organization, i.e., accessibility to higher management positions for people recruited in culturally different spaces.
5. Steadily monitor the local political developments and proactively seek ways to emphasize the advantages of the expansion for the foreign country's population to avoid an abrupt end to the SME's activity due to political changes.

Chapter 7

Conclusion

The present book intended to provide a comparative historical longitudinal case study that would look at the role of human capital, and of language skills in particular, and a global mindset in successful intercultural management. The Society of Jesus – to be more precise, the fathers who served it in the culturally different contexts of Japan and Peru during the sixteenth and early seventeenth centuries – was considered to act as a modern-day SME, which is why a closer look at the historical cases allows an evaluation of the impact that language skills and a global mindset can have for successful intercultural management in culturally diverse market contexts, especially for globalizing SMEs whose managers intend to expand to unknown markets.

The case studies provided insights into the historical developments within the order provinces of Japan and Peru. Both histories were divided into three periods: 1) an entry period, 2) a consolidation period, and 3) a period of decline. Personal "manager" data for the active fathers, comprising more than 200 individual data sets, was collected and evaluated with regard to existent language skills, a global mindset, and possible conflicts with the local authorities. It was shown that language skills were important but to a relatively low extent in the entry period, when conflicts were usually the consequence of competition with representatives of other religious organizations: Buddhist monks in Japan and the colonial government and the Inquisition in Peru. The entry period, nevertheless, was easier in the latter case, as the Peruvian context provided the Jesuits with a "market situation" that was determined by colonial agents who shared the same cultural traditions and value system. In Japan, the missionaries had to rely on support from local translators before the first Jesuits could master the languages. Nevertheless, the global mindset of men like Francis Xavier provided the order with successful intercultural management and made the penetration and start of the mission in Japan possible.

The consolidation period, under "enlightened" men like Alessandro Valignano and José de Acosta, showed that a global mindset seemed to be more important than language skills to stimulate the successful conversion of indigenous people to Christianity, but both men also realized that for long-term success, in Japan in general and in Peru with regard to the indigenous tribes' conversion, studying the language(s) was essential, which is why they encouraged the fathers in the respective contexts to study them. In Japan, Valignano even formulated the concept of "cultural accommodation" because he realized that the Christian missionaries could not ultimately succeed without adjusting themselves to a Japanese way of life. Valignano consequently stressed the importance of language skills in combination with a global mindset and came into conflict with Francisco Cabral, the first Jesuit in Japan who did not share such an approach for the Jesuit missionaries (Schütte, 1951; 1975). The pressure to culturally acclimate in Peru was not as pressing as in Japan, especially not in the cities, where the Jesuit colleges recreated European-like environments. In the peripheral regions of the large Peruvian province, however, the *reducciones* and the evangelization of indigenous people, to whom the basics of the Christian religion had to be explained, demanded a specific capacity with regard to language skills. The Jesuits who served in these regions were consequently much more familiar with indigenous languages. This divide in the Peruvian case would eventually also lead to a struggle between the two factions: the city-based pro-European faction and the periphery-based pro-indigenous faction.

In the period of decline, these two factions' opinions would collide, and the Jesuits would struggle over the appropriate course to take to address language education and questions related to a certain dogmatic flexibility. In Japan, in the meantime, the situation had worsened when first Toyotomi Hideyoshi and later Tokugawa Ieyasu began to sign decrees against Christianity in Japan. While Valignano, through negotiations with Toyotomi Hideyoshi, was able to secure the Jesuit mission's existence in the island country, the missionaries were eventually expelled in 1614 and could not do anything about it, even though most of the Jesuits there had applied Valignano's accommodation strategy and had also studied the language. While the Peruvian case ended due to a bureaucratic reconfiguration that allowed the Jesuits to continue their local work as part of a different colonial structure, the Japanese case ended violently, and Jesuits who did not leave the country as ordered were killed.

Taking the two cases into closer consideration, one can say that language education is without any doubt important and serves beyond the practical use of translating words. It is far more than that, as it helps to explain and understand cultural differences and the basic elements of the religion that were supposed to be offered to possible converts. In both cases, the language skills of the Jesuits were essential to secure success during the consolidation period. Nevertheless, it was also shown that language skills alone often do not suffice and that it is the global mindset that is even more important, especially since successful negotiators who understood the existence of cultural diversity and its possible impact were much more likely able to gain the support of local authorities than those who spoke the language but were not open-minded enough to reach some compromises that were dictated by the local context.

Ideally, an SME today would try to combine language capacity and a global mindset with regard to their managers' most wanted skill set. Only a combination of the two will secure much better intercultural management, especially concerning markets that do not share a Western lingua franca, like Japan or modern China. Companies should choose wisely when deciding whom to send to a newly opened market into which the SMEs have expanded, as these managers will be important to secure a successful market entry and positive long-term development.

The Jesuit Order, in both cases, failed to include the indigenous element in their market strategy sufficiently, as Japanese and Peruvian locals were not allowed into the higher ranks in large numbers, and so the Jesuits kept a "foreign image" in the eyes of the local authorities. Especially with regard to the latter, it is recommended to include local managers in company structures early on, as such symbiotic strategies might also secure the SME from future antagonism, though this could not have been fully solved or prevented in the Japanese and Peruvian cases.

As has been shown, there are particular external factors that need to be monitored by globally expanding SMEs. In this regard, language skills and a global mindset are important, as they allow the local management to establish ties with foreign authorities and gain their trust. Including the local workforce in higher management positions, as has been outlined before, will increase this trust. Such measures can never fully prevent a negative outcome but will, without any doubt, increase the chances of a successful expansion.

Initially, the question was raised as to what insight modern SMEs could gain from a historical case study. As has been shown, there is much to learn from the past, especially about successful intercultural management strategies. The Jesuits were among the first to expand to culturally unfamiliar regions of the world. They wanted to spread Christianity across the globe, but they also often had to act as managers who had to deal with issues that are not so very different from those SME managers have to deal with today. The choice of managers is actually a critical decision for globalizing SMEs, and it is recommended, based on the present case study, to choose them properly, especially with a view to having a global mindset and the existence of, or at least the willingness to study toward, a language proficiency that can have so many positive effects, just as the Jesuits' language skills had in Japan and Peru alike.

It is often argued that historical experiences offer something to learn from for our days, and, as has been shown in this comparative historical longitudinal case study, the Jesuits and their experiences in Japan and Peru show what can happen if expanding organizations do not keep in mind that it is the combination of a global mindset and language skills that allow companies to successfully expand in the first place as well as to secure their position during a consolidation period or to defend their market share in times of crisis.

The present study intended to compare the intercultural management of the Jesuit Order in two culturally different contexts in the sixteenth and seventeenth centuries. Studies like these should take a look at interculturality from both sides of the actual inter- or transcultural process at hand, but the sources often only provided the Jesuit perspective on the existent debates about cultural assimilation and intercultural management practices. It is, therefore, a limitation of the study that it remains culturally one-sided in the sense that interculturality could only be studied from one perspective, i.e., the Jesuit one.

Another limitation might be the focus on only two case studies, especially since the Jesuits operated globally, and it would have made sense 1) to include more cases in the analysis and 2) to follow some Jesuit managers across the different stations of their managerial career to strengthen the understanding and evaluability of their intercultural competences further.

Regardless of these limitations, the insights and results presented here provide a better understanding of intercultural management in early modern times, but there remain topics that should be further investigated. It would make sense to broaden the comparative perspective further and include Mexico and China, to name just two possible examples, in order to add data to the analysis and look for further similarities and possible differences. The approach used here would then be further globalized, and additional data sets would help strengthen the management recommendations given here based on the two compared cases. There is still much to learn from the historical "managers" in question, and the numerous and diverse sources the Jesuits have left will allow us more critical evaluations in the future. The present book was a first step to make use of these materials for modern-day managers and those whose success relies on them and their successful performance, which will, without any doubt, remain related to a positive understanding of interculturality and the synergies it might create.

Works Cited

Acosta, J. de. (1590). *Historia natural y moral de las Indias, en que se tratan de las cosas notables del cielo, y elementos, metales, plantas, y animales dellas, y los ritos, y ceremonias, leyes, y gouierno, y guerras de los Indios*. Iuan de Leon.

Acosta, J. de. (1605). *America, Oder wie mans zu Teutsch nennet Die Neuwe Welt/ oder West India*. Cornelium Sutorium.

Acosta, J. de. (1670). *De promulgando evangelio apud Barbaros, sive de procurando indorum salute*. Laurent Anisson.

Acosta, J. de. (1987) [1588]. *Historia natural y moral de las Indias*. Historia.

Acosta Rodríguez, A. (2014). *Prácticas coloniales de la Iglesia en el Perú: Siglos XVI y XVII*. Aconcagua Libros.

Adelaar, W. F. H. (2020). Linguistic Connections between the Altiplano Region and the Amazonian Lowlands. In A. J. Pearce, D. G. Beresford-Jones, & P. Heggarty (Eds.), *Rethinking the Andes-Amazonia Divide: A Cross-Disciplinary Exploration* (pp. 239–249). University College London Press.

Adler, N. J. (1983). A Typology of Management Studies Involving Culture. *Journal of International Business Studies, 14*(2), 29–47.

Adler, P. S., & Kwon, S. W. (2002). Social Capital Prospects for a New Concept. *Academy of Management Review, 27*, 17–40.

Aharoni, Y., & Brock, D. M. (2010). International Business Research: Looking Back and Looking Forward. *Journal of International Management, 16*(1), 5–15.

Ahi, A., Baronchelli, G., Kuivalainen, O., & Piantoni, M. (2017). International Market Entry: How Do Small and Medium-Sized Enterprises Make Decisions? *Journal of International Marketing, 25*(1), 1–21.

Alberro, S. (1992). *Les Espagnols dans le Mexique colonial: Histoire d'une acculturation*. A. Colin.

Alden, D. (1996). *The Making of an Enterprise: The Society of Jesus in Portugal, Its Empire, and Beyond 1540-1750*. Stanford University Press.

Álvarez-Taladriz, J. L. (1973). *Documentos franciscanos de la cristiandad de Japón (1593-1597): San Martín de la Ascensión y Fray Marcelo de Ribadeneira: Relaciones e informaciones*. Eikodo.

Alves Filho, P. E., & Milton, J. (2005). Inculturation and Acculturation in the Translation of Religious Texts: The Translations of Jesuit Priest José de Anchieta into Tupi in 16th Century Brazil. *Target, 17*(2), 275–296.

Amaro-Bebio, V. (2016). *Kōshi Nagasaki ni okeru kirishitan shisetsu ni kansuru kenkyū*. Tōkyō Daigaku.

Ambrogio, O., & Newson, L. A. (2020). Administration and Native Perceptions of Baptism at the Jesuit Peripheries of Spanish America (16th-18th centuries). In *Cultural Worlds of the Jesuits in Colonial Latin America* (pp. 149–169). University of London Press.

Anagnostou, S. (2005). Jesuits in Spanish America: Contributions to the Exploration of the American Materia Medica. *Pharmacy in History, 47*(1), 3–17.

Andersson, S., & Wictor, I. (2003). Innovative Internationalization in New Firms: Born Globals – The Swedish Case. *Journal of International Entrepreneurship*, *1*(3), 249–276.

Andresen, M., & Bergdolt, F. (2017). A Systematic Literature Review on the Definitions of Global Mindset and Cultural Intelligence: Merging Two Different Research Streams. *International Journal of Huma Resource Management*, *28*(1), 170–195.

An'no, M. (2014). Kyōkairyō Nagasaki: Iezusukai to Nihon. Kōdansha.

Anonymous. (1768). *Memorie per servir all'istoria del disacciamento dei Gesuiti, dai regni delle due Sicilie*.

App, U. (1997a). St. Francis Xavier's Discovery of Japanese Buddhism: A Chapter in the European Discovery of Buddhism (Part 1: Before the Arrival in Japan, 1547-1549). *The Eastern Buddhist, New Series*, *30*(1), 53–78.

App, U. (1997b). St. Francis Xavier's Discovery of Japanese Buddhism: A Chapter in the European Discovery of Buddhism (Part 2: From Kagoshima to Yamaguchi, 1549-1551). *The Eastern Buddhist, New Series*, *30*(2), 214–244.

Arimura, R. (2014). The Catholic Architecture of Early Modern Japan: Between Adaptation and Christian Identity. *Japan Review*, *27*, 53–76.

Armas Medina, F. (1953). *Cristianización del Perú, 1532–1600*. Consejo Superior de Investigaciones Científicas – Escuela de Estudios Hispano-Americanos.

Armstrong, M. (2006). *A Handbook of Human Resource Management Practice* (10. Aufl.). Kogan Page Publishers.

Arrelucea-Barrantes, M. (2012). Work, Family, and Honor: Understanding Colonial Slavery in Peru. *Review (Fernand Braudel Center)*, *35*(3–4), 273–296.

Avon, D., & Rocher, P. (2017). Historiography of the Society of Jesus: The Case of France after the Order's Restoration in 1814. In *Jesuit Historiography Online*. http://dx.doi.org/10.1163/2468-7723_jho_COM_192562

Balandier, G. (2001). La situation coloniale: Approche théorique. *Cahiers internationaux de sociologie*, *110*(1), 9–29.

Barmeyer, C. (2018). *Konstruktives Interkulturelles Management*. Vandenhoeck & Rupprecht.

Barmeyer, C., Bausch, M., & Moncayo, D. (2019). Cross-Cultural Management Research: Topics, Paradigms, and Methods—A journal-Based Longitudinal Analysis between 2001 and 2018. *International Journal of Cross Cultural Management*, *19*(2), 218–244.

Barmeyer, C., Bausch, M., & Mayrhofer, U. (2021). *Constructive Intercultural Management: Integrating Cultural Differences Successfully*. Edward Elgar.

Barmeyer, C., & Franklin, P. (2016a). Applying Competencies and Resources: Handling Cultural Otherness as the Second Step Towards Generating Complementarity and Sinergy from Cultural Diversity. In C. Barmeyer & P. Frankling (Eds.), *Intercultural Management: A Case-Based Approach to Achieving Complementarity and Synergy* (pp. 137–147). Palgrave Macmillan.

Barmeyer, C., & Franklin, P. (Eds.). (2016b). Intercultural Management. A Case-Based Approach to Achieving Complementarity and Synergy. Palgrave Macmillan.

Barmeyer, C., & Franklin, P. (2016c). Understanding Otherness and Discord: A Necessary but Insufficient First Step Towards Generating Complementarity and

Sinergy from Cultural Diversity. In C. Barmeyer & P. Frankling (Eds.), *Intercultural Management: A Case-Based Approach to Achieving Complementarity and Synergy* (pp. 15–27). Palgrave Macmillan.

Barmeyer, C., & Mayrhofer, U. (2008). The Contribution of Intercultural Management to the Success of International Mergers and Acquisitions: An Analysis of the EADS Group. *International Business Review, 17*(1), 28–38.

Barmeyer, C., & Mayrhofer, U. (2010, December 9). *Does Culture Shape the Balance of Power in Multinational Companies? The Case of the EADS Group.* 36th Annual EIBA (European International Business Academy) Conference, Porto, Portugal. https://halshs.archives-ouvertes.fr/halshs-00638849

Barmeyer, C., & Mayrhofer, U. (2014). How Has the French Context Shaped the Organization of the Airbus Group? *International Journal of Organizational Analysis, 22*(4), 426–448.

Barmeyer, C., & Mayrhofer, U. (2020). Contextualizing Intercultural Competences: Genesis, Concepts, and Research Agenda. In B. Grasser, S. Loufrani-Fedida, & E. Oiry (Eds.), *Managing Competences: Research, Practice, and Contemporary Issues* (pp. 233–251). CRC Press.

Bartel-Radic, A. (2006). Intercultural Learning and Global Teams. *MIR: Management International Review, 46*(6), 647–677.

Bartel-Radic, A., & Lesca, N. (2011). Do Intercultural Teams Need "Requisite Variety" to be Effective? *International Management, 15*(3), 89–104.

Bartel-Radic, Anne. (2013). 'Estrangeirismo' and flexibility: Intercultural learning in Brazilian MNCs. *Management International, 17*(4), 239–253.

Bartel-Radic, Anne, Moos, J. C., & Long, S. K. (2015). Cross-Cultural Management Learning through Innovative Pedagogy: An Exploratory Study of Globally Distributed Student Teams. *Decision Sciences Journal of Innovative Education, 13*(4), 539–562.

Barthel, M. (1991). *Die Jesuiten: Giftmischer oder Heilige?* Nikol.

Barthes, R. (1977). *Elements of Semiology, transl. By Annette Lavers and Colin Smith.* Hill and Wang.

Bartoli, D. (1858). *The Life of St. Francis Xavier Apostle of the Indies and Japan.* T. Jones.

Basadre, J. (1947). *Meditaciones sobre el destino histórico del Perú.* Huascarán.

Bauer, R. & Marroquín Arredondo, J. (2019). Introduction: An Age of Translation. In Marroquín Arredondo, J. & Bauer, R. (Eds.). *Translating Nature: Cross-Cultural Histories of Early Modern Science* (pp. 1–23). University of Pennsylvania Press.

Beck, T. (2013). Bank Financing for SMEs: Lessons from the Literature. *National Institute Economic Review, 225*, R23–R28.

Berk, A. (2017). Small Business Social Responsibility: More than Size. *The Journal of Corporate Citizenship, 67*, 12–38.

Bhagat, R. S., & Steers, R. M. (Eds.). (2009). *Cambridge Handbook of Culture, Organizations and Work.* Cambridge University Press.

Bijaoui, I. (2016). *SMEs in an Era of Globalization: International Business and Market Strategies.* Palgrave Macmillan.

Black, J. S. (1990). The Relationship of Personal Characteristics with the Adjustment of Japanese Expatriate Managers. *Management International Review*, 30(2), 119–134.

Bodkin, M. (1952). Xavier in Japan. *Studies: An Irish Quarterly Review*, 41(163–164), 281–292.

Bonfour, A. (2007). *The Management of Intangibles: The Organisation's Most Valuable Assets*. Routledge.

Boscariol, M. A. (2013). *No que toca a língua e adaptação na metodologica de trabalho jesuíta no Japão: Gaspar Vilela, Alessandro Valignano e João Rodrigues Tçuzu (1549-1620)*. Universidade de São Paulo.

Boscariol, M. A. (2016). Da menoridade do outro e do portarem-se como meninos: Cartas das missões jesuítas no Brasil e no Japão do ano de 1549. *Revista Oriente*, 24, 90–101.

Boscariol, M. A. (2017). From Brazil to Japan: The Jesuits under the Portugues Patronage's Authority from the Cases of Juan de Azpilicueta Navarro and Francis Xavier (16th Century). *Bulletin of Portuguese-Japanese Studies*, 2(3), 53–73.

Boswell, G. (2003). Letter Writing among the Jesuits: Antonio Possevino's Advice in the 'Bibliotheca Selecta' (1593). *Huntington Library Quarterly*, 66(3–4), 247–262.

Bouhours, D. (1743). *The life of Saint Francis Xavier, of the Society of Jesus, Apostle of the Indies and of Japan*. Ignatius Kelly.

Boxer, C. R. (1951). *The Christian Century in Japan, 1549-1650*. University of California Press.

Brewer-García, L. (2012). Bodies, Texts, and Translators: Indigenous Breast Milk and the Jesuit Exclusion of Mestizos in Late Sixteenth-Century Peru. *Colonial Latin American Review*, 21(3), 365–390.

Brockey, L. (2000). Largos caminhos e vastos mares: Jesuit Missionaries and the journey to China in the Sixteenth and Seventeenth Centuries. *Bulletin of Portuguese-Japanese Studies*, 1, 45–72.

Brodrick, J. (1950). *Petrus Canisius: 1521–1597* (Bde. 1–2). Heder.

Brodrick, J. (1952). *Saint Francis Xavier (1506–1552)*. Burns, Oates and Washbourne.

Brosseder, C. (2012). Cultural Dialogue and Its Premises in Colonial Peru: The Case of Worshipping Sacred Objects. *Journal of the Economic and Social History of the Orient*, 55(2–3), 383–414.

Brosseder, C. (2014). *The Power of Huacas: Change and Resistance in the Andean World of Colonial Peru*. University of Texas Press.

Brouthers, K. D., Nakos, G., & Dimitratos, P. (2015). SME Entrepreneurial Orientation, International Performance, and the Moderating Role of Strategic Alliances. *Entrepreneurship Theory and Practice*, 39(5), 1161–1187.

Brown, K. W. (1987). Jesuit Wealth and Economic Activity within the Peruvian Economy: The Case of Colonial Southern Peru. *The Americas*, 44(1), 23–43.

Bucheli, M., & Wadhwani, R. D. (Eds.). (2015). *Organizations in Time: History, Theory, Methods*. Oxford University Press.

Bücker, J., & Poutsma, E. (2010). How to Assess Global Management Competencies: An Investigation of Existing Instruments. *Management Revue*, 21(3), 263–291.

Buckley, P. J. (2018). *The Global Factory: Networked Multinational Enterprises in the Modern Global Economy.* Edward Elgar.

Burford, G., Kissmann, S., Rosado-May, F. J., Alvarado Dzul, S. H., & Harder, M. K. (2012). Indigenous Participation in Intercultural Education: Learning from Mexico and Tanzania. *Ecology and Society, 17*(4). http://dx.doi.org/10.5751/ES-05250-170433

Burgaleta, C. (1999). José de Acosta, S.J. (1540-1600): His Life and Thought. Loyola Press.

Buschmann, R.F., Slack, E.R., & Tueller, J.B. (Eds.). (2014). *Navigating the Spanish Lake: The Pacific in the Iberian World, 1521–1898.* University of Hawai'i Press.

Business Case Studies. (2019, February 13). *3 Classic Business Case Studies All Business Students Should Know.* https://businesscasestudies.co.uk/3-classic-business-case-studies-all-business-students-should-know/.

Campos, A. C. d. S. (2007). *Nuvens douradas e paisagens habitadas: A arte Namban e a sua circulação entre a Ásia e a América: Japão, China e Nova-Espanha (c. 1550- c. 1700).* Universidade Nova de Lisboa.

Cancino, C. A. (2014). Rapid Internationalization of SMEs: Evidence from „Born Global" Firms in Chile. *Innovar: Revista de ciencias administrativas y sociales, 24*, 141–151.

Canepa, T. (2016). *Silk, Porcelain and Lacquer: China and Japan and their Trade with Western Europe and the New World, 1500-1644.* Paul Holberton Publishing.

Cañibano, L., García-Ayuso Covarsí, M., Sánchez, M. P., & Olea, M. (1999). *Measuring Intangibles to Understand and Improve Innovation Management: Preliminary Results.* https://www.oecd.org/sti/ind/1947863.pdf

Caraccioli, M. J. (2021). *Writing the New World Book: The Politics of Natural History in the Early Spanish Empire.* University Press of Florida.

Caraman, P. (1975). *The Lost Paradise: An Account of the Jesuits in Paraguay, 1607-1768.* Sidgwick & Jackson.

Carlsmith, C. (2002). Struggling toward Success: Jesuit Education in Italy, 1540-1600. *History of Education Quarterly, 42*(2), 215–246.

Carrasco M., R. (2018). Jesuit Mission and the Globalization of Knowledge of the Americas: Florian Paucke's Hin und Her in the Province of 'Paraquaria' During the Eighteenth Century. In C. Roldán, D. Brauer, & J. Rohbeck (Eds.), *Philosophy of Globalization* (pp. 205–224). De Gruyter.

Casalini, C., & Pavur, C. (Eds.). (2016). *Jesuit Pedagogy, 1540-1616: A Reader.* Institute of Jesuit Sources.

Casillas, J. C., & Acedo, F. J. (2013). Speed in the Internationalization Process of the Firm. *International Journal of Management Reviews, 15*(1), 15–29.

Casillas, J. C., & Moreno-Menéndez, A. M. (2014). Speed of the Internationalization Process: The Role of Diversity and Depth in Experiential Learning. *Journal of International Business Studies, 45*(1), 85–101.

Catto, M. (2010). Missioni e globalizzazioni: L'adattamento come identità della Compagnia di Gesù. In M. Catto (Ed.), *Evangelizzazione e globalizzazione: Le missioni gesuitiche nell'età moderna tra storia e storiografia* (pp. 1–16). Società editrice Dante Alighieri.

Cauti, F.I. (2005). *Extremo Oriente y Perú en el siglo XVI.* Fondo Editorial de la Pontificia Universidad Católica del Perú.

Cavusgil, S. (1984). Differences among Exporting Firms Based o their Degree of Internationalization. *Journal of Business Research, 12*(2), 195–208.

Cavusgil, S. T., & Zou, S. (1994). Marketing Strategy-Performance Relationship: An Investigation of the Empirical Link in Export Market Ventures. *Journal of Marketing, 58,* 1–21.

Chakravarti, A. (2018). *The Empire of Apostles: Religion, Accomodatio, and the Imagination of Empire in Early Modern Brazil and India.* Oxford University Press.

Chanlat, J. F., & Pierre, P. (2018). *Le management interculturel: Évolution, tendances et critiques.* Éditions EMS.

Charles, J. (2003). *Indios Ladinos: Colonial Andean Testimony and Ecclesiastical Institutions (1583-1650).* Yale University.

Charles, J. (2004). Polémicas en torno a los catequistas andinos en el virreinato peruano (siglos XVI-XVII). *Historica, 28*(2). http://revistas.pucp.edu.pe/index.php/historica/article/view/1

Charles, J. (2007). 'More ladino than necessary': Indigenous Litigants and the Language Policy Debate in Mid-Colonial Peru. *Colonial Latin American Review, 16*(1), 23–47.

Charles, J. (2014). Trained by Jesuits: Indigenous Letrados in Seventeenth-Century Peru. In G. Ramos & Y. Yannakakis (Eds.), *Indigenous Intellectuals: Knowledge, Power, and Colonial Culture in Mexico and the Andes* (pp. 60–78). Duke University Press.

Chemmanur, T. J., Kong, L., Krishnan, K., & Yu, Q. (2019). Top Management Human Capital, Inventor Mobility, and Corporate Innovation. *Journal of Financial and Quantitative Analysis, 54*(6), 2383–2422.

Chetty, S., Ojala, A., & Leppäaho, T. (2015). Effectuation and Foreign Market Entry of Entrepreneurial Firms. *European Journal of Marketing, 49*(9–10), 1436–1459.

Chevalier, F. (1970). *Land and Society in Colonial Mexico, transl. By Lesley B. Simpson.* University of California Press.

Chiao, Y.-C., Lo, F.-Y., & Yu, C.-M. (2010). Choosing Between Wholly-Owned Subsidiaries and Joint Ventures of MNCs from an Emerging Market. *International Marketing Review, 27*(3), 338–365.

Child, J., & Hsieh, L. H. Y. (2014). Decision Mode, Information and Network Attachment in the Internationalization of SMEs: A Configurational and Contingency Analysis. *Journal of World Business, 49*(4), 598–610.

Chin, Y. W., & Lim, E. S. (2018). Policies and Performances of SMEs in Malaysia. *Journal of Southeast Asian Economies, 35*(3), 470–487.

Church-Morel, A., & Bartel-Radic, A. (2014). 'Not All Multilingual Teams Are Created Equal': Concepualizing Language Diversity Management, *XXIII Conférence Internationale de Management Stratégique, Rennes.*

Cieslik, H. (1954). Balthasar Gago and Japanese Christian Terminology. *Missionary Bulletin, 8.* http://pweb.sophia.ac.jp/britto/xavier/cieslik/ciejmj02.pdf

Cieslik, H. (1959). P. Pedro Kasui (1587-1639). Der letzte japanische Jesuit der Tokugawa-Zeit. *Monumenta Nipponica, 15*(1–2), 35–86.

Cieslik, H. (1962). Zur Geschichte der kirchlichen Hierarchie in der alten Japanmission. *Neue Zeitschrift für Missionswissenschaft, 18,* 42–58, 81–107, 177–195.

Cieslik, H. (1973). The Case of Christovao Ferreira. *Monumenta Nipponica, 29,* 1–54.

Clarence-Smith, W. G. (2020). Jesuits and Mules in Colonial Latin America: Innovators or Managers? In L. A. Newson (Ed.), *Cultural Worlds of the Jesuits in Colonial Latin America* (pp. 209–227). University of London Press.

Clossey, L. (2008). *Salvation and Globalization in the Early Jesuit Missions.* Cambridge University Press.

Coello de la Rosa, A. (2005). Más allá del Incario: Imperialismo e historia en José de Acosta, SJ (1540–1600). *Colonial Latin American Review, 14*(1), 55–81.

Coello de la Rosa, A. (2007). Los jesuitas y las misiones de frontera del alto Perú: Santa Cruz de la Sierra (1587-1603). *Revista Complutense de Historia de América, 33,* 151–175.

Coello de la Rosa, A. (2022). Introduction: Jesuits in Asian-Pacific Borderlands. *Journal of Jesuit Studies* 9(2), 173–179.

Cole, J.A. (1985). *The Potosí Mita, 1573-1700: Compulsory Indian Labor in the Andes.* Stanford University Press.

Collani, C. v. (2010). Matteo Ricci: Zum 400. Todestag des Pioniers der neuzeitlichen Chinamission. *Stimmen der Zeit, 5.* https://www.herder.de/stz/hefte/archiv/135-2010/5-2010/matteo-ricci-zum-400-todestag-des-pioniers-der-neuzeitlichen-chinamission/

Colmenares, G. (1969). *Haciendas de los Jesuítas en el Nuevo Reino de Granada, siglo XVIII.* Universidad Nacional de Colombia.

Como, M. I. (2008). *Shōtoku: Ethnicity, Ritual, and Violence in the Japanese Buddhist Tradition.* Oxford University Press.

Compañía de Jesus. (1575). *Cartas que los Padres y Hermanos de la Compañia de Jesús que andan en los Reynos de Japón escrivieron a los de la misma Compañia desde el año de mil y quinientos y quarenta y nueve, hasta el de mil y quinientos y setenta y uno.* Iñiquez de Lequerica.

Contente Domingues, F. (2003). Vasco da Gama's Voyage: Myths and Realities in Maritime History. *Portuguese Studies, 19,* 1–8.

Cooper, M. (1973). *Rodrigues the Interpreter: An Early Jesuit in Japan and China.* Weatherhill.

Cooper, M. (Eds.). (2001). *João Rodrigues's Account of Sixteenth-Century Japan.* Hakluyt Society.

Coraiola, D. M., Foster, W. M., & Suddaby, R. (2015). Varieties of History in Organization Studies. In P. G. McLaren, A. J. Mills, & T. G. Weatherbee (Eds.), *The Routledge Companion to Management and Organizational History* (pp. 206–221). Routledge.

Correia, P. (2003). Father Diogo de Mesquita (1551-1614) and the cultivation of Western plants in Japan. *Bulletin of Portuguese-Japanese Studies, 7,* 73–91.

Cricelli, L., Greco, M., & Grimaldi, M. (2013). The Assessment of the Intellectual Capital Impact on the Value Creation Process: A Decision Support Framework for Top Management. *International Journal of Management and Decision Making, 12*(2), 146–164.

Cui, A. P., Walsh, M. F., & Gallion, D. (2011). Internationalization Challenges for SMEs and Global Marketing Managers: A Case Study. *International Journal of Business and Social Research, 1*(1), 57–69.

Cui, A. P., Walsh, M. F., & Zou, S. (2014). The Importance of Strategic Fit Between Host-Home Country Similarity and Exploration Exploitation Strategies on Small and Medium-Sized Enterprises' Performance: A Contingency Perspective. *Journal of International Marketing, 22*(4), 67–85.

Curvelo, A. (2001). Nagasaki: An European Artistic City in Early Modern Japan. *Bulletin of Portuguese-Japanese Studies, 2*, 23–35.

Cushner, N. P. (1967). Merchants and Missionaries: A Theologian's View of Clerical Involvement in the Galleon Trade. *The Hispanic American Historical Review, 47*(3), 360–369.

Cushner, N. P. (1980). *Lords of the Land: Sugar, Wine, and Jesuit Estates of Coastal Peru, 1600-1767*. SUNY Press.

Cushner, N.P. (1983). *Farm and Factory: The Jesuits and the Development of Agrarian Capitalism in Colonial Quito, 1600–1767*. SUNY Press.

Cushner, N. P. (2006). *Why Have You Come Here? The Jesuits and thhe First Evangelization of Native America*. Oxford University Press.

da Gama, V. (2009). *Em nome de Deus: The Journal of the First Voyage of Vasco da Gama to India, 1497-1499* (G. J. Ames, ed.). Brill.

Danieluk, R. (2019). The Role and Significance of Father Visitor in the Society of Jesus. In T. M. McCoog (Eds.), *With Eyes and Ears Open: The Role of Visitors in the Society of Jesus* (pp. 31–48). Brill.

de Acuña, C. (1641). *Nuevo Descubrimiento del gran Rio de las Amazonas*. Imprenta del Reyno.

de Anchieta, J. (1595). *Arte De Grammatica Da Lingoa mais vsada na costa do Brasil*. Mariz.

de Betanzos, J. (1996). *Narrative of the Incas, ed. And transl. By Roland Hamilton and Dana Buchanan*. University of Texas Press.

de Cieza de Léon, P. (1554). *Crónica del Perú*. Martin Nucio.

de Ribadeneira, Pedro. (2014). *The Life of Ignatius of Loyola*. The Institute of Jesuit Sources.

de Sousa, L. (2010). *The Early European Presence in China, Japan, the Philippines and Southeast Asia (1555-1590): The Life of Bartolomeu Landeiro*. Tipografia Ka Va/Macao Foundation.

Debergh, M. (1980). Deux nouvelles études sur l'hisotire du Christianisme au Japon 1: Bases Doctrinales et Images du sacrement de l'eucharistie à l'Époque des premières missions chrétiennes au Japon. *Journal Asiatique, 268*, 397–416.

Debergh, M. (1984). Deux nouvelles études sur l'hisotire du Christianisme au Japon, 2: Les pratiques de purification et de pénitence au Japon vues par les missionaires Jésuites aux XVIe et XVIIe siècles. *Journal Asiatique, 272*, 167–217.

Decker, S. (2013). The Silence of the Archives: Business History, Post-Colonialism and Archival Ethnography. *Management & Organizational History, 8*(2), 155–173.

Dehergne, J. (1973). *Répertoire des Jésuites de Chine de 1552 à 1800.* Institutum Historicum S.I.

del Valle, I., More, A., & O'Toole, R. S. (2020). Introduction: Iberian Empires and a Theory of Early Modern Globalization. In *Iberian Empires and the Roots of Globalization* (pp. 1–21). Vanderbilt University Press.

Dejo, J., S.J. et al. (2021) [1704]. *Diego de Altamirano's Historia de la provincia Peruana de la Compañía de Jesús.* UARM.

Dejo, J., S.J. (2023). Spiritual Discourse in the Jesuit Missions: The Role of Nature in the Evangelization of Peru (Sixteenth–Seventeenth Centuries). *Journal of Jesuit Studies* 10(2), 238–257.

Delgado García, J. (1985). *El Beato Francisco Morales, O.P., mártir del Japón (1567–1622) su personalidad histórica y misionera.* Inst. Pontificio de Teologia/Misionología.

Depuy, H. F. (1921). An Early Account of the Establishment of Jesuit Missions in America. *Mass Proceedings of the American Antiquarian Society, 30,* 62–80.

Dias, D., Zhu, C. J., & Samaratunge, R. (2017). Examining the Role of Cultural Exposure in Improving Intercultural Competence: Implications for HRM Practices in Multicultural Organizations. *The International Journal off Human Resource Managament, 31*(2), 1–20.

D'Iribarne, P. (1994). The Honour Principle in the Bureaucratic Phenomenon. *Organization Studies, 15*(1), 81–97.

D'Iribarne, P. (2009). National Cultures and Organisations in Search of a Theory: An Interpretative Approach. *International Journal of Cross Cultural Management, 9*(3), 309–321.

D'Iribarne, P., Chevrier, S., Henry, A., Segal, J.-P., & Treguer-Felten, G. (2020). *Cross-Cultural Management Revisited: A Qualitative Approach.* Oxford University Press.

D'Iribarne, P., Henry, A., Segal, J.-P., Chevrier, S., & Globokar, T. (1998). *Cultures et mondialisation: Gérer par-delà les frontières.* Editions du Seuil.

Disney, A. R. (2010). *Twilight of the Pepper Empire: Portuguese Trade in Southwest India in the Early Seventeenth Century.* Manohar Publishers.

Doi, T. (1939). Das Sprachstudium der Gesellschaft Jesu in Japan im 16. Und 17. Jahrhundert. *Monumenta Nipponica, 2*(2), 437–465.

Dominguez, N., & Mayrhofer, U. (2017). Internationalization Stages of Traditional SMEs: Increasing, Decreasing and Re-Increasing Commitment to Foreign Markets. *International Business Review, 26*(6), 1051–1063.

Dominguez, N., & Mayrhofer, U. (2018a). Introduction. In N. Dominguez & U. Mayrhofer (Eds.), *Key Success Factors of SME Internationalisation: A Cross-Country Perspective* (pp. 1–3). Emerald.

Dominguez, N., & Mayrhofer, U. (2018b). *Key Success Factors of SME Internationalisation.* Emerald.

Dominguez, N., & Mayrhofer, U. (2018c). Succeeding in the Chinese Market: The Case of the French Company Mixel Agitators. In N. Dominguez & U. Mayrhofer (Eds.), *Key Success Factors of SME Internationalisation: A Cross Country Perspective* (pp. 195–204). Emerald.

Donnelly, J. P. (Ed.). (2006). *Jesuit Writings of the Early Modern Period, 1540-1640.* Hackett Publishing.

Dubois, A., & Gadde, L.-E. (2002). Systematic Combining: An Abductive Approach to Case Research. *Journal of Business Research, 55*, 553–560.

Duignan, P. (1958). Early Jesuit Missionaries: A Suggestion for Further Study. *American Anthropologist, 60*(4), 725–732.

Dunning, J. H. (1992). *Multinational Enterprise and the Global Economy.* Prentice Hall.

Dürr, R. (2017). Akkommodation und Wissenstransfer: Neuerscheinungen zur Geschichte der Jesuiten in der Frühen Neuzeit. *Zeitschrift für Historische Forschung, 44*(3), 487–509.

Durston, A. (2007). *Pastoral Quechua: The History of Christian Translation in Colonial Peru, 1550-1650.* University of Notre Dame Press.

Ebisawa, A. (1944). *Kirishitan no shakai katsudō oyobi Nanban igaku.* Fuzanbō.

Ebisawa, A. (1960). *Christianity in Japan: A Bibliography of Japanese and Chinese Sources.* International Christian University.

Ebisawa, A. (1971). *Kirishitanshi no kenkyū.* Shin Jinbutsu Ōraisha.

Ebisawa, A. (1991). *Kirishitan Nanban bungaku nyūmon.* Kyōbunkan.

Echavone, A. (1955). Origen y evolución de la idea jesuitica de "Reducciónes" en las misiones del Virreinato del Peru. *Missionalia Hispanica, 34*, 95–144.

Eco, U. (1979). *A Theory of Semiotics.* Indiana University Press.

Egaña, A. de. (1954). *Monumenta Peruana: vol. 1: (1565-1575).* Monumenta Historica Soc. Iesu.

Egaña, A. de. (1958a). *Monumenta Peruana: vol. 2: (1576-1580).* Monumenta Historica Soc. Iesu.

Egaña, A. de. (1958b). *Monumenta Peruana: vol. 3: (1581-1585).* Monumenta Historica Soc. Iesu.

Egaña, A. de. (1966). *Monumenta Peruana: vol. 4: (1586-1591).* Monumenta Historica Soc. Iesu.

Egaña, A. de. (1970). *Monumenta Peruana: vol. 5: (1592-1595).* Monumenta Historica Soc. Iesu.

Egaña, A. de. (1974). *Monumenta Peruana: vol. 6: (1596-1599).* Monumenta Historica Soc. Iesu.

Egaña, A. de, & Fernandez, E. (1981). *Monumenta Peruana: vol. 7: (1600-1602).* Monumenta Historica Soc. Iesu.

Egido, T., Burrieza Sanchez, J., & Revuetta Gonzalez, M. (2004). *Los Jesuitas en España y en el mundo hispánico.* Pons.

Ehalt, R. d. S. (2009). Revisiting the First Jesuit Library in Japan: An Analysis of the Purpose of Nunes Barreto's Library in Kyushu (1556). *Review of Culture, 32*, 42–51.

Ehalt, R. d. S. (2017). *Jesuits and the Problem of Slavery in Early Modern Japan.* Tokyo University of Foreign Studies.

Ekberg, C. J. (2000). *French Roots in the Illinois Country: The Mississippi Frontier in Colonial Times.* University of Illinois Press.

Elison, G. (1973). *Deus Destroyed: The Image of Christianity in Early Modern Japan.* Harvard University Press.

Ellis, P. (2000). Social Ties and Foreign Market Entry. *Journal of International Business Studies, 31*(3), 443–469.

Ellis, P., & Pecotich, A. (2001). Social Factors Influencing Export Initiation in Small and Medium-Sized Enterprises. *Journal of Marketing Research*, *38*(1), 119–130.

Ellis, R. R. (2003). 'The Best Thus Far Discovered': The Japanese in the Letters of Francisco Xavier. *Hispanic Review*, *71*(2), 155–169.

Elo, M., Benjowsky, C., & Nummela, N. (2015). Intercultural Competences and Interaction Schemes: Four Forces Regulating Dyadic Encounters in International Business. *Industrial Marketing Management*, *48*(5), 38–49.

Engelhard, J. (1997). *Interkulturelles Management: Theoretische Fundierung und funktionsbereichsspezifische Konzepte*. Springer.

Engelhard, J. (2018). Interkulturelles Management. In *Gabler Wirtschaftslexikon*. https://wirtschaftslexikon.gabler.de/definition/interkulturelles-management-40858

England, G. W., & Lee, R. (1974). The Relationship between Managerial Values and Managerial Success in the United States, Japan, India, and Australia. *Journal of Applied Psychology*, *59*(4), 411–419.

Eriksson, T., Nummela, N., & Saarenketo, S. (2014). Dynamic Capability in a Small Global Factory. *International Business Review*, *23*(1), 169–180.

Estenssoro Fuchs, J. C. (2003). *Del paganismo a la santidad: La incorporación de los indios del Perú al catolicismo (1532–1750)*. IFEA.

European Commission. (2021). *SME Definition*. Internal Market, Industry, Entrepreneurship and SMEs. https://ec.europa.eu/growth/smes/sme-definition_en

Evers, N., & O'Gorman, C. (2011). Improvised Internationalization inn New Ventures: The Role of Prior Knnowledge and Networks. *Entrepreneurship and Regional Development*, *23*(7–8), 549–574.

Fang, T. (2010). Asian Management Research Needs More Self-Confidence: Reflection on Hofstede 2007 and Beyond. *Asia Pacific Journal of Management*, *27*(1), 155–170.

Farge, W. J. (2002). *The Japanese Translations of the Jesuit Mission Press, 1590–1614: De imitatione Christi and Guía de pecadores*. Edwin Mellen.

Farmer, R. N., & Richman, B. M. (1965). *Comparative Management and Economic Progress*. Richard D. Irwin.

Feld, H. (2006). *Ignatius von Loyola: Gründer des Jesuitenordens – Eine Biographie*. Böhlau.

Feldmann, H. (1993). As disputas de São Francisco Xavier com bonzos e nobres do Japão relatadas por Luís Fróis S.J. e João Rodrigues S.J. In P. Milward (Eds.), *Portuguese Voyages to Asia and Japan in the Renaissance Period* (pp. 282–297). Sophia University.

Fernández Duro, C. (1896). Pedro Sarmiento de Gamboa, El Navegante. *Boletín de la Real Academia de la Historia*, *28*(4), 273–287.

Fernandez, E. (1986). *Monumenta Peruana: Bd. 8: (1603-1604)*. Monumenta Historica Soc. Iesu.

Fernando, L. (2016). Jesuits and India. In *Oxford Handbooks Online*. https://www.oxfordhandbooks.com/view/10.1093/oxfordhb/9780199935420.001.0001/oxfordhb-9780199935420-e-59

Ferro, J. P. (1993). A epistolografia no quotidiano dos missionários Jesuítas now séculos XVI e XVII. *Lusitania Sacra, 5,* 137–158.

Fink, G., & Meierwert, S. (2004). Issues of Time in International, Intercultural Management: East and Central Europe from the Perspective of Austrian Managers. *Journal of East European Management Studies, 9*(1), 61–84.

Flyvbjerg, B. (2006). Five Misunderstandings About Case-Study Research. *Qualitative Inquiry, 12*(2), 219–245.

Forrestal, A., & Smith, S. A. (2016). Re-thinking Missionary Catholicism for the Early Modern Era. In A. Forrestal & S. A. Smith (Eds.), *The Frontiers of Mission: Perspectives on Early Modern Missionary Catholicism* (pp. 1–21). Brill.

Franklin, P. (2007). Differences and Difficulties in Intercultural Management Interaction. In H. Kotthoff & H. Spencer-Oatey (Eds.), *Handbook of Intercultural Communication* (pp. 263–284). De Gruyter.

Fraser, V. (1992). Architecture and Ambition: The Case of the Jesuits in the Viceroyalty of Peru. *History Workshop, 34,* 16–32.

Friedrich, M. (2009a). Government and Information-Management in Early Modern Europe. The Case of the Society of Jesus (1540–1773). *Journal of Early Modern History 12*(6), 1–25.

Friedrich, M. (2009b). Governing the Early Modern Society of Jesus. Concepts, Structures, Issues, and Critical Voices. *Studies in Jesuit Spirituality* 41(1), 1–42.

Friedrich, M. (2018). *Die Jesuiten: Aufstieg, Niedergang, Neubeginn.* Piper.

Friedrich-Stegmann, H. (2018). Dos testimonios alemanes sobre la expulsión de los jesuitas españoles. *Espacio, Tiempo y Forma, Servie IV: Historia Moderna, 31,* 183–194.

Fróis, L. (1976). *História de Japam: Bd. 5 vols.* (J. Wicki, ed..). Biblioteca nacional.

Fróis, L. (2004). *Topsy-turvy 1585: A Translation and Explication of Luis Frois S.J.'s Tratado (treatise) listing 611 ways Europeans and Japanese are contrary* (R. D. Gill, ed.). Paraverse Press.

Fujita, N. S. (1991). *Japan's Encounter with Christianity: The Catholic Mission in Pre-Modern Japan.* Paulist Press.

Fujitani, J. (2016). Penance in the Jesuit Mission to Japan, 1549-1562. *Journal of Ecclesiastical History, 67*(2), 306–324.

Fukahori, A. (2016). *Ongaku-men kara miru Iezusu-kai no Tōyō senkyū: 16 seiki nakaba kara 17 seiki shoki ni okeru Goa, Nihon, Makao wo taishū toshite.* Aichi Kenritsu Geijutsu Daigaku.

Furuya, N., Stevens, M. J., Bird, A., Oddou, G., & Mendenhall, M. (2009). Managing the Learning and Transfer of Global Management Competence: Antecedents and Outcomes of Japanese Repatriation Effectiveness. *Journal of International Business Studies, 40*(2), 200–215.

Gabrielsson, P., & Gabrielsson, M. (2013). A Dynamic Model of Growth Phases and Survival in International Business-to-Business New Ventures: The Moderating Effect of Decision-Making Logic. *Industrial Marketing Management, 42*(8), 1357–1373.

Gannon, M. J., & Newman, K. L. (Eds.). (2002). *The Blackwell Handbook of Cross-Cultural Management.* Blackwell.

García Echevarría, S. (1999). Competitiveness and Changing Process in a Global Economy. In J. Engelhard & W. A. Oechsler (Eds.), *Internationales Management:*

Auswirkungen globaler Veränderungen auf Wettbewerb, Unternehmensstrategie und Märkte (pp. 47–74). Springer.

Gehl, P. F. (2003). Religion and Politics in the Market for Books: The Jesuits and Their Rivals. *The Papers of the Bibliographical Society of America*, 97(4), 435–460.

Ghelarducci, V. (2020). 'Con intençión de haçerlos Christianos y con voluntad de instruirlos': Spiritual education among American Indians in Anello Oliva's Historia del Reino y Provincias del Perú. In Linda A. Newson (Ed.), *Cultural Worlds of the Jesuits in Colonial Latin America* (pp. 171–188). University of London Press.

Gibbert, M., Ruigrok, W., & Wicki, B. (2008). What Passes as Rigorous Case Study? *Strategic Management Journal*, 29, 1465–1474.

Giudicelli, C. (2011). Las tijeras de San Ignacio: Misión y clasificación en los confines coloniales. In G. Wilde (Ed.), *Saberes de la conversión: Jesuitas, indígenas e imperios coloniales en las fronteras de la cristiandad* (pp. 347–371). SB Editorial.

Godfrey, P. C., Hassard, J., O'Connor, E. S., Rowlinson, M., & Ruef, M. (2016). What is Organizational History? Toward a Creative Synthesis of History and Organization Studies. *Academy of Management Review*, 41(4), 590–608.

Godwin-Jones, R. (2019). In a World of SMART Technology, Why Learn Another Language? *Journal of Educational Technology & Society*, 22(2), 4–13.

Gomes, L., & Ramaswamy, K. (1999). An Empirical Examination of the Form of the Relationship between Multinationality and Performance. *Journal of International Business Studies*, 30(1), 173–188.

Gonoi, T. (1983). *Tokugawa shoki kirishitanshi kenkyū*. Yoshikawa Kōbunkan.

Gonoi, T. (1990). *Nihon Kirisutokyōshi*. Yoshikawa Kōbunkan.

Gonoi, T. (2002). *Nihon kirishitanshi no kenkyū*. Yoshikawa Kōbunkan.

Gradie, C. M. (1988). Spanish Jesuits in Virginia: The Mission That Failed. *The Virginia Magazine of History and Biography*, 96(2), 131–156.

Green, B. (2016). Colonial Theodicy and the Jesuit Ascetic Ideal in José de Acosta's Works on Spanish America. In R. A. Markys (Ed.), *Exploring Jesuit Distinctiveness: Interdisciplinary Perspectives on Ways of Proceeding within the Society of Jesus* (pp. 114–136). Brill.

Grendler, P. F. (2019). Jesuit Schools and Universities in Europe 1548-1773. *Brill Research Perspectives in Jesuit Studies*, 1(1), 1–118. https://doi.org/10.1163/25897454-12340001

Griffiths, N. (1996). *The Cross and the Serpent: Religious Repression and Resurgence in Colonial Peru*. University of Oklahoma Press.

Grimaldi, M., Corvello, V., De Mauro, A., & Scarmozzino, E. (2017). A Systematic Literature Review on Intangible Assets and Open Innovation. *Knowledge Management Research and Practice*, 15, 90–100.

Grosskopf, S., & Barmeyer, C. (2021). Learning from Multi-Paradigmatic Sensitivity in Cross-Cultural Management? Empirical and Theoretical Considerations. *International Journal of Cross Cultural Management*, XX(X), 1–22. https://doi.org/10.1177/14705958211019437

Guillermou, A. (1993). *Ignatius von Loyola* (3. Aufl.). Rowohlt.

Gutiérrez Estévez, M. (2013). Otra vez sobre sincretismo. In Sánchez Paredes, J. & Curatola Petrocchi, M. (Eds.). *Los rostros de la tierra encantada: Religión, evangelización y sincretismo en el Nuevo Mundo* (pp. 503–522). Ifea-puc.

Hagemann, E. (1942). The Persecution of the Christians in Japan in the Middle of the Seventeenth Century. *Pacific Historical Review, 11*(2), 151–160.

Hagen, B., Denicolai, S., & Zucchella, A. (2014). International Entrepreneurship at the Crossrooads between Innovation and Internationalization. *Journal of International Entrepreneurship, 12*(2), 111–114.

Hallberg, K. (2001). *A Market-Oriented Strategy for Small and Medium-Scale Enterprises* (IFC Discussion Paper Nr. 48).

Hampe M., T. (1982). La Encomienda en el Peru en el siglo XVI. *Historica, 6*(2), 173–216.

Hartmann, P. C. (2008). *Die Jesuiten* (2nd edition). C.H. Beck.

Harvey, C., & Press, J. (1996). *Databases in Historical Research: Theory, Methods and Applications*. MacMillan.

Haub, R. (2004). *Petrus Canisius: Botschafter Europas*. Lahn-Verlag.

Healy, G. R. (1958). The French Jesuits and the Idea of the Noble Savage. *The William and Mary Quarterly, 15*(2), 143–167.

Hehrlein, Y. (1992). *Mission und Macht: Die politisch-religiöse Konfrontation zwischen dem Dominikanerorden in Peru und dem Vizekönig Francisco de Toledo (1569-1581)*. Matthias-Grünewald-Verlag.

Heid, H. (1997). *Von Erfarung aller Land: Reiseberichte aus der Zeit des 16. bis zur Mitte des 19. Jahrhunderts in der Historischen Bibliothek der Stadt Rastatt*. Stadt Rastatt.

Hennart, J.-F., & Slangen, A. H. (2015). Yes, We Really Do Need More Entry Mode Studies! A Commentary on Shaver. *Journal of International Business Studies, 46*(1), 114–122.

Hermel, P., & Khayat, I. (2011). The Role of Resources: Micro-Firms Internationalization in the French Context. *Journal of Small Business and Enterprise Development, 18*(2), 298–310.

Hesselink, R. H. (2015). *The Dream of Christian Nagasaki: World Trade and the Clash of Cultures, 1560–1640*. McFarland.

Heuts, K. (2015). Validation and Propagation: Mutio Vitelleschi's Letters from Surviving Japan Mission Jesuits (1625–1627). *MaRBLe Research Papers, 6*, 97–114.

Hickson, D. J., Hinings, C. R., McMillan, C., & Schwitter, J. P. (1974). The Culture-Free Context of Organization Structure: A Tri-National Comparison. *Sociology, 8*(1), 59–80.

Higashibaba, I. (2001). *Christianity in Early Modern Japan: Kirishitan Belief and Practice*. Brill.

Hilmersson, M., & Johanson, M. (2016). Speed of SME Internationalization and Performance. *MIR: Management International Review, 56*(1), 67–94.

Hoey, J. B., III. (2010). Alessandro Valignano and the Restructuring of the Jesuit Mission in Japan, 1579-1582. *Eleutheria, 1*(1), 23–42.

Hofstede, G. (1980). *Culture's Consequences: International Differences in Work-related Values*. Sage.

Hofstede, G., Hofstede, G. J., & Minkov, M. (2010). *Culture and Organizations: Software of the Mind*. McGraw Hill.
Holzmüller, H. H. (1997). Kulturstandards: Ein operationales Konzept zur Entwicklung kultursensitiven Managements. In J. Engelhard (Ed.), *Interkulturelles Management: Theoretische Fundierung und funktionsbereichsspezifische Konzepte* (pp. 55–74). Springer.
Hosne, A. C. (2013). *The Jesuit Missions to China and Peru, 1570-1610: Expectations and Appraisals of Expansionism*. Routledge.
Hosne, A. C. (2014). Friendship among Literati: Matteo Ricci SJ (1552–1610) in Late Ming China. *Transcultural Studies*, *1*, 190–214.
Hoyt, S. (2015). Viracocha: Christ among the Ancient Peruvians? *BYU Studies Quarterly*, *54*(1), 105–134.
Hruby, J. (2013). *Das Global Mindset von Managern*. Springer.
Hruby, J. (2014). *Global Mindsets: Überblick und Bedeutung für Unternehmen und Organisationen*. Springer Gabler.
Hruby, J., Jorge de Melo, R., Samunderu, E., & Hartel, J. (2019). Unpacking the Complexities of Global Mindset: A Multi-Lens Analysis. In J. S. Osland, M. E. Mendenhall, & M. Li (Eds.), *Advances in Global Leadership* (vol. 11, pp. 97–144). Emerald.
Hsia, R.-P. (2010). *A Jesuit in the Forbidden City: Matteo Ricci, 1552–1610*. Oxford University Press.
Hsia, R.-P. (2014). Jesuit Foreign Missions: A Historiographical Essay. *Journal of Jesuit Studies*, *1*(1), 47–65.
Hsia, R.-P. (2015). The Catholic Historical Review: One Hundred Years of Scholarship on Catholic Missions in the Early Modern World. *The Catholic Historical Review*, *101*(2), 223–241.
Huiyi, W. (2017). 'The Observations We Made in the Indies and in China': The Shaping of the Jesuits' Knowledge of China by Other Parts of the Non-Western World. *East Asian Science, Technology, and Medicine*, *46*, 47–88.
Hyland, S. (2003). *The Jesuit and the Incas: The Extraordinary Life of Padre Blas Valera, S.J.* University of Michigan Press.
Imai, R. (1971). *Sengoku jidai*. Sekai Bunkasha.
Imago primi saeculi Societatis Iesu a prouincia Flandro-Belgica eiusdem Societatis repraesentata. (1640). Balthasar Moretus.
Imbruglia, G. (1992). Ideali di civilizzazione: La Compagnia di Gesù e le missioni (1550–1600). In A. Prosperi & W. Reinhard (Eds.), *Il nuovo mondo nella coscienza italiana e tedesca del Cinquecento* (S. 287–308). Il Mulino.
Imbruglia, G. (2014). A Peculiar Idea of Empire: Missions and Missionaries of the Society of Jesus in Early Modern History. In M. A. Bernier, C. Donato, & H.-J. Lüsebrink (Eds.), *Jesuit Accounts of the Colonial Americas: Intercultural Transfers Intellectual Disputes, and Textualities* (S. 21–49). University of Toronto Press.
Ingelhart, R., & Welzel, C. (2005). *Modernization, Cultural Change, and Democracy: The Human Development Sequence*. Cambridge University Press.
Irwin, C. (2019). Catholic Presence and Power: Jesuit Painter Bernardo Bitti at Lake Titicaca in Peru. *Journal of Jesuit Studies*, *6*(2), 270–293.

Itier, C. (2021). 'Huaca,' un concepto andino mal entendido. *Chungara revista de antropología chilena, 53*(3), 480–490.

Ivens, B., & Mayrhofer, U. (2003). Les facteurs de réussite du marketing relationnel. *Décisions Marketing, 31,* 39–47.

Jacob, F. (2014). Tokugawa Ieyasu: Reichseiniger, Shōgun oder Japans "Diktator"? In *Diktaturen ohne Gewalt? Wie Diktatoren ihre Macht behaupten* (pp. 79–102). K&N.

Jacob, F. (2017). Technological Spatialities: The Impact of Geography and Technology During the Imjin War (1592-1598). In S. Danielsson & F. Jacob (Eds.), *War and Geography: The Spatiality of Organized Mass Violence* (pp. 25–38). Schöningh.

Jaeger, A. M., Kim, S. S., & Butt, A. N. (2016). Leveraging Values Diversity: The Emergence and Implications of a Global Managerial Culture in Global Organizations. *MIR: Management International Review, 56*(2), 227–254.

Jain, S., & Ahuja, S. K. (2019). Impact of Human Capital Management Practices on Employee Job Performance. *Proceedings of 10th International Conference on Digital Strategies for Organizational Success.* https://ssrn.com/abstract=3307706.

Jenster, N. P., & Steiler, D. (2011). 'Turning Up the Volume' in Inter-Personal Leadership: Motivating and Building Cohesive Global Virtual Teams During Times of Economic Crises. In W. H. Mobley, M. Li, & Y. Wang (Eds.), *Advances in Global Leadership* (vol. 6, pp. 267–297). Emerald Group Publishing.

Jesuita Anónimo. (1968) [1594]. *Relación de las costumbres antiguas de los naturales del Perú.* Ediciones Atlas.

Johanson, J., & Vahlne, J. (1977). The Internationalization Process of the Firm: A Model of Knowledge Development and Increasing Foreign Market Commitments. *Journal of International Business Studies, 8*(1), 23–32.

Johnson, J., & Tellis, G. J. (2008). Drivers of Success for Market Entry into China and India. *Journal of Marketing, 72,* 1–13.

Johnston, S. M. (2016). Pre-Suppression Jesuits in German-Speaking Lands. In *Jesuit Historiography Online.* http://dx.doi.org/10.1163/2468-7723_jho_COM_19 2578

Jorissen, E. (1988). *Das Japanbild im „Traktat" (1585) des Luis Frois.* Aschendorff.

Kalafsky, R. V. (2017). Export Programs and SME Market Choice: Evidence from North West England. *GeoJournal, 82*(6), 1135–1144.

Kaller, M., & Jacob, F. (2019). *Transatlantic Trade and Global Cultural Transfers since 1492: More than Commodities.* Routledge.

Karsten, L. (2014). Time as a Periodization of Management Practices. *Management & Organizational History, 9*(4), 414–432.

Kataoka, R. I. (1985). *La Vita e la Pastorale di Luis Cerqueira SJ Vescovo del Giappone 1598-1614.* Pontificia University Gregoriana.

Kataoka, Y. (1970). *Nagasaki no junkyōsha.* Kadokawa Shoten.

Kataoka, Y. (1979). *Nihon kirishitan junkyōshi,*. Jiji Tsūshinsha.

Katoriku Bunka Kyōkai. (1949). *Nichi-Ō bunka kōshō bunken mokuroku: Sabieru torai yonhyakunen kinen.* Kokuritsu Kokkai Toshokan.

Kawalilak, C., & Lock, J. (2018). Advancing Cross/Intercultural Awareness and Responsiveness in Higher Education Contexts. *The Journal of Educational Thought (JET), 51*(3), 235–238.

Kelley, L., & Worthley, R. (1981). The Role of Culture in Comparative Management: A Cross-Cultural Perspective. *The Academy of Management Journal, 24*(1), 164–173.

Kelly, J. E., & Thomas, H. (Eds.). (2019). *Jesuit Intellectual and Physical Exchange between England and Mainland Europe, c.1580-1789*. Brill.

Kessler, V. (2019). How to Integrate Spirituality, Emotions and Rationality in (Group) Decision-Making. In Kok, J. & van den Heuvel, S.C. (Eds.). *Leading in a VUCA World: Integrating Leadership, Discernment and Spirituality* (pp. 105–118). Cham.

Ketelaar, J. E. (1990). *Of Heretics and Martyrs in Meiji Japan: Buddhism and Its Persecution*. Princeton University Press.

Kigama, K. (2014). Tsugarushi to kirishitan: Tsugaru Tamenobu no kirisutokyō he no sekkin. *Hachinohe Gakuin Daigaku Kiyō, 49*, 15–36.

Kiryakova-Dineva, T., & Hadzhipetrova-Lachova, M. (2017). Intercultural Management: Main Aspects and Perspectives for the Practice of International Organizations. *Entrepreneurship, 5*(1), 97–105.

Klaiber, J. L. (2009). *The Jesuits in Latin America, 1549–2000: 450 Years of Inculturation, Defense of Human Rights, and Prophetic Witness*. Institute of Jesuit Sources.

Knight, G. A., & Cavusgil, S. T. (1996). The Born Global Firm: A Challenge to Traditional Internationalization Theory. In S. T. Cavusgil & T. Madsen (Eds.), *Advances in International Marketing* (Bd. 8, S. 11–26).

Koschorke, K. (1998). *Christen und Gewürze: Konfrontation und Interaktion kolonialer und indigener Christentumsvarianten*. Vandenhoeck & Ruprecht.

Koselleck, R. (2010). *Vergangene Zukunft: Zur Semantik geschichtlicher Zeiten*. Suhrkamp.

Kriegbaum, B. (2006, März 29). *Die Jesuitenreduktionen (1609-1767)* [Vortrag beim Dies academicus der Theologischen Fakultät zum Ignatianischen Jahr]. https://www.uibk.ac.at/theol/leseraum/texte/637.html

Kunttu, A., & Torkkeli, L. (2015). Service Innovation and Internationalization in SMEs: Implications for Growth and Performance. *Management Revue, 26*(2), 83–100.

Laanti, R., Gabrielsson, M., & Gabrielsson, P. (2007). The Globalization Strategies of Business-to-Business Born Global Firms inn the Wireless Technology Industry. *Industrial Marketing Management, 36*(8), 1194–1117.

Landin Carrasco, A. (1946). *Life and travels of Pedro Sarmiento de Gamboa*. Historical Institute of the Navy.

Lane, H. W. (1980). Systems, Values and Action: An Analytic Framework for Intercultural Management Research. *Management International Review, 20*(3), 61–70.

Laures, J. (1959). Die Kirche von Chikugo. *Monumenta Nipponica, 15*(3–4), 380–414.

Lawrence, W. W. (2012). Coping with External Pressures: A Note on SME Strategy. *Social and Economic Studies, 61*(1), 161–170.

le Bris, D., Goetzmann, W. N., & Pouget, S. (2017). The Present Value Relation Over Six Centuries: The Case of the Bazacle Company. *Journal of Financial Economics, 132*(1), 248–265.

Lefebvre, E., & Lefebvre, L. A. (2001). Innovative Capabilities as Determinants of Export Performance and Behavior: A Longitudinal Study of Manufacturing SMEs. In A. Kleinknecht & P. Mohnen (Eds.), *Innovation and Firm Performance: Ecometric Explorations of Survey Data* (pp. 281–309). MacMillan.

Leinsle, U. G. (2014). Der Widerstand gegen Perera und seine Physik in der oberdeutschen Jesuitenprovinz. *Quaestio, 14*, 51–68.

Levy, O., Beechler, S., Taylor, N., & Boyacigiller, N. A. (2007). What We Talk about when We Talk about „Global Mindset": Managerial Cognition in Multinational Corporations. *Journal of International Business Studies, 38*(2), 231–258.

Lewis, J. B. (Ed.). (2015). *The East Asian War, 1592-1598: International Relations, Violence and Memory*. Routledge.

Li, L., & Quian, G. (2008). Partnership or Self-Reliance Entry Modes: Large and Small Technology-Based Enterprises' Strategies in Overseas Markets. *Journal of International Entrepreneurship, 6*(4), 188–208.

Li, S. (2001). *Stratégies missionnaires des Jésuites Français en Nouvelle-France et en Chine au XVIIieme siècle*. L'Harmattan.

Liebowitz, J. (2000). *Building Organizational Intelligence: A Knowledge Management Primer*. CRC Press.

Little, D., & Thorne, S. L. (2017). From Learner Autonomy to Rewilding: A Discussion. In M. Cappellini, T. Lewis, & A. R. Mompean (Eds.), *Learner Autonomy and Web 2.0* (pp. 12–35). Equinox.

Liu, Y. (2011). The True Pioneer of the Jesuit China Mission: Michele Ruggieri. *History of Religions, 50*(4), 362–383.

Lopetegui, L. (1942). *El Padre José de Acosta y las misiones*. Instituto Gonzalo Fernández de Oviedo.

López-Gay, J. (2000). Father Francisco Passio (1554-1612) and His Ideas about the Sacerdotal Training of the Japanese. *Bulletin of Portuguese-Japanese Studies, 3*, 27–42.

Louart, P., & Martin, A. (2012). Small and Medium-Sized Enterprises and their Attitudes towards Internationalization and Innovation. *International Business Research, 5*(6), 14–23.

Loureiro, R. M. (2000). Turning Japanese? The Experiences and Writings of a Portuguese Jesuit in 16th Century Japan. In D. Couto & F. Lachaud (Eds.), *Empires éloignés: L'Europe et le Japon (XVIe-XIXe siècles)* (S. 155–168). École française d'Extrême-Orient.

Loyola, I. (1951) Spiritual exercises. Translated by Louis J. Puhl. http://spex.ignatianspirituality.com.

Lozano, P. (1754). *Historia de la Compañia de Jesus en la Provincia Del Paraguay* (Bd. 1). Manuel Fernandez.

Lu, J. W., & Beamish, P. W. (2001). The Internationalization and Performance of SMEs. *Strategic Management Journal, 22*(6–7), 565–586.

Luhmann, N. (2011). *Organisation und Entscheidung*, third edition. Springer VS.

MacCormack, S. (1991). *Religion in the Andes: Vision and Imagination in Early Colonial Peru.* Princeton University Press.

MacCormack, S. (2004). Religion and Society in Inca and Spanish Peru. In E. Phipps (Ed.), *The Colonial Andes: Tapestries and Silverwork, 1530-1830.* Metropolitan Museum of Art.

Macintosh, N. & Quattrone, P. (2010). *Management Accounting and Control Systems: An Organizational and Sociological Approach,* second edition. Wiley.

Maclean, M., Harvey, C., & Clegg, S. (2016). Conceptualizing Historical Organization Studies. *Academy of Management Review, 41*(4), 609–632.

Majocchi, A., Mayrhofer, U., & Camps, J. (2013). Joint Ventures or Non-Equity Alliances? Evidence from Italian Firms. *Management Decisions, 51*(2), 380–395.

Málaga Medina, A. (1974). Las reducciones en el Perú durante el gobierno del virrey Francisco de Toledo. *Anuario de estudios americanos, 31,* 818–842.

Maldavsky, A. (2012). *Vocaciones inciertas. Misión y misioneros en la provincia jesuita del Perú en los siglos XVI y XVII.* CSIC-IFEA Universidad Ruiz de Montoya.

Maldavsky, A. (2018). The Andes. In R.-P. Hsia (Ed.), *A Companion to Early Modern Catholic Global Missions* (pp. 41–72). Brill.

Maloney, M. R., & Zellmer-Bruhn, M. (2006). Building Bridges, Windows and Cultures: Mediating Mechanisms between Team Heterogeneity and Performance in Global Teams. *MIR: Management International Review, 46*(6), 697–720.

Mannheim, B. (1991). *The Language of the Inka since the European Invasion.* University of Texas Press.

Marcuse, L. (2008). *Ignatius von Loyola: Ein Soldat der Kirche.* Diogenes.

Martin, L. (2001). *La conquista intelectual del Perú: El Colegio jesuita de San Pablo, 1568-1767.* Editorial Casiopea.

Marzal, M. (1985). *El sincretismo iberoamericano* Pontificia Universidad Católica del Perú.

Marzal, M. (1988). *La transformación religiosa peruana.* Pontificia Universidad Católica del Perú.

Matsuda, K. (1947). *Kirishitan daimyō, Ōtomo Sōrin no shōgai.* Chūō Shuppansha.

Maurice, M., & Sorge, A. (Eds.). (2000). *Embedding Organizations: Societal Analysis of Actors, Organizations and Socio-Economic Contexts.* John Benjamins.

Mayrhofer, U. (2004). International Market Entry: Does the Home Country Affect Entry-Mode Desicisions? *Journal of International Marketing, 12*(4), 71–96.

Mayrhofer, U. (2017). *Management interculturel: Comprendre et gérer la diversité culturelle Label Fnege 2018 dans la catégorie Manuel.* Vuibert.

McCoog, T. M. (2019). *Pre-suppression Jesuit Activity in the British Isles and Ireland.* Brill.

McGinness, A. B. (2018). The Historiography of the Jesuits in Brazil Prior to the Suppression. In *Jesuit Historiography Online.* http://dx.doi.org/10.1163/246 8-7723_jho_COM_209645

Medina, F. B. (2001). Ruiz de Portillo, Jerónimo. In C. O'Neill & J. M. Domínguez (Eds.), *Diccionario Histórico de la Compañía de Jesús* (vol. 4, pp. 3437–3438). Institutum Historicum Societatis Iesu-Universidad Pontificia Comillas.

Mignini, F. (2019). *New Perspectives in the Studies on Matteo Ricci.* Quodlibet.

Mignolo, W. D. (2000). *Local Histories/Global Designs: Coloniality, Subaltern Knowledges and Border Thinking.* Princeton University Press.

Mignolo, W. D., & Ennis, M. (2001). Coloniality at Large: The Western Hemisphere in the Colonial Horizon of Modernity. *CR: The New Centennial Review, 1*(2), 19–54.

Millones, L. (2007). Mesianismo en América hispana: El Taki Onqoy. *Memoria Americana* 15, 7–39.

Mills, A. J., & Novicevic, M. N. (2020). *Management and Organizational History: A Research Overview.* Routledge.

Mills, K. (1997). *Idolatry and its Enemies: Colonial Andean Religion and Extirpation, 1640–1750.* Princeton University Press.

Mills, K. (2007). The Naturalization of Andean Christianities. In R.-P. Hsia (Ed.), *The Cambridge History of Christianity: Bd. 6: Reform and Expansion, 1500–1660* (pp. 508–539). Cambridge University Press.

Mione, A. (2015). The Value of Intangibles in a Situation of Innovation: Questions Raised by the Case of Standards. *Journal of Innovation Economics & Management, 17,* 49–68.

Moran, J. F. (1993). *The Japanese and the Jesuits: Alessandro Valignano in Sixteenth Century Japan.* Routledge.

More, A. (2020). Jesuit Networks and the Transatlantic Slave Trade: Alonso de Sandoval's Naturaleza, policía sagrada y profana (1627). In I. del Valle, A. More, & R. S. O'Toole (Eds.), *Iberian Empires and the Roots of Globalization* (pp. 131–157). Vanderbilt University Press.

Mörner, M. (1973). The Spanish American Hacienda: A Survey of Recent Research and Debate. *Hispanic American Historical Review, 53*(2), 183–216.

Morris, J. H. (2018). *Rethinking the History of Conversion to Christianity in Japan: 1549-1644.* University of St. Andrews.

Mujica, R. (2016). *La imagen transgredida: Ensayos de iconografía peruana y sus políticas de representación simbólica.* Congreso de la República.

Müller, S. (1996). Auslandsorientierung als Zielsetzung der Personalentwicklung. In A. Thomas (Ed.), *Psychologie interkulturellen Handelsn* (pp. 341–364). Hogrefe.

Mullett, M. A. (1999). *The Catholic Reformation.* Routledge.

Murai, S. (1998). *Nihon kinsei kokka no shōso.* Tōkyōdō Shuppan.

Murai, S. (1999). Ichi kirishitan bushi no kiseki. *Nihon Josei Daigaku Shigaku Kenkyūkai, 40,* 71–90.

Murai, S. (2000). *Tennō to kirishitan kinsei.* Yūzankaku Shuppan.

Murai, S. (2002). *Kirishitan kinsei to minshū no shūkyō.* Yamakawa Shuppansha.

Nagahara, K. (1978). *Sengoku jidai.* Yoshikawa Kōbunkan.

Nebgen, C. (2007). *Missionarsberufungen nach Übersee in drei deutschen Provinzen der Gesellschaft Jesu im 17. Und 18. Jahrhundert.* Schnell&Steiner.

Negandhi, A. R. (1975). Comparative Management and Organization Theory: A Marriage Needed. *Academy of Management Journal, 18*(2), 334–344.

Negandhi, A. R. (1983). Cross-Cultural Management Research: Trend and Future Directions. *Journal of International Business Studies, 14*(2), 17–28.

Negandhi, A. R., & Prasad, S. B. (1971). *Comparative Management*. Appleton-Century-Crofts.

Nejime, K. (2014). Alessandro Valignano (1539-1606) between Padua and Japan. *Gakushūin Joshi Daigaku-kyō, 16*, 43–52.

Newitt, M. D. D. (2005). *A History of Portuguese Overseas Expansion, 1400-1668*. Routledge.

Newson, L.A. (2020). Introduction. In L.A. Newson (Ed.), *Cultural Worlds of the Jesuits in Colonial Latin America* (pp. 1–7). University of London Press.

Ng, K.-Y., Tan, M., & Ang, S. (2011). Global Culture Capital and Cosmopolitan Human Capital: The Effects of Global Mindset and Organizational Routines on Cultural Intelligence and International Experience. In A. Burton-Jones & J.-C. Spender (Eds.), *The Oxford Handbook of Human Capital*. Oxford University Press. https://www.oxfordhandbooks.com/view/10.1093/oxfordhb/97801995 32162.001.0001/oxfordhb-9780199532162-e-4

Niina, K. (2017). *Shimazu Takahisa: Sengoku Daimyō Shimazu-shi no tanjō*. Ebisu Kōshō Shuppan.

Nobili, R. de. (1971). *On Adaptation, trans. Of Narratio fondamentorum quibus Madurensis Missionis institutum coeptus est et hucusque consistit*. De Nobili Research Institute.

Nofuji, T., & Uchijima, M. (Eds.). (2017). *Shimabara Hantō no shinkō to rekishi: Ikki to sono go no Matsudaira-shi chisei*. Seinan Gakuin Daigaku Hakubutsukan.

Nonaka, I., & Reinmoeller, P. (1999). Knowledge Creation Architecture: Constructing the Places for Knowledge Assets and Competitive Advantage. In J. Engelhard & W. A. Oechsler (Eds.), *Internationales Management: Auswirkungen globaler Veränderungen auf Wettbewerb, Unternehmensstrategie und Märkte* (pp. 21–46). Springer.

Nonnemann, W. (2009). On the Economics of the Socialist Theocracy of the Jesuits in Paraguay (1609–1767). In M. Ferrero & R. Wintrobe (Eds.), *The Political Economy of Theocracy* (pp. 119–142). Palgrave Macmillan.

Nummela, N., Saarenketo, S., Jokela, P., & Loane, S. (2014). Strategic Decision-Making of a Born Global: A Comparative Study from Three Small Open Economies. *Management International Review, 54*(4), 527–550.

Nummela, N., Saarenketo, S., & Puumalainen, K. (2004). A Global Mindset: A Prerequisite for Successful Internationalization? *Canadian Journal of Administrative Sciences, 21*(1), 51–64.

Oberg, W. (1963). Cross-Cultural Perspective on Management Principles. *Academy of Management Journal, 6*(2), 141–143.

Oberholzer, P. (Eds.). (2015). *Diego Laínez (1512-1565) and his Generalate*. Institutum Historicum Societas Iesu.

Oehme, M., & Bort, S. (2015). SME Internationalization Modes in the German Biotechnology Industry: The Influence of Imitation, Network Position, and International Experience. *Journal of International Business Studies, 46*(6), 629–655.

Ogawa, S. (2010). On the Decay, Preservation and Restoration of Imported Portuguese Christian Missionary Vocabulary in the Kyushu District of Japan since the 16th Century. *Slavia Centralis, 3*(1), 150–161.

Ōhashi, Y. (1996). New Perspectives on the Early Tokugawa Persecution. In J. Breen & M. Williams (Eds.), *Japan and Christianity: Impacts and Responses* (pp. 46–62). St. Martin Press.

Ōhashi, Y. (2016). 16-19 seiki Nihon ni okeru kirishitan no juyō kinsei senpuku. *Kokubungaku kenkyū shiryōkan kiyō, 12,* 123–134.

Olin, J. C. (1979). The Idea of Pilgrimage in the Experience of Ignatius Loyola. *Church History, 48*(4), 387–397.

Oliveira e Costa, J. P. (1993). *Portugal e O Japão: O Século Namban.* Imprensa Nacional Casa da Moeda.

Oliveira e Costa, J. P. (1998). *O Cristianismo no Japão e o Episcopado de D. Luis Cerqueira.* Universidade Nova de Lisboa.

O'Malley, J. W. (1994). *The First Jesuits.* Harvard University Press.

O'Malley, J. W. (Eds.). (1999). *The Jesuits: Cultures, Sciences, and the Arts, 1540–1773.* Toronto University Press.

O'Malley, J. W. (2013). *Saints or Devils Incarnate? Studies in Jesuit History.* Brill.

Omata Rappo, H. (2020a). *Des Indes lointaines aux scènes des collèges: Les reflets des Martyrs de la mission japonaise en Europe (XVIe–XVIIIe siècle).* Aschendorff.

Omata Rappo, H. (2020b). Death on the Cross: The Beatification of the Twenty-Six Martyrs of Nagasaki (1627) and the Iconography of the Crucifixion. In Quiles García, F. Et al. (Eds.). *A la luz de Roma: Santos y santidad en el Barroco Iberoamericano, vol. iii: Tierra de santidad* (pp. 129–150). Enredars.

Omata Rappo, H. (2023). From the Cross to the Pyre: The Representation of the Martyrs of Japan in Jesuit Prints. *Journal of Jesuit Studies* 10(3), 456–486.

O'Reilly, T. (2020). The Spiritual Exercises and Illuminism in Spain: Dominican Critics of the Early Society of Jesus. *Journal of Jesuit Studies* 7(3), 377–402.

Oswald, J., & Rummel, P. (Eds.). (1996). *Petrus Canisius, Reformer der Kirche. Festschrift zum 400. Todestag des zweiten Apostels Deutschlands.* Sankt Ulrich.

Oviatt, B., & McDougall, P. (2005). Defining International Entrepreneurship and Modeling the Speed of Internationalization. *Entrepreneurship: Theory and Practice, 29*(5), 537–553.

Oviatt, B., & McDougall, P. (1994). Toward a Theory of International New Ventures. *Journal of International Business Studies, 25*(1), 45–64.

Oviatt, B., & McDougall, P. (1995). Global Start-Ups: Entrepreneurs on a Worldwide Stage. *Academy of Management Executive, 9*(2), 30–44.

Pacheco, D. (1971). Diogo de Mesquita, S.J. an the Jesuit Mission Press. *Monumenta Nipponica, 26*(3–4), 431–443.

Pacheco, D. (1973). *El hombre que forjó a Nagasaki. Vida del P. Cosme de Torres, S. J.* Apostoloda de la Prensa.

Pacheco, D. (1974). Xavier and Tanegashima. *Monumenta Nipponica, 29*(4), 477–480.

Pacheco, D. (1977). Iglesias de Nagasaki durante el "Siglo Cristiano", 1568-1620. *Boletín de la Asociación Española de Orientalistas, 13,* 49–70.

Pacheco, D. (1989). *Fundação do Porto de Nagasaki e a sua cedência à Sociedade de Jesus.* Centro de Estudos Marítimos de Macau.

Padberg, J. S. (1997). *Three Forgotten Founders of the Society of Jesus.* Society of Jesus.

Page, C. (2017). *La biografía del jesuita Marciel de Lorenzana, precursor de las misiones del Paraguay escrita por el P. Diego de Boroa*. Báez ediciones.
Page, C. (2018). Relación de las misiones del Paraguay del P. Marciel de Lorenzana (1621). *IHS: Antiguos Jesuitas en Iberoamérica*, 6(1), 128–157.
Paul, H. (2014). Christopher Columbus and the Myth of "Discovery". Transccript.
Pauluzzo, R., & Shen, B. (2018). *Impact of Culture on Management of Foreign SMEs in China*. Springer.
Pearce, A. J. (2020). Colonial Coda: The Andes–Amazonia Frontier under Spanish Rule. In A. J. Pearce, D. G. Beresford-Jones, & P. Heggarty (Eds.), *Rethinking the Andes–Amazonia Divide: A Cross-Disciplinary Exploration* (S. 313–324). University College London Press.
Pennec, H. (2003). *Des jésuites au royaume du Prêtre Jean (Éthiopie): Stratégies, rencontres et tentatives d'implantation 1495-1633*. Fundação Calouste Gulbenkian.
Perez Fernandez, I. (1988). *Bartolomé de Las Casas en el Perú. El espíritu lascasiano en la primera evangelización del imperio incaico (1531–1573)*. Centro de estudios regionales andinos Bartolomé de las Casas.
Pérez, L. (1920). Memoriales y otros documentos del P. Francisco de Montilla. *Archivum Franciscanum Historicum, 13*, 181–214.
Pérez, L. (1923). *Cartas y relaciones del Japon: Persecución y martirio de los misioneros franciscanos*. G. López del Horno.
Pérez Tudela y Buesco, J. (1998). *Obras clásicas para la historia de Iberoamérica*. Fundación Histórica Tavera.
Peterson, M. F., & Søndergaard, M. (Eds.). (2008). *Foundations of Cross Cultural Management: Vol. 4 vols*. Sage.
Pfefferman, T. (2016). Reassembling the Archives: Business History Knowledge Production from an Actor-Network Perspective. *Management & Organizational History, 11*(4), 380–398.
Piekkari, R., & Zander, L. (2005). Language and Communication in International Management. *International Studies of Management and Organization, 35*(1), 3–9.
Polgár, L. (1986). *Bibliographie sur l'histoire de la Compagnie de Jésus (1901-1980)*, vol. 2: Les pays. Amérique, Asie, Afrique, Océanie. IHSI.
Polo, F. C., & Rodríguez, C. R. (2014). Una revisión histórico-descriptiva de las empresas pioneras en el tratamiento de intangibles. *Intangible Capital, 10*(1), 125–154.
Porras Barrenechea, R. (1962). *Los cronistas del Perú (1528-1650)*. Sanmartí y Cía.
Prange, C., & Zhao, Y. (2018). Strategies for Internationalisation: How Chinese SMEs Deal with Distance and Market Entry Speed. In N. Dominguez & U. Mayrhofer (Eds.), *Key Success Factors of SME Internationalisation: A Cross Country Perspective* (pp. 205–224). Emerald.
Presbitero, A. (2021). Enhancing Intercultural Task Performance: Examining the Roles of Social Complexity Belief and Cultural Intelligence. *Personnel Review*. https://doi.org/10.1108/PR-03-2020-0198.

Quattrone, P. (2004). Accounting for God: Accounting and Accountability Practices in the Society of Jesus (Italy, XVI-XVII centuries). *Accounting, Organizations and Society, 29*(7), 647–683.

Quinn, P. A. (1981). Ignatius Loyola and Gian Pietro Carafa: Catholic Reformers at Odds. *The Catholic Historical Review, 67*(3), 386–400.

Radulet, C. (1994). O 'Cerimonial' do P. Alessandro Valignano: Encontro de culturas e missionação no Japão. In R. Carneiro (Ed.), *O Século Cristão do Japão: Actas do Colóquio Comemorativo dos 450 anos de amizade Portugal-Japão (1453-1993)* (pp. 55–69). Centro de Estudos dos Povos e Culturas de Expressão, Universidade Católica Portuguesa.

Rahner, K. (1979). *Ignatius of Loyola*. Collins.

Ramada Curto, D. (2005). The Jesuits as Intermediaries in Early Modern World. *Archivum Historicum Societatis Iesu, 74*(147), 3–22.

Ramsey, J. R., Aad, A. A., Jian, C., Barakat, L., & Drummond, V. (2016). Emergence of Cultural Intelligence and Global Mindset Capital: A Multilevel Model. *Multinational Business Review, 24*(2), 106–122.

Rasheed, H. S. (2005). Foreign Entry Mode and Performance: The Moderating Effects of Environment. *Journal of Small Business Management, 43*(1), 41–54.

Rasiah, R., & Thangiah, G. (2017). Government Policies, Regional Trading Agreements and the Economic Performance of Local Electronics Component Producing SMEs in Malaysia. *Journal of Southeast Asian Economies, 34*(2), 302–321.

Rask, M. (2014). Internationalization through Business Model Innovation: In Search of Relevant Design Dimensions and Elements. *Journal of International Entrepreneurship, 12*, 146–161.

Rassekh, F. (1998). The Convergence Hypothesis: History, Theory and Evidence. *Open Economies Review, 9*, 85–105.

Redondo Bonet, L. (2011). *Iezusu-kai no konseki: Nihon de okonawareta Iezusu-kai no āto seminariyo seido ni kansuru ikkōsatsu*. Tōkyō Geijutsu Daigaku.

Reinhard, W. (1976). Gelenkter Kulturwandel im Siebzehnten Jahrhundert: Akkulturation in den Jesuitenmissionen als universalhistorisches Problem. *Historische Zeitschrift, 223*(3), 529–590.

Ribadeneira, P. (1592). *Vida del. P. Francisco de Borja*. P. Madrigal.

Rieter, F. J. (1995). *They Built Utopia: The Jesuit Missions in Paraguay 1610–1768*. Scripta Humanistica.

Rocha, H. M. d. S. d. R. d. (2014). *O Oriente no Ocidente: O Japão na cultura portuguesa do século XVI - a visão de Luís Fróis nas Cartas de Évora*. Universidade Lusíada de Lisboa.

Rodrigues, J. (1604). *Arte da lingoa de Iapam*. Collegio de Iapão da Companhia de Iesu.

Rodrigues, J. (1976). *Pari-bon Nippo jisho/Vocabulario da lingoa de Iapam* (H. Ishizuka, ed.). Benseisha.

Roemer, B. B. (1946). *Foundations of the Jesuits in the Viceroyalty of Peru (1568-1605)*. Loyola University.

Rogge, J. (Ed.). (2013). *Making Sense as a Cultural Practice: Historical Perspectives*. Transcript.

Rojo-Mejuto, N. (2018). Los inicios de la lexicografía hispano-japonesa. *Revista de Lexicografía, 24*, 143–169.

Romani, L., Barmeyer, C., Primecz, H., & Pilhofer, K. (2018). Cross-Cultural Management Studies: State of the Field inthe Four Research Paradigms. *International Studies of Management and Organization, 48*(3), 1–17.

Romero, C. A. (Ed.). (1943). *Las crónicas de los Molinas: "Destrucción del Perú".* Domingo Miranda.

Roofe, M. E., & Stone Roofe, A. E. (2016). A Commentary on SMEs in Brazil: Lessons for Jamaica and the Caribbean. *Social and Economic Studies, 65*(2–3), 161–175.

Root, F. R. (1977). *Entry Strategies for Foreign Markets: From Domestic to International Business.* AMACOM.

Ross, A. C. (1994). *A Vision Betrayed: The Jesuits in Japan and China, 1542-1742.* Orbis Books.

Rowlinson, M., Hassard, J., & Decker, S. (2014). Research Strategies for Organizational History: A Dialogue Between Historical Theory and Organization Theory. *Academy of Management Review, 39*(3). https://doi.org/10.5465/amr.2012.0203.

Rubiés, J.-P. (2012). Real and Imaginary Dialogues in the Jesuit Mission of Sixteenth-century Japan. *Journal of the Economic and Social History of the Orient, 55*(2–3), 447–494.

Ruiz de Montoya, A. (1640). *Arte y vocabulario de la lengua Guarani.* J. Sánchez.

Russo, A., & Perrini, F. (2010). Investigating Stakeholder Theory and Social Capital: CSR in Large Firms and SMEs. *Journal of Business Ethics, 91*(2), 207–221.

Şahin, F., & Gürbüz, S. (2020). Entrepreneurial Orientation and International Performance: The Moderating Role of Cultural Intelligence. *Journal of Management & Organization, 26*(2), 263–287.

Saint Francis Xavier and the Roots of Christianity in Japan. (2015, August 27). Nippon.com.

Saito, A., Rosas Lauro, C., Ravi Mumford, J., Wernke S.A., Zuloaga Rada M., & y Spalding K. (2014). Nuevos avances en el estudio sobre las reducciones toledanas. *Bulletin of the National Museum of Ethnology, 39*(1), 123–167.

Saito, A., & Rosas Lauro, C. (Eds.). (2017). *Reducciones. La concentración forzada de las poblaciones indígenas en el virreinato del Perú.* Fondo editorial de la Pontificia Universidad Católica del Perú.

Saka-Helmhout, A. (2011). Comparative Historical Analysis in International Management Research. In R. Piekkari (Ed.), *Rethinking the Case Study in International Business and Management Research* (pp. 383–407). Edward Elgar.

Saladin, I. (2020). *Karten und Mission: Die jesuitische Konstruktion des Amazonasraums im 17. Und 18. Jahrhundert.* Mohr Siebeck.

Sánchez, M. P., Chaminade, C., & Olea, M. (2000). Management of Intangibles: An Attempt to Build a Theory. *Journal of Intellectual Capital, 1*(4), 312–327.

Sanchez Salgado, R. (2017). Professionnalisation ou amateurisme? Projets financés par UE dans le domaine d'emploi et la profession interculturelle. *Politique Européenne, 57*, 54–83.

Sarmento de Matos, J. (1989). *Sons de Lisboa: Uma Biografia de Valentim de Carvalho*. Dom Quixote.

Scarino, A. (2010). Assessing Intercultural Capability in Learning Languages: A Renewed Understanding of Language, Culture, Learning, and the Nature of Assessment. *The Modern Language Journal*, 94(2), 324–329.

Schauwecker, D. (2015). *Vom Wunder zur Magie Frühe japanische Christenwunder in west-östlicher Literatur* (Beiträge des Arbeitskreises Japanische Religionen). Universität Tübingen. https://publikationen.uni-tuebingen.de/xmlui/handle/10900/67489

Schilling, D. (1940). Neue Funde zu den Christlichen Druckereien Japans im 17. Jahrhundert. *Monumenta Nipponica*, 3(2), 648–653.

Schöndorf, H., & Funiok, R. (Eds.). (2018). *Ignatius von Loyola und die Pädagogik der Jesuiten: Ein Modell für Schule und Persönlichkeitsbildung*. Peter Lang.

Schurhammer, G. (1928). *Das kirchliche Sprachproblem in der japanischen Jesuitenmission de 16. Und 17. Jahrhunderts: Ein Stück Ritenfrage in Japan*. Deutsche Gesellschaft für Natur-u. Völkerkunde Ostasiens.

Schurhammer, G. (1929). *Die Disputationen des P. Cosme de Torres S.J. mit den Buddhisten i Yamaguchi im Jahre 1551*. Deutsche Gesellschaft für Natur- u. Völkerkunde Ostasiens.

Schütte, J. F. (1951). *Valignanos Missionsgrundsätze für Japan* (vol. 1). Edizioni di Storia e Letteratura.

Schütte, J. F. (1967). Die Wirksamkeit der Päpste für Japan im ersten Jahrhundert der japanischen Kirchengeschichte (1549-1650): Versuch einer Zusammenfassung. *Archivum Historiae Pontificiae*, 5, 175–261.

Schütte, J. F. (1975). *Monumenta Historica Japoniae, vol. 1: Textus catalogorum Japoniae aliaeque de personis domibusque S.J. in Japonia informationes et relationes, 1549-1654*. Monumenta Historica Soc. Iesu.

Schwarzkopf, S. (2013). 'Culture' and the Limits of Innovation in Marketing: Ernest Dichter, Motivation Studies and Psychoanalytic Consumer Research in Great Britain, 1950s–1970s. *Management & Organizational History*, 2(3), 219–236.

Schwemmer, P. (2014). My Child Deus: Grammar versus Theology in a Japanese Christian Devotional of 1591. *Journal of Jesuit Studies*, 1(3), 465–482.

Scott, H. V. (2009). *Contested Territory: Mapping Peru in the Sixteenth and Seventeenth Centuries*. University of Notre Dame Press.

Segovia Gordillo, A. (2020). Las gramáticas misioneras sobre la lengua quechua a través de sus paratextos. *Nueva Revista de Filología Hispánica*, 68(2), 451–497.

Sestu, M. C., Majocchi, A., & D'Angelo, A. (2018). Entry Mode Strategies: Are SMEs Any Different? In N. Dominguez & U. Mayrhofer (Eds.), *Key Success Factors of SME Internationalisation: A Cross Country Perspective* (pp. 63–80). Emerald.

Shore, P. (2007). Recent Studies in Jesuit History. *Journal of Religious History*, 31(3), 316–323.

Sievernich, M. (2002). Von der Akkomodation zur Inkulturation: Missionarische Leitideen der Gesell schaft Jesu. *Zeitschrift für Missionswissenschaft und Religionswissenschaft*, 86, 260–276.

Sievernich, M. (2005). Mission und Missionen der Gesellschaft Jesu. In J. Meier (Ed.), *Sendung, Eroberung, Begegnung: Franz Xaver, die Gesellschaft Jesu und die katholische Weltkirche im Zeitalter des Barock* (pp. 7–30). Harrassowitz.

Sioris, G. A. (1997). Luís Fróis: Chronicler and Interpreter of Japan, a Jesuit Between Two Countries. In Comissão Territorial de Macau para as Comemorações dos Descobrimentos Portugueses (Eds.), *Luís Fróis: Proceedings of the International Conference, United Nations University, Tokyo, September 24-26, 1997* (pp. 3–17). Embassy of Portugal in Japan.

Siu, W., & Liu, Z. (2005). Marketing in Chinese Small and Medium Enterprises (SMEs): The State of the Art in a Chinese Socialist Economy. *Small Business Economics, 25*(4), 333–346.

Smith, G. E. (2007). Management History and Historical Context: Potential Benefits of Its Inclusion in the Management Curriculum. *Academy of Management Learning & Education, 6*(4), 522–533.

Smith, P. B., Peterson, M. F., & Thomas, D. C. (2008). *The Handbook of Cross-Cultural Management Research*. Sage.

Soto Antuñedo, W. (2016a). Alonso de Barzana S.I Apóstol de Andalucía y Sudamérica. *Archivo Teológico Granadino, 79*, 5–130.

Soto Antuñedo, W. (2016b). El deseo de las Indias: Las cartas indípetas de Alonso de Barzana SJ (1530–1598). *Archivum Historicum Societatis Iesu, 85*, 405–444.

Soto Antuñedo, W. (2018). *Alonso de Barzana SJ, (1530-1590): El Javier de las Indias Occidentales*. Loyola & Mensajero.

Sousa, Lúcio de. (2010). *The Early European Presence in China, Japan, the Philippines and Southeast Asia (1555-1590): The Life of Bartolomeu Landeiro*. Fundação Macau.

Sousa Pinto, P. J. d. (2012). *The Portuguese and the Straits of Melaka, 1575-1619: Power, Trade, and Diplomacy*. NUS Press.

Spencer-Oatey, H., & Franklin, P. (2009). *Intercultural Interaction: A Multidisciplinary Approach to Intercultural Communication*. Palgrave Macmillan.

Stahl, G. K., & Tung, R. L. (2015). Towards a More Balanced Treatment of Culture in International Business Studies: The Need for Positive Cross-Cultural Scholarship. *Journal of International Business Studies, 46*(4), 391–414.

Steinkerchner, S. (2020). Introduction: Dominicans and Jesuits, through the Centuries. *Journal of Jesuit Studies* 7(3), 357–376.

Stern, S. (1982). *Peru's Indigenous Peoples and the Challenge of Spanish Conquest: Huamanga to 1640*. University of Wisconsin Press.

St-Pierre, J., Lacoursière, R., & Veileux, S. (2018). Québec SME Risk Managemet and Exports to Asian Countries. In N. Dominguez & U. Mayrhofer (Eds.), *Key Success Factors of SME Internationalisation: A Cross Country Perspective* (pp. 175–193). Emerald.

Strasser, U. (2020). *Missionary Men in the Early Modern World: German Jesuits and Pacific Journeys*. Amsterdam University Press.

Stutz, C., & Sachs, S. (2018). Facing the Normative Challenges: The Potential of Reflexive Historical Research. *Business & Society, 57*(1). https://doi.org/10.11 77/0007650316681989.

Subhan, Q. A., Mahmood, T., & Sattar, A. (2014). Innovation and Economic Development: A Case of Small and Medium Enterprises in Pakistan. *Pakistan Economic and Social Review, 52*(2), 159–174.

Suddaby, R. (2016). Toward a Historical Consciousness: Following the Historic Turn in Management Thought. *M@n@gement, 19*(1), 46–60.

Sumati, V. (2011). Born Global Acquirers from Indian IT: An Exploratory Case Study. *International Journal of Emerging Markets, 6*(4), 351–368.

Swope, K. (2016). *A Dragon's Head and a Serpent's Tail: Ming China and the First Great East Asian War, 1592 1598*. University of Oklahoma Press.

Takahashi, M. (2001). A Portuguese Clavichord in Sixteenth-Century Japan? *The Galpin Society Journal, 54*, 116–123.

Takase, K. (2013). Kirishitan jidai Iezusu-kai korejio (Yamaguchi, Hirado, Ikitsuki, Chijiwa, Arie, Kazusa, Amakusa) ni tsuite. *Shigaku, 82*(3), 235–309.

Takase, K. (1993). *Kirishitan no seiki: Zabieru tonichi kara sakoku made*. Yoshikawa Kōbunkan.

Takase, K. (1994). *Kirishitan jidai taigai kankei*. Yoshikawa Kōbunkan.

Taylor, S., Bell, E., & Cooke, B. (2009). Business History and the Historiographical Operation. *Management & Organizational History, 4*(2), 151–166.

Teece, D. J. (2010). Business Model, Business Strategy and Innovation. *Long Range Planning, 43*(2–3), 172–194.

Telles, B. (1645). *Chronica da Companhia de IESU, na provincia de Portugal, e o que fizeram d'este Reyno, os Religiosos que na mesma Provincia entràram, nos annos em que viveo S. Inacio de Loyola, Nosso Fundador*. Paulo Craesbeeck.

Thanh, H. V. (2016). Un équilibre impossible: Financer la mission jésuite du Japon, entre Europe et Asie (1579-1614). *Revue d'histoire moderne et contemporaine (1954-), 63*(3), 7–30.

Thanh, H. V. (2018). L'économie des objets de dévotion en terres de mission. *Archives de sciences sociales des religions, 63*(183), 207–226.

Thomas, A. (1988). Untersuchungen zur Entwicklung eines interkulturellen Handlungstrainings in der Managerausbildung. *Psychologische Beiträge, 30*, 147–165.

Thomas, D. C. (2014). Cross-Cultural Management. In *Oxford Bibliographies*. https://www.oxfordbibliographies.com/view/document/obo-9780199846740/obo-9780199846740-0074.xml

Thomas, D. C., & et al. (2015). Cultural Intelligence: A Theory-Based, Short Form Measure. *Journal of International Business Studies, 46*(9), 1099–1118.

Thurner, M. (2009). The Founding Abyss of Colonial History: Or "The Origin and Principle of the Name of Peru". *History and Theory, 48*(1), 44–62.

Thurner, M. (2011). *History's Peru: The Poetics of Colonial and Postcolonial Historiography*. University of Florida Press.

Tōkyō Daigaku Shiryō Hensanjo (Eds.). (1990). *Iezusukai Nihon shokanshū*. 2 vols. Tōkyō Daigaku Shiryō Hensanjo.

Torkkeli, L., Nummela, N., & Saarenketo, S. (2018). A Global Mindset: Still a Prerequisite for Successful SME Internationalisation? In N. Dominguez & U. Mayrhofer (Eds.), *Key Success Factors of SME Internationalisation: A Cross Country Perspective* (pp. 7–24). Emerald.

Torres, A. M. (1932). *El Padre Valverde: Ensayo biográfico y crítico*. Editorial Ecuatoriana.
Torres Saldamando, E. (1906). Padre Jerónimo Ruiz de Portillo, primer Provincial en el Perú. *Revista Histórica, 1*, 445–455.
Toyama, M. (2011). *Chūsei Nagasaki no kisoteki kenkyū*. Shibunkaku Shuppan.
Tremml-Werner, B. (2015). *Spain, China, and Japan in Manila, 1571-1644*. Amsterdam University Press.
Trigault, N. (1623). *De Christianis apud Japonios triumphis sive de gravissima ibidem contra Christi fidem persecutione exorta anno MDCXII usque ad annum MDCXX*. Sadeler.
Tronu Montane, C. (2012a). Mercaderes y frailes españoles en el Japón del Siglo de Oro. In M. J. Zamora Calvo (Ed.), *Japón y España: Acercamientos y desencuentros (siglos XVI y XVII)* (S. 255–265). Satori.
Tronu Montane, C. (2012b). *Sacred Space and Ritual in Early Modern Japan: The Christian Community of Nagasaki (1569-1643)*. SOAS University of London.
Tronu Montane, C. (2012c). The Jesuit Accommodation Method in 16th and 17th Century Japan. In J. Martínez Millán, H. Pizarro Llorente, & E. Jiménez Pablo (Eds.), *Los Jesuitas: Religión, política y educación (Siglos XVI-XVIII)* (pp. 1617–1642). UNE.
Tronu Montane, C. (2015). The Rivalry between the Society of Jesusand the Mendicant Orders in Early Modern Nagasaki. *Agora: Journal of International Center for Religious Studies, 12*. https://www.researchgate.net/publication/278715051_The_rivalry_between_the_Jesuits_and_the_Mendicant_orders_in_Nagasaki_at_the_end_of_the_sixteenth_century_and_the_beginning_of_the_seventeenth_century.
Tutino, J. (2021). Capitalism, Christianity, and Slavery: Jesuits in New Spain, 1572–1767. *Journal of Jesuit Studies* 8(1), 11–36.
Tylenda, J. N. (2001). *A Pilgrim's Journey: The Autobiography of Ignatius of Loyola*. Ignatius Press.
Üsdiken, B., & Kipping, M. (2021). *History in Management and Organization Studies: From Margin to Mainstream*. Routledge.
Valignano, A. (1601). *Libro primero del principio y progresso de la religión Christiana en Jappón y de la especial providencia de que Nuestro Señor usa con aquella nueva iglesia*. British Museum Additional manuscript 9857.
Valignano, A. (1943). *Les Instructions du Père Valignano pour l'ambassade japonaise en Europe* (P. Abranches & H. Bernard, eds.). Sophia University.
Valignano, A. (1946). *Il Cerimoniale per i missionari del Giappone: Advertimentos e avisos acerca dos costumes e catangues de Jappão di Alexandro Valignano* (J. F. Schütte, ed.). Edizioni di Storia e Letteratura.
Valignano, A. (1954). *Sumario de las cosas de Japón (1583)* (J. L. Alvarez-Taladriz, ed.). Sophia University.
Vande Walle, W. F. (1996). The Language Barrier in the History of Japanese-European Relations. *Kyoto Conference on Japanese Studies 1994, 3*, 345–356. https://doi.org/10.15055/00003569.
Van Lent, W., & Durepos, G. (2019). Nurturing the Historic Turn: "History as Theory" versus "History as Method." *Journal of Management History, 25*(4), 429–443.

Vargas Ugarte, R. (1963). *Historia de la Compañía de Jesús en el Perú: Bd. 4. vols.* Aldecoa.

Venn, H. (1862). *The Missionary Life and Labours of Francis Xavier Taken from His Own Correspondence: With a Sketch of the General Results of Roman Catholic Missions Among the Heathen.* Longman, Green, Longman, Roberts, & Green.

Vitelleschi, M. (1632). *Iaerliicksche brieven van Iaponien der jaren 1625. 1626. 1627.* Jan Cnobbaert.

Vlam, G. A. H. (1979). The Portrait of S. Francis Xavier in Kobe. *Zeitschrift für Kunstgeschichte, 42*(1), 48–60.

Wadhwani, R. D. (2016). Historical Methods for Contextualizing Entrepreneurship Research. In F. Welter & W. B. Gartner (Eds.), *A Research Agenda for Entrepreneurship and Context* (pp. 134–145). Edward Elgar.

Wadhwani, R. D., & Decker, S. (2017). Clio's Toolkit: The Practice of Historical Methods in Organization Studies. In S. Jain & R. Mir (Eds.), *Routledge Companion to Qualitative Research in Organization Studies* (pp. 113–127). Routledge.

Watanabe, A. (2023). *Japan on the Jesuit Stage: Two 17th-Century Latin Plays with Translation and Commentary.* Bloomsbury.

Weaver, B. J. M. (2018). Rethinking the Political Economy of Slavery: The Hacienda Aesthetic at the Jesuit Vineyards of Nasca, Peru. *Post-Medieval Archaeology, 52*(1), 117–133.

Welch, C., Piekkari, R., Plakoyiannaki, E., & Paavilainen-Mäntymäki, E. (2011). Theorising from Case Studies: Towards a Pluralist Future for International Business Research. *Journal of International Business Studies, 42*, 740–762.

Whitley, R. (1999). *Divergent Capitalisms: The Social Structuring and Change of Business Systems.* Oxford University Press.

Wicki, J. (1968). *Documenta Indica: Bd. 10: (1575-1577).* Monumenta Historica Soc. Iesu.

Willert, P. F. (1887). The Jesuits and the Renaissance. *The English Historical Review, 2*(6), 336–338.

Winnerling, T. (2014). *Vernunft und Imperium: Die Societas Jesu in Indien und Japan, 1542–1574.* Vandenhoeck & Rupprecht.

Wirtz, P. (2020, January 29). Ce que la gouvernance des ordres catholiques dit de la pérennité des organisations. *The Conversation.* https://theconversation.com/ce-que-la-gouvernance-des-ordres-catholiques-dit-de-la-perennite-des-organisations-130493

Wohltmann, H.-W. (2018). Humankapital. In *Gabler Wirtschaftslexikon.* https://wirtschaftslexikon.gabler.de/definition/humankapital-32920

Wolde Aregay, M. (1998). The Legacy of Jesuit Missionary Activities in Ethiopia from 1555 to 1632. In G. Haile, A. Lande, & S. Rubenson (Eds.), *The Missionary Factor in Ethiopia: Papers from a Symposium on the Impact of European Missions on Ethiopian Society, Lund University, August 1996* (pp. 53–55). Peter Lang.

Wong, T. (2017). *Matteo Ricci's Xiqin Quyi: A Jesuit's Expert Musicking in Ming China.* Georg-August-Universität Göttingen.

Xavier, St. F. (1552). *Letter from Japan, to the Society of Jesus in Europe, 1552.* https://my.tlu.edu/ICS/icsfs/EurosinAsiaSources9pg.pdf?target=f95413e2-209d-4e7f-a324-456e70da7a3d

Yamamoto, Y. (2012). Scholasticism in Early Modern Japan. *Mediaevalia: Textos e estudos, 31,* 251–279.

Zamora, J. P. d. (1997). *Historia de la pérdida y descubrimiento del galeón „San Felipe"* (J. Martínez Pérez, ed.). Institución „Gran Duque de Alba" de la Diputación Provincial de Ávila.

Zampol D'Ortia, L. (2020). The Dress of Evangelization: Jesuit Garments, Liturgical Textiles, and the Senses in Early Modern Japan. *Entangled Religions, 10.* https://doi.org/10.13154/er.10.2020.8438

Zavala, A. J., & Tamiyo, K. O. (2012). Yaso kunjin kitô genbun: Texto original de las oraciones del catequista cristiano (1658-1712). *Relaciones: Estudios de historia y sociedad, 33*(131), 183–241.

Zhang, X., Ma, Z., Wang, Y., Li, X., & Huo, D. (2016). What Drives the Internationalization of Chinese SMEs? The Joint Effect of National Entrepreneurship Characteristics, Network Ties and Ownership. *International Business Review, 25*(2), 522–534.

Zhou, L., Wu, W., & Luo, X. (2007). Internationalization and the Performance of Born-Global SMEs: The Mediating Role of Social Networks. *Journal of International Business Studies, 38*(4), 673–690.

Zott, C., & Amit, R. (o. J.). Business Model Design: An Activity System Perspective. *Long Range Planning, 43*(2–3), 216–226.

Zou, S., & Cavusgil, S. T. (2002). The GMS: A Broad Conceptualizationn of Global Marketing Strategy and Its Effect on Firm Performance. *Journal of Marketing, 66,* 40–56.

Zubillaga, F. (1943). Métodos misionales de la primera Instrucción de San Francisco de Borja para la América española. *Archivum Historicum Societatis Iesu, 12,* 58–88.

Županov, I. G. (2016). The Historiography of the Jesuit Missions in India (1500–1800). In *Jesuit Historiography Online.* http://dx.doi.org/10.1163/2468-7723_jho_COM_192579.

Appendices

9.1. Appendix 1: Jesuit Missionaries in Japan 1549-1614[1]

The following people could be identified in the regular reports (collected in MHJ) as Jesuits who had served in Japan between 1549 and 1614. Information has been gathered for Padres, usually the leading members of the mission during their time of service. The different spellings are a consequence of the ones provided in the original source, which had been kept here for reasons of documentation accuracy. In the data set and the manager portfolios presented in the case studies, they have, however, been anglicized.

9.1.1. Entry Period (1549-1563)

1553
P[adre]. Cosmo de Torres
P. Baltasar Gago
Juan Hernandes
Pero de Alcáceva
Duarte da Silva

1555
O P. M. Melchior [Núnez Barreto]
Cosmo de Torres
P. Balthesar Guago
P. Gaspar Vilella
Joam Fernández
António Díaz
Fernán Méndez
Melchior Díaz
Luís Fróis
Estávan de Góis
Duarte da Silva

1558
P. Cosmo de Torres
P. Baltezar Gago
P. Gaspar Vilella
I[rmão] (brother) Joáo Fernández
I. Duarle da Sylva
I. Luís d'Aimeyda
I. Ruy Pereyra

1559
P. Cosmo de Torres
P. Baltezar Gago
P. Gaspar Vilella
I. Yoão Fernández
I. Duarte da Silva
l. Luís Dalmeida
l. Ruy Pereira
l. Guilherme

1561
P. Cosmo de Torres
P. Baltasar Gago
P. Gaspar Vilella
I. João Fernández
I. Lourenço

---

[1] The information is provided according to the MJH, part 1 "A Fundata Missione Japonica Usque Ad Exilium," 1-609.

I. Gilherme [Pereira]
I. Duarte da Silva
I. Rui Pireyra
I. Luís Dalmeyda

1562/63
P. Cosmus Torres, Superior
P. Ludovicus Fróis

P. Gaspar Vilela
P. Joannes Baptisla
Fr[ater] Joannes Fernández
Fr. Duardus Selva
Fr. Ludovicus Almeida
Fr. Guilhermus
Fr. Laurentius

9.1.2. Consolidation Period (1564-1587)

1564
P. Cosme de Torres
P. Belchior de Figeiredo
P. Luis Fróes
P. Joam Cabral
P. Baltesar da Costa
P. João Baptista [de Monte]
P. Gaspar Vilela
I. Joam Fernández
I. Luis Dalmeida
I. Gilherme [Pereira]
I. Aires Sanches
I. Jácome Gonçálvez
I. Miguel Vaz

P. Organtino
P. Luis Fróis
P. Balthasar de Acosta
P. Melchior de Figueredo
P. Juan Baptista [de Monte]
P. Balthasar López
P. Balthasar [= Sebastião] González
P. Gaspar Coello
P. Juan Viejo
H[ermano] Miguel Vázquez
H. Arias Sánchez
H. Diego Hernández
H. Antonio Núñez
H. Guillelmo

1571
P. Francisco Cabral, Superior
P. Organtino
P. Luis Fróis
P. Balthezar da Costa
P. Belchior de Figeiredo
P. Joam Baptista [de Monte]
P. Sebastião Gonçálvez
P. Gaspar Coelho
P. Ballbezar Lopes
I. Migel Vaaz
I. Luís Dalmeida
I. Aires Sanches
I. Gilherme [Pereira]

1575
P. Francisco Cabral, Superior
P. Luis Fróes
P. Bastião Gonçálvez
P. Gaspar Coelho
P. Balthezar da Costa
P. Belchior de Figueiredo
P. João Baptista [de Monle]
P. Balthezar López
P. Organtino
I. Guilherme
I. Luís d'Almeida
I. Aires Sanches
I. Miguel Vaaz

1572
P. Francisco Cabral, Superior

Appendices

1576[2]
P. Francisco Cabral, Superior
P. Gaspar Coelho
P. Organtino
P. Bastião Gonçálvez
P. Luís Fróis
P. Belchior de Figueyredo
P. Balthezar López
P. João Francisco [Stephanoni], Italiano
P. Christóvão de Lyão
P. Afonso Gonçálvez
P. António López
P. João Baptista [de Monte], Ferrarez.
P. Pero Ramón
P. Balthezar López [o Grande]
P. Belchior de Moura
P. Gregório Céspedes
P. Gonçallo Rabello
P. André Pinto
I. Francisco Laguna
I. Francisco Carrión
I. Diogo da Mesquita
I. Symeão Dalmeiyda
I. Álvaro Dias
I. Diogo Pereyra
I. Bertolameo Redondo
I. Luis Dalmeyda
I. Áyres Sanches
I. Miguel Vaz
I. Guilherme
I. João, japponese, com outros dous Irmãos noviços (Japanese, with two other novice brothers).

P. Bispo da China [D. Belchior Carneiro]

1581[3]
Bungo
P. Francisco Cabral (Superior)
P. Pedro Remão (Master of the novices)
P. Francisco de Laguna
I. Gaspar Martins
I. João de Crastro
I. Domingos Fernández
I. André Dória
I. João de Torres (Japanese)

Portuguese Novices
I. Joáo Bernardes
I. Jerónymo Correa
I. Simáo Gonçálvez
I. Pedro Carrasco
I. Francisco Dória

Japanese Novices
I. Lino
I. Simão
I. Lião de Tacata
I. Jião
I. Ignácio
I. Bélchior

Collegio de S. Paulo (Búgo)
P. Belchior de Figueiredo, Reitor
P. Antonino, Meslre
P. Álvaro Díaz

---

[2] Starting in 1576, the reports provide some information about the language skills in two categories, namely "Confessáo na língoa da terra" (Confession in the language of the land) for fathers (padres) and "Sabem a língoa" (Know the language) for the brothers (irmãos).
[3] In 1581, the list of Jesuits in Japan is for the first time listed according to the places and their respective "Casa," where the Jesuits were active. It shows that the missionary activities were spread, although sometimes only a few missionaries served in rather "peripheral" regions.

I. Manoel Borralho, so t oministro, Porluges
I. Jofo Paulo (Japanese)
I. Miguel (Japanese)
I. Miguel Soares
I. Pedro Coelho
I. Amador de Góis
I. João Rodríguez
I. Luis D'Abreu

Yu
P. Gonçalo Rabello
I. Mathias (Japanese, preacher)

Noççu
P. João Bautista
I. Fanca Lião (Japanese, preacher)

Meacò (Yamaxirò)
P. João Francisco
I. Berlholameu Redondo
I. Cosme (Japanese, preacher)

Anzuchiyama (Nabunága)
P. Organtino
P. Carrião
P. Diogo de Misquita
I. Simeão
I. Diogo Pereira
I. Lourenço (Japanese, preacher)
I. Vicente (Japanese, preacher)

Sonocúni [= Tsunokuni]
P. Joseph Furtanele
I. Jerónymo Vaz

Vacay
P. Gregório de Céspedes
I. Paulo (Japanese, preacher)

Árima (Figen)
P. Melchior de Moura
P. Christóvão de Moreira
I. João de Milão
I. Ambrósio da Cruz
I. Jorge (Japanese)

Árima (Árie)
P. Alonso González
I. António Alvarez
I. Roque (Japanese, preacher)

Cochinóççu
P. Balthesar López
I. Guilhelme

Omura
P. Lucena
I. Francisco Fernández

Curi
P. Christóvão Lião
I. Nicolao (Japanese)

Nágasaqui
P. Gaspar Coelho
P. Luís Fróes
P. Miguel Vaz
P. Aries Sanches
I. Ambrósio Fernández
I. Roque (Japanese, preacher)

Firando
P. Balthesar López
P. Bastião Gonçálvez

Ura (Amacúsa)
P. Júlio Piano

Fondo
P. António López
I. Gomes (Japanese)

Appendices

Cutami
P. Luis D'Almeida

1583
P. Gaspar Coelho
P. Luís Fróis
P. Pedro Gomes
P. Organtino
P. Melchior de Figeiredo
P. Bastiáo Gonçálvez
P. João Baptista de Monte
P. Melchior de Moura
P. Pedro Ramón
P. Baltezar Lopes (Firando)
P. Ayres Sanches
P. Afonso de Lusena
P. Christóvão de Lião
P. Jorge de Carvalhal
P. Antóni Lopes
P. Álvoro Dias
P. Francisco Pássio
P. Damião Marín
P. Baltezar Lopes (Arima)
P. Alfonso González
P. Julioo Piani
P. Francisco de Laguna
P. Christóvão Moreira
P. Antonino Prenestino
P. Gonsallo Rabelo
P. Joseph Fortaneti
P. João Francisco
P. Francisco Carrião
P. Gregório de Céspedes

European irmãos
I. Miguel Soares
I. Amador De Góis
I. João Rodriges
I. Pero Coelho
I. Joã de Milão
I. António Álvarez
I. Manoel Borralho
I. Jerónimo Correa
I. Luís D'Abreu
I. Simão Gonçalvez
I. Francisco Dória
I. André Dória
I. Ambrózio da Crus
I. Francisco Pires
I. João Niculao
I. Jerónimoo Vaz
I. Simeão D'Almeida
I. Jácome de Navais
I. Domingos Dias
I. Gaspar Carvalho
I. Francisco Fernandes
I. Domingos Fernández
I. Guilherme
I. João Bernardes
I. Ambrózio Fernández
I. Jerardino
I. Diogo Prereira
I. Bertolameru Redondo
I. João de Crasto
I. Gaspar Martínez

Japanese irmãos
I. Niculao
I. Afonso
I. Gomes
I. Jião
I. Ynácio
I. Bastião
I. Simão
I. Gaspar
I. André
I. Thomé
I. Lourenso
I. Damião
I. Roque
I. Yofo Paulo
I. Vicente
I. João de Torres
I. Paulo

I. Cosme
I. Miguel
I. Mathias
I. Francão Lião
I. Simão
I. Liãoo do Tacata
I. Romão
I. Melchior
I. Lino

1587[4]
P. Gaspar Coelius
P. Aloicius Fróis
F. Damianus de Chicugen (Japanese)

Ximi
P. Melchior de Mora
P. Antonius Fernández
P. Marcus Ferrarius
P. Alvarus Diaz,
F. Joanes de Milano
F. Antonius Álvarez
F. Jacobus de Navais
F. Joanes Bernárdez
F. Dominicus Diaz
F. Linus (Japanese)

Chingivana
P. Balthasar López
F. Alonsus (Japanese)

Ariensi and Cochinocensi
P. Petrus Paulus [Navarro]
F. Rocus (Japanese)
F. Gulielmus [Pereira]

Nangasaquensis
P. Antonius López
P. Joanes de Crasto

P. Sebastianus Gonçales
P. Julius Pianus
F. Gómez (Japanese)
F. Ambrosius Fernández

Domus Omurensis
P. Alfonsus de Lucen
P. Christophorus de Leone [de León]
P. Franciscus Rodríguez
F. Franciscus Fernández
F. Nicolaus (Japanese)

Domus Firandensis
P. Joanes Baptista
P. Aries Sanches
F. Leo de Tacata (Japanese)

Domus Amacuçanensis
P. Alfonsus González
P. Balthasar López
F. Franciscus Pírez
F. Sebastianus [Kimura] Firandensis (Japanese)

Fundensi [= Hondo (Amakusa)]
P. Antonius Franciscus Chritana
F. Thoma Firandensis (Japanese)

In regione Bunguense. In Collegio Funayensi.
P. Petrus Gómez
P. Franciscus Calderonus
P. Joanes Rodríguez [Giram]
P. Fulvius Gregorius
F. Joanes de Torres
F. Balthasar Correa
F. Michael Soares
F. Joanes Rodríguez [Tçuzu]
F. Petrus Coelius

---

[4] In 1587 more than 100 Jesuits were listed for the first time.

Appendices

F. Amator de Góis
F. Hieronymus Correa
F. Aloicius de Abreo
F. Andreas de Ória
F. Franciscus de Óória
F. Gaspar Carvalius
F. Joanes Gómez
F. Philippus Gómez
F. Franciscus Carvalius
F. Simon de Ōmura (Japanese)
F. Petrus [Chikuan] de Cochin (Japanese)

Sucumensi [= Tsukumi (Bungo)]
P. Franciscus Laguna
F. Paulus [Ryōin] de Amacuça

Nochuensi [= Notsu (Bungo)]
P. Joannes Franciscus Stephanonius
F. Michael de Cansuça [Katsusa]

Usuquensis
P. Petrus Ramonus
P. Franciscus Pérez
P. Theodoro Mantels
F. Emanuel Borralius
F. Joanes Gerardinus
F. Yofu Paulus (Japanese)
F. Romanus (Japanese)

Japanese Novices
F. Matheus [Tokumaru] de Tacata
F. Thomas de Figén
F. Linus de Figén
F. Dominicus de Firando
F. Cosmus [Tomunaga] de Nangaye
F. Simeon de Bungo
F. Fabianus de Goquinay
F. Joanes de Vomi
F. Joanes de Sunocùni
F. Thomas [Kimura] de Çunocùni
F. Michael [Kimura] de Çunocùni

F. Paulus [Miki] de Çunocùni

Yuénsi [Yu-no-in (Bungo)]
P. Gonçalus Rebellus
F. Simon de Goquinay (Japanese)

Xinganensi [= Shiga (Bungo)]
P. Joanes Rodríguez
F. Thoma Bunguensis (Japanese)

Miochensi [= Myoken (Buzen)]
P. Georgius Carvalhal
F. Fanca Leo (Japanese)

Amangucensi [= Yamaguchi (Suwo)]
P. Cristophorus de Morera
F. Gaspar [Sadamatsu) de Ōmura (Japanese)

Iio [= Iyo (Shikoku)]
P. Franciscus Carrionus
F. Sebastianus de Osay (Japanese)

Vosaca
P. Organtinus
P. Gregorius de Céspedes
P. Damianus Marinus
F. Hieronymus Vaz
F. Joannes Nicolaus
F. Vincenlius de Vacasa (Japanese)
F. Guianes [Mori] de Çunocùni

Sacayensi Residentia
P. Franciscus Passius
P. Celsus Confalonerus
F. Bartholomeus Rodondus
F. Laurentius de Figén (Japanese)

Residentia Meacensi
P. Petrus Crassus
P. Antoninus
F. Didacus Pereira

F. Cosmus [Takai] de Meaco (Japanese)

Tacasuchensi [= Takatsuki (Settsu)]
P. Gil de Mata

F. Ignalius de Miaco (Japanese)

Acacensi [= Akashi (Harima)]
P. Joseph Fornatelus
F. Andrcas de Amacuça (Japanese)

9.1.3. Period of Decline (1588-1614)

Decline (1588-1614)
1589[5]
Cazzuça
P. Gaspar Coelho
P. Luís Fróis
I. Vomi João
I. Ambrósio Fernández
I. André Douria

Arima
P. Francisco Laguna
P. Celso
I. João Bernardes
I. Romão de Bungo

Quchinoççu
P. Gonçalo Rebelo
I. Guilherme

Arie
P. Francisco Calderón
P. Francisco Peres
I. Ambrósio de Bayrros
I. Fransicso Douria
I. Francisco Carvalho
I. Francisco Pires
I. Thomé de Firando
I. Simão de Vomura
I. Miguel Colaço

I. Miguel do Cami [Kimura]
I. Thoma do Cami [Kimura]
I. Jorge do Cami
I. Ximizu João do Cami
I. Miqui Paulo do Cami
I. Jião do Facata
I. Marino do Tacaqu
I. Francisco de Fiunga
I. Bastião de Bungo
I. Semião de Bungo
I. Matheus de Bungo
I. Cosme de Nagaye
I. Jião do Cami
I. Roque
I. João Nicolao
I. Luis de Nagasaqui
I. Jácome de Navais
P. António Fernández
I. Paulo de Bungo

Mie and Ximabara
P. Álvaro Dias
I. Domingos Dias
I. Basitam de Firand[o]
I. Pedro de Cu
Seminário de Fachiravo
P. Damião Marín
I. João Rodriguez
I. Diogo Pereira

---

[5] The report lists 116 Jesuits – Padres 37, Irmãos de Europa 19, and Irmãos japõis 60 and for the first time a majority of the Jesuits were Japanese, although almost all were listed as irmãos. The upper management consequently remained in the hands of Jesuit padres from Europe, mostly Portugal and Spain.

I. Phelipe Gómez

Amacuça
P. Afonço González
P. João Francisco
P. Marcos Ferraro
I. Bertholomeu Redondo
I. Simão do Fingo

Cavachinoura
P. Pedro Ramón
P. António Francisco
I. Gaspar Carvalho
I. Lião do Cami
I. Luís do Cami
I. Fabião do Cami
I. João de Torres de Yamaguchi
I. Nicolao do Cami
I. António de Firando
I. Yofo Paulo de Vacaça
I. Augustinho de Vomura
I. Amador de Nagasaqui
I. Mathias do Tacaqu
I. Thome de Sonogui
I. Melchior de Nagasaqui
I. António do Cami
I. Francisco do Cami
I. Máncio de Amacubo
I. Paulo de Sonongui
I. Máximo do Cami
I. Lionardo de Firando
I. Jullião do Cami
I. Miguel do Ysaphay
I. Aleixo de Bungo
I. Lião do Tacata
I. Ignátio do Cami
I. Thoma

Ilha de Yoyeno
P. Balthazar Lopes
P. Gregório Fúlvio
I. Miguel de Cazzuça

Nagasaqui
P. Pedro Gómez
P. Organtino
P. João de Castro
P. Antóio López
P. Pero Paulo
P. Gregório Céspedes
I. Balthazar Correa
I. Gómez de Yamaguchi
I. Cosme de Miaco
I. Vicente de Vacaça

Conga
P. Egídio, olim Gil, da Mata
I. Lourenço

Vomura
P. Afonço de Lucena
P. João Rodriguez
P. Francisco Rodríguez
P. Theodoro Manteles
I. Francisco Fernández
I. Nicolao de Yamaguchi
I. Adão

Vomura (terras)
P. Bastião Gonçalvez
I. João Gerardino
I. Gaspar de Vomura

Ilhas de Firando
P. Francisco Carreón
P. Jorge de Carvalhal
P. Aires Sanches
I. Domingos de Firando
I. André de Amacuça

Ilhas do Goto
P. Josepho Fornalete
P. Balthazar López
I. Paulo de Amacuça

Bugo
P. Francisco Pássio
P. Christóvão Morera
I. Francão Lião do Bandou

1592/93
Nagasaqui (Casa de Misericórdia)
P. António Lopes
P. Joam de Crasto
P. Damiam Marim
P. António Cordeiro
I. Ambrósio Fernández
I. Sungui Gomes
I. Yofo Paulo

Nagasaqui (Casa de Todos os Sanctos)
P. Pero Gómez
P. Francisco Pásio
P. Pero da Crus
P. Pero Paulo
I. Joam Rodríguez
I. Mateus de Couros
I. Guaspar de Paiva
I. Miqui Paulo

Conga
P. Joam Baptista
I. Same Luís

Conura
P. Júlio Piani
I. Sadamacççu Guaspar

Toquiççu (Nagasaqui)
P. Bastiam Goncçálvez

Residencia de Firando
P. Joseph Fornalete
I. Simión de Bungo

Sacaguchi
P. Afonso de Lucena
P. Baltezar Lopes
I. Joam de Torres
I. Francisco Fernamdes
I. Yquiççuqui Toma
I. Gonoy Paulo
I. Adam

Curi
P. Joam Rodriguez
I. Yamaguchi Niculao

Sonógui
P. Manoel Borralho
I. Canzusa Miguel

Collégio e Casa de povação de Amaqusa
P. Francisco Calderón
P. Diogo de Misquita
P. Celço Cofalonério
P. Alonso González
P. Marcos Feraro
P. Niculao de Avilla
P. Manoel Barreto
P. Francisco Pírez
I. Guaspar Carvalho, Portugues
I. Francisco Luís
I. Felipe Gómez
I. Francisco Douria (Malacan)
I. Ambrósio de Barros (Indian)
I. Casaria Juliam
I. Foriye Lionardo
I. Sungui Tomé
I. Yxinda Amador
I. Nixi Romão
I. Moriyama Miguel
I. Tocumaru Mateus
I. Cusano André
I. Itto Máncio
I. Casaria Justo

I. Sanga Matias
I. Ychiqu Miguel
I. Nacavo Matias
I. Itto Justo
I. Chinjiva Miguel
I. Nacaura Juliam,
I. Nagavara Niculao
I. Quimura Miguel
I. Nixi Francisco
I. Ycaruga Máximo
I. Macara Francisco
I. Tanabe Liam
I. Unguio Fabiam
I. Tacay Cosme
I. Fara Martinho
I. Firamdo Tomás
I. Conga Marino
I. Nagasaqui Luís
I. Fiunga Francisco
I. Mizuguchi Agostinho
I. Yyo Melchior
I. Bastiam de Firado
I. Ariye Simón
I. Maççuvoca André
I. Joam Baptista
I. Joam Bernardes
I. Pedro

Xiqui
P. Pero Morejón, Castelhano
I. Bertolameu Redondo
I. Joam Niculao
I. Cçuchimochi Heitor
I. Votavo Máncio
I. Máncio Joam

Somotto
P. António Alvares
I. Xingua Aleixo

Conzura
P. Álvoro Días (Indian)

I. Firata Jorge

Oyano
P. Baltezar Lopes
I. Facata Giam

Arima
P. Melchior de Moura
P. Gregório de Céspedes
P. Joam Francisco
I. Diogo Pireira (Indian)
I. Tamura Romão

Canzuça
P. António Francisco
I. Guilherme,
I. Tomunaga Cosme
I. Afonso

Chinjiva
P. Gonçalo Rebello,
I. Cudo Paulo

Ximabara
P. António Fernandes
I. Roque

Ariye
P. Ruy Barreto
I. Yama Joao

Siminário de Fachirao
P. Pero Ramón
P. Joam de Millam (Indian)
P. Francisco Rodríguez
I. Domingos Días
I. Ballezar Correa
I. Miguel Colaço
I. Jácome de Navais (Indian)
I. Taquxima Joam
I. Tocumari Liam
I. Quimura Toma

Bungo
P. Christóvão Moreira
P. Gregório Fúlvio
I. Fancan Liao

Miaco
P. Organtino
P. Francisco Peres
I. Vicente,
I. Amaqua Paulo
I. Mori Giam,
P. Gil da Mata (sent to Rome)

1603
Collégio de Nangasaqui
Reverendíssimo Bispo Dom Luís Cerqueira (Bishop of Japan, since 1598)
P. Francisco Pássio
P. Diego Mesquita
P. Gaspar Carvalho
P. João Rodriguez
P. Belchior de Moura
P. Mattheus de Couros
P. Pero da Cruz
P. João Rodriguez Jirão
P. Manoel Barreto
P. António Francisco
P. Baltasar López
P. João Francisco Stefanónio
P. Rui Gómez
P. Nicolao de Ávila
P. Gaspar de Crasto
P. João Nicolao
I. Ambrósio Faz
I. Bartolomé Redondo
I. Balthasar Correa
I. Manoel Ferreira
I. Gaspar de Paiva
I. Diogo Pereira
I. João Baptista [Pece]
I. Sangui Gómez

I. Confan Lião
I. Fara Martinho do Compo
I. Çumgi Thomé
I. Fogin António
I. Cosme Tacai
I. Fiunga Francisco
I. Pero João
I. Tadeu
I. Moriama Miguel
I. Ichico Miguel

Focami [Kōnoura]
P. Bartolomé Gómez
I. Conga Julio

Uchime [Tokitsu]
P. António Álvarez
I. Casaria Justo

Conga e Ysafay
P. Rui Barreto
I. Roque

Casa da Provação de Todos os Santos
P. Celso Confaloneiro
P. Gabriel de Matos
I. Agostinho de Teves
I. João Alberto
I. Manoel d'Oliveira
I. Manoel Gonçalvez
I. Francisco Lobo
I. Francisco d'Oliveira
I. Manoel Rodríguez
I. Omachi Lourenço
I. Nixi António
I. Vota Agostinho
I. Foin Gaspar
I. Xibata Diogo
I. Catano Diogo
I. Quimora Leonardo
I. Cato Inácio
I. Fita Matias

Appendices

I. Misochuchi Máncio

Vomura
P. Afonso de Lucena
P. Gonçalo Rebello
P. Nicolao da Costa
I. Francisco Fernández
I. Vicente Carruba
I. Sandamaque Gaspar

Susta [Suzuta]
P. Baltasar López
I. Nixi Romão

Cori
P. António Fernández
I. Xingui Aleixo

Sonongui
P. Maoel Boralho

Collégio de Arima
P. Francisco Calderão
P. João Pomeiro
P. Álvaro Diaz
P. Júlio Piani
P. Luís Niabara
P. Bartolomé de Sequeira
I. Romão
I. Ximixu Raphael
I. Simiao
I. Guilbelme

Arima (Seminário conjunto ao Collégio)
P. João de Milão
P. Pero Rodriguez
I. Constantino Dourado
I. Cuia [?] Pero

Amzuça
P. António Cordeiro

I. Domingos Díaz
I. Songa Matthias

Arie
P. Carlos Spínola
I. Sanga Mathias

Ximambara
P. João Batista Baessa
I. Jama João

Taira e Saigo
P. Francisco Pírez

Chimgiua
P. Ambrósio de Bairros
I. Yo Xisto

Ilhas de Amacusa e Xiqui
P. Garcia Garcés
P. João Frias
I. Guenga Joseph

Cauachinura
P. Chimora Bastião

Conzura
P. Marcos Ferraro
I. Cavachi Máximo

Casa Reitoral de Miaco
P. Organtino Soldo
P. Francisco de Paiva
I. Join Vicente
I. Firata Jorge
I. Ungio Fabião
I. More Gião

No Miaco d'arriba
P. Baltasar de Torres
I. Michio Miguel

Fuximi (Fortress Daifu)
P. Gerónimo Rodriguez
I. Fanca Lião
I. Amacusa Paulo

Ozaca
P. Pero Morejão
P. Gerónimo d'Ángeles
I. Bungo Bartolameu

Facata (Chicogem)
P. Pero Ramón
I. Nangavara Nicola

Cocora (Bujem)
P. Gregório de Céspedes
I. João de Torres
I. Saito André

Bungo e Amaguche
P. Pero Paulo
I. Amacusa André

1606/7[6]
Collégio de Nangasaqui
P. Diogo de Misquita
P. Bertholameu de Cequeira
P. João Rodriguez Girão
P. Belchior de Moura
P. António Francisco
P. Francisco de Payva
P. Francisco Luís
P. Gonçalo Rebello
P. João Francisco
P. João Nicolao
P. João Rodriguez
P. João Coelho
P. Manoel Barreto
P. Manoel Borralho

P. Nicolao d'Avila
P. Organtino
I. Ambrósio Fernández
I. Gaspar de Payva
I. Cosme (Japanese)
I. Xibata Diogo
I. Fiunga Francisco (Japanese)
I. Gomes (Japanese)
I. Domingos Díaz
I. Gião (Japanese)
I. Leonardo (Japanese)
I. Miguel Moriyama (Japanese)
I. Fara Martinho (Japanese)
I. Mathias (Japanese)
I. Máncio Firabaxi (Japanese)
I. Pero João, (Japanese, school master)
I. Tbomé Tçuji (Japanese)
I. Vicente Carruba

Na casa do Sor **Bispo**
P. João Baptista Baeça
I. Balthazar Correa
I. Leão Cofão (Japanese)

Residências sogeitas à Casa de Nangasaqi
Na Misericórdia
P. Gaspar Carvalho

Ospital
P. Rui Gómez
I. Francisco Fernández

Santa Clara de Uracami
P. António Álvarez

Fucafori
P. Gaspar de Crasto

---

[6] Due to timely proximity, three lists for 1606/7 have been fused here.

Appendices

Yangami
P. Baltasar López

Issafai
P. Ruy Barreto

Tone
P. Afonso de Lucena
I. Gaspar (Japanese)

Fudoyama
P. António Fernández
I. Aleixo (Japanese)

Casa de Provação em Todos-os-Santos
P. Celso Confaloneiro
P. Nicolao da Costa
I. Joao Bernárdez
I. Manoel Rodríguez
I. André Noma
I. Baltasar Tçurunda (Japanese)
I. Gonçalo Viera
I. Gaspar Toy
I. Jorge Joren
I. João de Ariye (Japanese)
I. Luís Naitó (Japanese)
I. Luís Matçuvo (Japanese)
I. Luis Xivozuca (Japanese)
I. Miguel Matçuda (Japanese)
I. Mathias Machida (Japanese)
I. Máncio Taichiqu (Japanese)
I. Paulo Sayto
I. Salvador de Barros
I. Thoma Funamoto
I. Thoma Izichi
I. Miguel Maqui
I. Julio (Japanese)
I. Romão Nixi

Arima
P. Francisco Calderón

P. Alvaro Días
P. Vicente Ribeiro
P. Joao Baptista Porro
P. Luís (Japanese)
I. Romao (Japanese)
I. Pedro Chicuam (Japanese)
I. Symeão (Japanese)

No Seminário
P. João Pomério
I. Máncio Ito (Japanese)
I. Juliao Nacaura (Japanese)
I. Constantino Dourado (Japanese)

Canzuça
P. António Cordeiro
P. Bastião (Japanese)
I. André (Japanese)

Ariye
P. João de Fonseca
I. Augustinho Vota (Japanese)

Ximabara
P. João Baptista Zola
P. Pedro Rodríguez
I. Roque (Japanese)
I. Sanga Mathias (Japanese)

Saigo
P. Francisco Pirez
I. Jozeph (Japanese)

Chijiva
P. Ambrósio
I. Justo Yamada (Japanese)

Xiqui
P. Garcia Garcés

Conzura
P. Marcos Ferraro

I. Ignácio (Japanese)

Saxinotçu
P. João de Frias
I. Máncio Mizzucuchi (Japanese)

Facata
P. Pedro Ramón
P. Pedro de Monte Agudo
I. Nicolao (Japanese)

Aquizuqui
P. Gabriel de Matos
I. Nixi António (Japanese)

Yamaguchi [leg.: Yanagava]
P. João Matheus
I. Yama João (Japanese)

Bujem [=Cocura]
P. Gregório de Céspedes
P. Camilo Constâncio
I. Diogo Pereira
I. João de Torres (Japanese)
I. André (Japanese)

Bungo
P. Pedro Paulo
P. João Vicente
I. Lorenço Vomachi (Japanese)

Miaco
P. Pedro Morejón
P. Carlos
I. Paulo Reoin (Japanese)
I. Fabião (Japanese)
I. Martinho Xiquimi (Japanese)

1 r. Thomás de Fig[uei]redo (Japanese)
I. Vicente Toin (Japanese)
I. Tadeu (Japanese)

Camiguiõ
P. Bento Fernández
I. Raphael (Japanese)

Fuximi
P. Hyerónimo de Ángelis
I. Fancão (Japanese)
I. Yuqi Diogo (Japanese)

Ozaca
P. Baltazar de Torres
I. Xisto (Japanese)

Sacay
P. Francisco Pacheco
I. Bartholameu (Japanese)

Foccoqu
P. Hyerónimo Rodríguez
I. Miguel Quimura (Japanese)

Firoxima
P. Matheus de Couros
P. João da Costa
I. Ixida António (Japanese)

1613[7]
Collegio de Nangasaqui & suas Residências
P. Valentim Carvalho, Provincial
P. Jerónimo Rodriguez
P. António Francisco

---

[7] Catálogo dos Padres e Irmáos da Provincia de Japao, feito em Fevereiro do anno de 1613. Pera ver Nosso Reverendo P.e Geral Claudio Aquaviva, MJH (1975: 552-558). 121 Jesuits are listed in total, including 62 padres.

P. Francisco Calderón
P. Gabriel de Matos
P. Carlo Spínola
P. Belchior de Moura
P. Francisco Pacheco
P. João Pomério
P. Manoel Barreto
P. Manoel Borralho
P. Nicolao Dávila
P. Rui Gomes
P. Ambrósio de Barros
P. Nicolao da Costa
P. Manoel Rodriguez
P. João Nicolao
P. Vicente Ribeiro
P. Francisco Lobo
P. Martinho Campo
I. João Bernardes
I. Manole Gonçalvez
I. Gaspar de Paiva
I. Diogo Pereira
I. João Bautista
I. Domingos Dias
I. Balthasar Correa
I. André Pinto
I. Francisco Calado
I. Ambrósio Fernández
I. Gomes (Japanese)
I. Cosme (Japanese)
I. Leonardo Qimura (Japanese)
I. Miguel Moriyama (Japanese)
I. Diogo Xibata (Japanese)
I. Christóvão (Japanese)
I. Xisto (Japanese)
I. André Saitó (Japanese)
I. Thomas Funamoto (Japanese)
I. Gaspar Sadamatçu (Japanese)
I. Mathias Machida (Japanese)
I. Thomás (Japanese)
I. Luís Xivozzuca (Japanese)
I. Máncio Taichicu (Japanese)
I. Pedro (Japanese)

I. André Noma (Japanese)
I. Máncio João (Japanese)

Residência anexa à casa da Misericórdia
P. Gaspar Carcalho
P. Álvaro Dias

Residência do Hospital
P. Diogo de Misquita
P. Gaspar de Crasto
P. Jácome António
I. Francisco Fernández
I. Miguel Xuccan (Japanese)

Uracami
P. António Árvarez
I. Justo Casariya (Japanese)

Fudōyama
P. António Fernández
P. Sebastião Qimura (Japanese)
I. Aleixo Xinji (Japanese)

Tone
P. Afonso de Lucena
I. Agustinho Ota (Japanese)

Isafay
P. João da Costa
I. André Amacusa (Japanese)

Arima
P. Mattheus de Couros
P. Francisco Pírez
P. João Rodriguez
P. Bartholameu Soares
P. Pero Martínez
P. Manoel Borges
I. Costantino (Japanese)
I. Miguel Maqi (Japanese)
I. Diogo Yuqi (Japanese)

I. Miguel Matçuda (Japanese)

Tacacu
P. Luís (Japanese)

Ariye
P. João de Fonseca

Cuchinotçu
P. Pero Marques

Xiqui
P. Garcia Garcés
P. Diodo Carvalho
I. Romão Nixi

Cózzura
P. Marcos Ferraro
P. João Bautista
I. Inácio Cató (Japanese)

Casa do Facata, e suas Residências
P. Celso Confalonério
P. Julião Nacaura (Japanese)
P. Thomé Tçuji Nagavara (Japanese)
I. Nicolao Nagavara (Japanese)

Amagui
P. Francisco Eugénio
I. Mathias Sanga (Japanese)

Yanagava
P. João Matheus Adami
I. João Yama (Japanese)

Bungo
P. Pero Paulo

Notçu
P. Bartholameu da Siqueira
I. Máncio Mizoguchi (Japanese)

Xinga
P. João Vicente Antolheti
I. Lourenço Omachi (Japanese)

Miyaco
P. Pero Morejón
P. Christóvão Ferreira,
P. Bento Fernández
P. Jerónimo de Ángelis
I. Jorge Tonno (Japanese)
I. Paulo (Japanese)
I. Luís Naitó (Japanese)
I. Lião Fancan (Japanese)
I. Máncio Firabayaxi (Japanese)
I. Martinho Xiqimi (Japanese)
I. Thadeu (Japanese)

Fuximi
P. João Baptista da Ilha
I. Luís Matçuvo (Japan)

Ozaca
P. João Bautista Porro
P. João Bautista de Baeça
I. Bartholameu (Japanese)

Sacay
P. Camilo Constâncio
I. Júlio Conga (Japanese)

Foccocu
P. Balthasar de Torres
I. Thomás Ijichi (Japanese)

Firoxima
P. Sebastião Vieira
P. António Ixida (Japanese)
I. Paulo Saitó
I. Balthasar Tçuruda (Japanese)

1614[8]

P. Afonso de Lucena
P. Álvaro Dias
P. Ambrosio de Barros
P. António Álvarez
P. António Fernández
P. António Francisco Critano
P. António Ixida
P. Belchior de Moura
P. Balthezar de Torres
P. Bertholameu de Siqueira
P. Bento Fernández
P. Bertolameu Soares
P. Carlo Espínola
P. Celso Confalonero
P. Christóvão Ferreira
P. Camillo Constanço
P. Diogo Carvalho
P. Francisco Calderón
P. Francisco Pírez
P. Francisco Luis
P. Francisco Pacheco
P. Francisco Eugénio
P. Francisco Lobo
P. Gaspar de Crasto
P. Gabriel de Matos
P. Garcia Garcéz
P. João Pomério
P. João Bautista Bayeça
P. João Rodriguez Girão
P. João Nicolao
P. João de Fonseca
P. João da Costa
P. Joāp Bautista Zola
P. João Vicente Antolhete
P. João Bautista
P. João Bautista Porro
P. Jácome António
P. Jerónimo Rodríguez
P. Jerónimo de Ángeles
P. João Mateus Adami
P. Julião Nacaura (Japanese)
P. Luiz (Japanese)
P. Manuel Borralho
P. Marcos Ferraro
P. Mateus de Couros
P. Manuel Gonçalvez
P. Manuel Borges
P. Manuel Rodríguez
P. Martinho Campo
P. Máncio Firabayaxi (Japanese)
P. Nicolai de Ávila
P. Nicolao da Costa
P. Pero (Pietro) Paulo Navarro
P. Pero Morejón
P. Pero Márquez
P. Pero Martins
P. Ruy Gómez
P. Sebastião Vieira
P. Sebastião Quimura (Japanese)
P. Thomé Tçuji (Japanese)
P. Valentim Carvalho
P. Vicente Ribeiro

---

[8] Only the 62 padres of the 115 Jesuits are listed here, as the irmãos are mostly the same as in 1613.

9.2. Appendix 2: Jesuit Missionaries in Peru (1568-1605)

9.2.1. Entry Period (1568-1575)

1569
P. Jherónimo Ruiz de Portillo, Provincial
P. Bracamonte
P. Luis López
P. Pedro Miguel de Fuentes
P. Cristóval Sanches
Don Joán Toscano
H[ermano] Francisco de Medina
H. Antonio González
H. Pedro Mexía
H. Leandro Felipe
H. Joán Gutiérrez
H. Hernando Despinar
H. Martín de Contreras
H. Juan Garcia
H. Pedro Llobet
H. Alonso Pérez
H. Juan Ruiz
H. Juan Ruiz[9]
H. Martin Miguel
H. Francisco de Heredia
H. Juan Pérez de Aguilar
H. Francisco de Espinosa
H. Juan Pérez de la Milla
H. Martin Piçarro
H. Joseph de Riberta
H. Blas Valera
H. Gonzálo Ruiz
H. Juan Rodriguez

1571
P. Gerónimo Ruiz de Portillo
P. Bartolomé Hernandez
P. Joán de Çúñiga

P. Diego de Bracamonta
P. Diego Ortún
P. Sebastián Amador
P. Joán Gomez
P. Luis López
P. Pedro Miguel de Fuentes
P. Barzana
P. Cristóval Sánchez
P. Mesía
H. Pedro Llobet
H. Joán de Casasola
H. Joán Garcia
H. Antonio Martínez
H. Diego Martínez
H. Francisco de Medina
H. Antonio de Ocanpo
H. Juan Gutiérrez
H. Hernando Despinar
H. Martín de Conreras
H. Alonso Pérez
H. Joán Ruiz
H. Juan Rodríguez
H. Juan Ruiz
H. Francisco de Heredia
H. Joán Perez de Aguilar
H. Blas Morán
H. Francisco López
H. Joán Sanchez
H. Baltazar Ruiz
H. Lendro Felipe
H. Básquez
H. Marco Antonio
H. Francisco Romero
H. Juan de Mendoça
H. Joán de Anaya

---

[9] He actually had the same name as the Hermano listed before.

Appendices

H. Martín Piçarro
H. Joseph de Ribera
H. Blas Valera
H. Gonçalo Ruiz
H. Joán de Lezarraga
H. Vicente Yáñez
H. Andrés de Montalvo

1572
Lima
P. Batolomé Hernández
P. Miguel de Fuentes
P. Sebastian Amador
P. Juan Gómez
P. Pedro Mexía
P. Diego Ortún
P. Antonio Martínez
P. Philipe
P. Cristóbal Sánchez
P. Diego Bracamonta
H. Juan Cassasola
H. Juan García
H. Hernando Despinar
H. Juan Gutiérrez
H. Miguel de Contreras
H. Martín Pizarro
H. Joseph de Rivera
H. Juan Ruiz
H. Juan Ruiz
H. Blas Balera
H. Francisco de Heredia
H. Juan Pérez de Aguilar
H. Francisco López
H. Juan Sánches de Menocal
H. Baltassar Ruiz
H. Vicente Yañez
H. Blas Morán
H. Juan de Anaya
H. Francisco Romero
H. Antonio Vázquez
H. Juan de Mendoza
H. Diego González Carasco

H. Marco Antonio
H. Juan de Añasco
H. Santiago Pérez

Cuzco
P. Luis López
P. Alonso Barzana
H. Francisco de Medina
H. Diego Martínez
H. Antonio González de Ocampo
H. Pedro Lobet
H. Alonso Pérez
H. Francisco Despinosa

1573
P. Hiéronimo Ruiz de Portillo, provincial
P. Miguel de Fuentes
P. Bartolomé Hernández
P. Joseph de Acosta
P. Andrés López
P. Joán Gómez
P. Antonio Martínez
P. Pedro Mezia
P. Cristoval Sánchez
H. Francisco López
H. Joán García
H. Pedro Lobet
H. Joán Gutiérrez
H. Martín Piçarro
H. Martín de Contreras
H. Joán Ruiz
H. Alonso Pérez
H. Joán Ruiz
H. Blas Valera
H. Joán Pérez de Aguilar
H. Joán de Anaya
H. Joán Sánchez
H. Balthassar Ruiz
H. Vicente Yáñez
H. Antonio Vázquez

Novicios
H. Diego González Carrasco
H. Pedro de Rojas
H. Pedro de Añasco
H. Sanctiago Pérez
H. Diego Flores
H. Alonso del Aguila
H. Joán Miguel
H. Estevan Izquierdo
H. Francisco de Carrión

Santiago
P. Diego Hortún
H. Francisco de Heredia

Cuzco
P. Luis López
P. Alonso de Barzana

9.2.2. Consolidation Period (1576-1599)

1583[10]
Padres
P. Balthasar Piñas
P. Joán de Montoya
P. Hierónimo Ruiz de Portillo
P. Alonso Ruiz
P. Joseph de Acosta
P. Alonso de Barçana
P. Miguel de Fuentes (inquisitioned)
P. Joán de Atiença
P. Joán Sebastián
P. Joseph Tiruel
P. Andrés López
P. Diego Martínez
P. Diego de Bracamonta
P. Diego de Vaena
P. Diego de Ortún
P. Joán Gomez
P. Antonio Martínez

P. Sebastián Amador
P. Leandro Philippe
H. Francisco de Medina
H. Diego Martínez
H. Antonio González
H. Antonio Martínez
H. Hernando de Espinar
H. Joseph de Ribera
H. Francisco de Espinosa
H. Blas Morán
H. Marco Antonio

Los embiados a la provincia de Chuquiavo
P. Joán de Zúñiga
H. Joán de Casasola
H. Gonzalo Ruiz

P. Leandro Philippe
P. Francisco de Medina
P. Antonio González
P. Blas Valera
P. Francisco Angulo
P. Estevan Cavello
P. Antonio López
P. Estevan de Avila
P. Dionisso Velazquez
P. Diego de Çúñiga
P. Diego Flores
P. Diego Paz
P. Ludovico Bertonio
P. Francisco de Portillo
P. Hernán Pérez
P. Alonso de Valdivieso
P. Agustín Sánchez
P. Luis de Estella
P. Joán de Aguilar

---

[10] MP 3 (1958): 1581-1585.

P. Vicente Yáñez
P. Pedro de Cartagena
P. Diego González
P. Martín Pizzaro
P. Christóval Hortiz
P. Andrés Hortiz
P. Ignaco Iñiguez
P. Pedro de Rojas
P. Joán Ruiz
P. Francisco de Herrera
P. Diego de Torres
P. Joán Beltran
P. Lope Delgado
P. Joán Fonte
P. Diego de Torres (actually same name)
P. Bernardino Papiol
P. Joán de Anaya
P. Estevan de Ochoa
P. Pedro Rodríguez
P. Bartholomé de Santiago
P. Joán Baptista Rufo
P. Pedro de Añasco

Hermanos
H. Joán de Hinojosa
H. Francisco Cardoso
H. Pedro de Castillo
H. Hernando Velázquez
H. Joán de Sanmartin
H. Hierónimo de Castro
H. Pedro de Oscos
H. Diego Ramírez
H. Bartolomé de Scobar
H. Diego de Agreda
H. Onofre Estevan
H. Julián Delgado
H. Hernando de Aguillera
H. Antonio de Illescas
H. Lorenço Barriales
H. Joán Vázquez
H. Gregorio Cisneros

H. Joán García
H. Joán de Casasola
H. Pedro Pablo
H. Luís de Soto
H. Diego Martínez
H. Bernardo Vitti
H. Francisco López
H. Marco Antonio
H. Francisco de Heredia
H. Benito González
H. Joán Romero
H. Alonso Pérez
H. Joán de Candía
H. Augustín de Peñasancta
H. Antonio Velásquez
H. Bartolomé Lorenço
H. Gregorio de Palencia
H. Joán Miguel
H. Joán Sanchez
H. Joán de Casarubios
H. Joán de Santiago
H. Joán de Plasencia
H. Joán Ruiz
H. Gaspar Pereira
H. Gonçalo de Velmonte
H. Pedro de Vargas
H. Pedro Sotila
H. Estevan Izquierdo
H. Martín Garay
H. Joán de Otalora
H. Joán Martínn
H. Joán Sánchez
H. Blas Morán
H. Hernando Nieto
H. Rodrigo Hernández
H. Santiago Pérez
H. Pedro de Vega
H. Antonio López
H. Domingo Bermeo
H. Diego González
H. Martín Picón
H. Gonçalo Ruiz

H. Anndrés de Rivas
H. Hierónimo Berdugo
H. Joán de Mosquera
H. Pedro de Madrid
H. Francisco de Carrión

Hermanos novicios
P. Hernando Guerra
H. Andrés de Sarabia
H. Joán de Villegas
H. Sanctos de Gabironda
H. Pedro de Salamanca
H. Ignatio Cataños
H. Pedro Barrassa
H. Francisco de Contreras
H. Martín de Soto
H. Francisco Hernández
H. Antonio Nuñez
H. Hernando Alonso
H. Joán Serrano
H. Pedro de Saraviarte

1591[11]
Collegio de Lima
P. Joán de Atiença, provincial
P. Joán Sebastián, rector
P. Hernando de Mendoça
P. Balthasar Piñas
P. Estevan de Avila
P. Francisco Zamorano
P. Pedro de Castillo
P. Diego Alvarez de Paz
P. Antonio González
P. Francisco de Herrera
P. Diego de Paz
P. Hernán Pérez
P. Joán de Avellaneda
P. Joan Manuel de Anaya
P. Luis de Valdivia

P. Paulo Joseph
P. Bartholomé de Escobar
P. Joán Pérez de Aguilar
P. Antonio de Vega
P. Joán de Alva
P. Joán de Olivares
P. Luis de Estella
P. Hernando Morillo

Hermanos theologos
H. Juan Romero
H. Francisco Ponce
H. Gaspar de Monrroy
H. Antonio Mexía
H. Cristóbal Narváez
H. Joán Rodríguez
H. Francisco Martínez
H. Alonso de Villalobos
H. Gerónimo de Montesinos
H. Hernando de Herrera
H. Joán López
H. Alonso Mexía
H. Hernando de la Cueva
H. Gonçalo Xuárez
H. Francisco Perlin
H. Luis de Santillán
H. Gabriel de Chabes

Hermanos artistas
H. Francisco Daça
H. Alonso Martín
H. Francisco Vázquez
H. Joán Baptista
H. Alonso Salvatierra
H. Rodrigo de Valverde
H. Pedro Sánchez
H. Martin Vázquez

---

[11] MP 4 (1966): 1586-1591.

Hermanos coadjutores
H. Gaspar Pereira
H. Juan de Casarubias
H. Alonso Pérez
H. Francisco López
H. Luis de Soto
H. Benito Gonçález
H. Francisco de Heredia
H. Bartholomé Lorenço
H. Joan Serrano
H. Andrés de Ribas
H. Pedro Pablo
H. Joán Díaz
H. Gaspar Antonio
H. Francisco Gómez
H. Francisco Hernández
H. Joán Zamorano
H. Joán de Virves
H. Cristóbal Vivas

Hermanos novicios
H. Joán de Pareja
H. Joán de Vargas
H. Eugenio Baltodano
H. Balthasar de los Reyes
H. Francisco de Aramburo
H. Cristóbal Garcés
H. Diego de Goicochea
H. Joán Mendo
H. Joán de Aguila
H. Francisco de Castro
H. Valerio del Castillo

Collegio del Cuzco
P. Diego de Torres
P. Francisco de Medina
P. Antonio López
P. Estevan Ochoa
P. Diego de Quïenca
P. Joán Pérez Menacho
P. Pedro Rodríguez
P. Gregorio de Cisneros

P. Diego Flores
P. Antonio Núñez
P. Antonio Vallejo

Hermanos escolares
H. Joán de Ibarra
H. Joán de Güémez
H. Joán de Heredia
H. Hernando de Salinas

Hermanos coadjutores
H. Marco Antonio
H. Pedro de Madrid
H. Gregorio de Palencia
H. Santos de Gavironda
H. Antonio Romano
H. Gonçalo Ruiz
H. Simón Hernández

Collegio de la ciudad de La Paz
P. Joán Beltrán, rector
P. Joan de Montoya
P. Joán Gómez
P. Bernardino Papiol
P. Diego Ramírez

Hermanos coadjutores
H. Joán Ruiz
H. Pedro de Vega
H. Santiago Pérez
H. Gerónimo Berdugo
H. Pedro de Benavides

Collegio de la ciudad de Ariquipa
P. Christóval de Ovan, rector
P. Joseph Tiruel
P. Juan Suárez de Lara
P. Martín Piçarro
P. Augustín Sánchez
P. Lorenço Barriales
P. Joán Alonso
P. Lope Delgado

Hermanos coadjutores
H. Antonio de Llanos
H. Joán García
H. Domingo Bermeo
H. Hernando Nieto
H. Martín de Garay
H. Joán Martín
H. Joán Plasencia
H. Joán Antonio de Cumes

Collegio de la Villa Imperial de Potosí
P. Diego de Torres Ruvio, rector
P. Manuel Vásquez
P. Valentín de Caravantes
P. Miguel de Urrea
P. Ruperto Arnono
P. Vicente Yáñez
P. Padre Gerónimo

Hermanos coadjutores
H. Blas Morán
H. Rodrigo Hernández
H. Francisco Deça
H. Juan Toledano
H. Luis Desquibel
H. Pedro de Sotilla
H. Joán Pérez
H. Alonso Crespo

Residencia de Juli
P. Antonio de Ayanz, superior
P. Luis Bertonio
P. Pedro Vicente
P. Gerónimo de Castro
P. Julián Delgado
P. Hierónimo de Andión
P. Hernando de Aguilera
P. Joán Baptista
P. Miguel Muñoz

Hermanos coadjutores
H. Diego Gonçalez
H. Diego Virues
H. Bernardo Viti

Collegio de la ciudad de Quito
P. Estevan Cavello, rector
P. Diego Gonçález
P. Alonso Ruiz
P. Joán Básquez
P. Joán Herrán
P. Onofre Estevan
P. Andrés Hernández
P. Joán Díaz
P. Hernando Morillo

Hermanos coadjutores
H. Joán de Santiago
H. Pedro de Vargas
H. Joán Sánchez Menocal
H. Joán Núñez
H. Pedro de Quirós
H. Cristóval Sánchez Carrasco
H. Alonso de León
H. Joán Perlín

Residencia de Panamá
P. Lucio Garcete, superior
P. Joán de León
P. Ignacio Cataño
P. Ignacio Jaymes

Hermanos coadjutores
H. Joán de Casasola
H. Diego de la Plaça
H. Pedro Sánchez de Salazar

Missiones de Santa Cruz
P. Diego Martínez, superior
P. Diego de Samaniego
P. Dionisio Velásquez
P. Andrez Ortiz Orruño

H. Joán Sánchez

Mission de Tucumán
P. Joan Fonte, superior
P. Francisco de Angulo
P. Alonso de Barçana
P. Pedro de Añasco
H. Joán de Villegas

1595[12]
Collegio de Lima
P. Joán Sebastián-Daraco, Rector, Provincial
P. Hernando de Mendoca
P. Estevan Cabello
P. Joán de León
P. Estevan de Avila
P. Alonso Messía
P. [Francisco Camorano]
P. Luis de Estela
P. Diego Alvarez de Paz
P. Juan Font
P. Diego de Paz
P. Antonio Gonçález
P. Hernán Pérez
P. Paulo Joseph-Ocaña
P. Joán de Anaya
P. Antonio de Ayanz
P. Joán Pérez Menacho
P. Bartolomé de Scobar
P. Andrés Hernández
P. Joán de Avellaneda
P. Christóval Narváez
P. Joán Suárez
P. Joán López de Almansa
P. Hernando de Herrera
P. Hernando de la Cueva
P. Francisco Perlín

P. Gonçalo Suárez
P. Alonso Messía
H. Andrés Ximenes
P. Joán Gómez
P. Francisco Zamorano
H. Francisco Daza
H. Francisco Vázquez
H. Alonso Martín
H. Alonso de Salvatierra
H. Martin Vásquez
H. Pedro Sanches
H. Pero de Vendoya
H. Joan Baptista Sorita
H. Joán de Ibarra
H. Joán de Heredia
H. Francisco de Arambulo
H. Valeriano del Castillo
H. Christóval García
H. Andrés Sanches
H. Pedro Alonso
H. Joán Sanches
H. Francisco López
H. Luis de Soto
H. Pedro Pablo
H. Bernardo Bitti
H. Francisco de Heredia
H. Alonso Pérez
H. Bartolomé Lorenco
H. Gaspar Pereira
H. Gaspar Antonio
H. Joán de Casarrubias
H. Estevan de Santacruz
H. Joán Martinez
H. Benito Gonçález
H. Joán Gonçales
H. Diego Phelipe
H. Christóval Vives
H. Pedro Salazar

---

[12] MP 5 (1970): 1592-1595. In 1595 the record for the first time listed more than 200 Jesuits in the Peruvian order province.

H. Josef Abitabili
H. Francisco Hernández
H. Francisco Gómez
H. Joán de Vargas
H. Gaspar Rodrigues
H. Christóval Garcés
H. Láçaro de Xarana
H. Pedro Navarro
H. Sebastián del Campo
H. Alonso Gómez
H. Christóval Robledo

Casa de probación
P. Christóval de Ovando
P. Joán Pérez de Aguilar
P. Joán de Truxillo
P. Alonso de Villalobos

Hermanos de 3a probación
H. Nicolás Mastrillo
H. Joán Perlín
H. Julio Pisce

Hermanos antiguos
H. Hernando de Salinas
H. Joán Díaz

Hermanos novicios
H. Cosme de Tevar
H. Sebastián Haçanero
H. Sebastián Suares
H. Joán Vallexo
H. Phelipe de Tapia
H. Pedro de Molina
H. Diego López
H. Francisco de Contreras
H. Francisco Cardoso
H. Pedro de Cuevas
H. Lorenco Guerrero
H. Pedro de Sarmiento
H. Alonso Gómez
H. Joán Iranzo

H. Pedro Martín
H. Sebastián Pablo de Prado
H. Francisco de Villegas

Collegio del Cuzco
P. Manuel Vázquez
P. Diego de Cuenca
P. Pedro del Castillo
P. Gregorio de Cisneros
P. Pedro Rodrigues
P. Diego de Flores
P. Antonio de Vega
P. Diego Ramires
P. Gonçalo de Lyra
P. Ignacio Catano
P. Antonio Vallejo
H. Francisco Martínez
H. Rodrigo de Peñafiel
H. Alexandro Faya
H. Martín de Aranda
H. Gonçalo Ruiz
H. Gregorio de Palencia
H. Pedro de Madrid
H. Sanctos de Gavironda
H. Pedro de Vocanegra
H. Alonso Ortiz
H. Joán de Pareja
H. Domingo Gonçales
H. Rodrigo Gómez
H. Andrés Sanches
H. Antonio de Cárdenas

Collegio de Ariquipa
P. Joán Beltrán
P. Alonso Ruiz
P. Joseph Tiruel
P. Franciseo de Medina
P. Agustín Sanches
P. Antonio Messía
P. Joán Alonso

Hermanos coadjutores
H. Joán García
H. Hernando Nieto
H. Joán Gómez
H. Gaspar Arroyo
H. Sebastián de Alarcón
H. Diego de Guaicochea
H. Miguel de Artiaga
H. Antón Martín
H. Joán de Virues
H. Joán Antonio Cumis
H. Joán Serrano

Collegio de Potosí
P. Estevan Ochoa
P. Antonio Martínez
P. Diego de Torres Rubio
P. Vicente Yáñez
P. Pedro de Oñate
P. Julián Delgado
P. Herónimo de Vega

Hermanos coadjutores
H. Blas Morán
H. Rodrigo Hernández
H. Alonso Crespo
H. Giorge Fernández
H. Andrés de Sarabiarte
H. Diego de Escudero
H. Gonçalo Vexarano

Collegio de la ciudad de La Paz
P. Valentín de Caravantes
P. Miguel de Urrea
P. Joan Baptista Rufo
P. Rodrigo Manrique
P. Joán de Güémez

Hermanos coadjutores
H. Joán Ruiz
H. Diego Gonçales
H. Pedro de Vega

H. Herónimo Verdugo
H. Francisco Deza
H. Joán Pelaes de Villegas
H. Francisco de Castro

Collegio de Quito
P. Diego de Torres
P. Diego Goncales (Holguín)
P. Joán Vásquez
P. Onofre Estevan
P. Joán Frías Errán
P. Joán Domingues
P. Joán Díaz

Hermanos coadjutores
H. Joán de Santiago
H. Marco Antonio
H. Joán Sanches Menocal
H. Pedro de Vargas
H. Christóval Sanches Carrascoso
H. García de Quirós
H. Joán Núñez
H. Hernando de Torres

Collegio de Chuquisaca
P. Lope Delgado
P. Martín Piçarro
P. Herónimo de Castro
P. Antonio Núñez
P. Pedro Rodrigues
P. Antonio Pardo
P. Antonio de Vivar

Hermanos coadjutores
H. Santiago Pérez
H. Estevan Isquierdo
H. Domingo Vermeo
H. Antonio Román
H. Joán Pérez
H. Eugenio Valtodano

Recidencia de Juli
P. Pedro Vicente
P. Antonio López
P. Joán de Alva
P. Ludovico Bertonio
P. Luis de Leiute
P. Gabriel de Chaves

Hermanos coadjutores
H. Diego de Virves
H. Pedro de Venavides

Residencia de Panamá
P. Herónimo de Avila
P. Ignacio Jaimes
P. Herónimo de Montesinos

Hermanos estudiantes y coadjutores
H. Joán de Aldana
H. Baltasar de los Reyes
H. Diego de la Plaça
H. Luis Méndez

Mission de Tucumán
P. Joán Romero
P. Alonso de Barçana
P. Francisco de Angulo
P. Pedro de Añasco
P. Joán López Viana
P. Marciel de Lorençana
P. Gaspar Monrroy

9.2.3. Period of Decline (1600-1605)
1601[13]
Collegio de Lima
P. Estevan Páez, visitador
P. Rodrigo de Cabredo, provincial
P. Joseph Tiruel
P. Juan de Olivares

Hermanos coadjutores
H. Joán del Aguila
H. Joán Toledano

Missión de Sancta Cruz
P. Diego Martínez
P. Diego de Samaniego
P. Dionisio Velásquez
P. Andrés Ortiz
P. Alonso de Miranda
P. Hierónimo de Andión
P. Angelo Monitola

Hermanos coadjutores
H. Joán Sanches
H. Bernardo de la Plaça

Missión de Chile
P. Balthasar Piñas
P. Luis de Valdivia
P. Hernando de Aguilera
P. Gabirel de Vega
P. Joán de Olivares
P. Luis de Santillán

Hermanos coadjutores
H. Miguel Teleña
H. Martín de Garay
H. Fabián García

P. Balthasar Piñas
P. Juan Sebastián
P. Estevan Avila
P. Diego de Torres
P. Juan Beltrán
P. Philipe Claver

---

[13] MP 7 (1981): 1600-1602.

Appendices

P. Juan Pérez Meoacho
P. Juan Gómez
P. Alonso de Miranda
P. Francisco Zamorano
P. Luis de Estella
P. Pedro de el Castillo
P. Diego Ramírez
P. Bartholomé de Escobar
P. Antonio Gonçales
P. Philippo Leandro
P. Joseph de Arriaga
P. Antonio Bivar
P. Francisco Perlín
P. Hierónirno de Montesinos
P. Andtés Ximenes
P. Juan López de Almansa
P. Alonso Messía
P. Juan de Aldana

Hermanos estudiantes
H. Balthasar de los Reyes
H. Alexandro Faya
H. Gaspar de Arroyo
H. Cosme de Chevar
H. Juan de Vallejo
H. Sebastián Xuares
H. Pbelippe de Tapia
H. Francisco de Contreras
H. Alonso de Sandoval
H. Manuel de Fonseca
H. Luis Ferrer
H. Diego de Mora
H. Gabriel Zerrato
H. Basilio de Vengochea
H. Alonso de Herrera
H. Pedro López
H. Francisco de Palma
H. Diego de Peñalosa
H. Antonio Vásquez
H. Augusdn Xuárez
H. Pedro Rodríguez
H. Pedro de Victoria

H. Augustln de Aguilar
H. Bernardo Castellanos
H. Francisco Ordóñez
H. Diego de Nágera
H. Lope de Mendoça
H. Juan Gonçales
H. Juan de Soxo
H. Hierónimo de Montalvo

Hermanos coadjutores
H. Gaspar Pereira
H. Luis de Soto
H. Pedro Pablo
H. Bernardo Vitti
H. Alonso Pérez
H. Francisco López
H. Francisco de Heredia
H. Juan de Casarrubias
H. Juan Mart1nez
H. Estevan de Santa Cruz
H. Gonçalo Velmonte
H. Benito Gonçalez
H. Santos de Gavironda
H. Juan del Barco
H. Juan de Vargas
H. Francisco Gómez
H. Gaspar Rodrlguez
H. Pedro de Salaçar
H. Francisco Deza
H. Diego de la Plaça
H. Francisco Hernández
H. Domingo Gonçález
H. Christóval Garcés
H. Jorge Femández
H. Manuel de Artiaga
H. Pedro de Cueva
H. Christóval Robledo
H. Juan Estevan-Llerena
H. Hernando de Torres
H. Hernando Xuárez
H. Pedro Martín
H. Alonso Pérez

List of Abbreviations

BG	=	born global
CIM	=	constructive intercultural management
DI	=	Documenta Indica
MHJ	=	Monumenta Historica Japoniae
MNC	=	multinational corporation
MP	=	Monumenta Peruana
MOS	=	Management and Organization Studies
SME	=	Small and medium-sized enterprise

www.ingramcontent.com/pod-product-compliance
Lightning Source LLC
Chambersburg PA
CBHW071354290426
44108CB00014B/1538